LANCASHIRE BOULDERING

Robin Müller

Published by Cottongrass Books.
Copyright © 2014 Cottongrass Books, Robin Müller. All rights reserved.
Printed and published with financial assistance from the BMC.

www.lancashirebouldering.com

Flapper, 5+ - Cow's Mouth p272

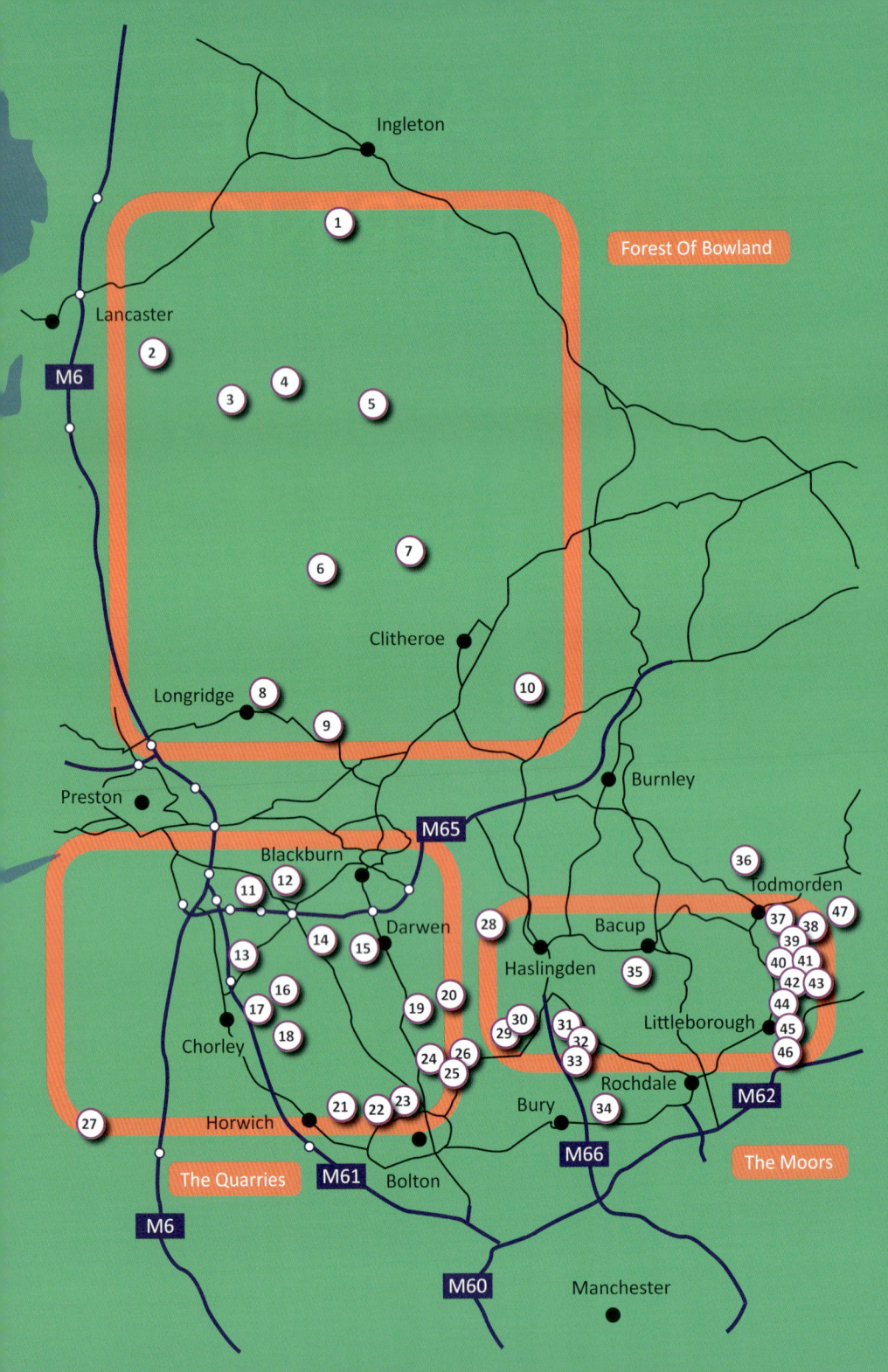

CONTENTS

Bowland Map		4
Quarries Map		6
Moors Map		8
Foreword		10
Important Things To Read		11
Where To Go first		12

Grades		13
How To Use The Book		15
Local Info		16
Climbing Walls		19
Wardens Of Rock		317
Timeline		318

Historical Overview		319
Interviews		320
Credits		328
Top 250 List		330
Index		332

BOWLAND

Chapter		Page
1	Great Stone Of Fourstones	22
2	Windy Clough	24
3	Thorn Crag	32
4	Wolfhole Crag	46
5	The Bull Stones	48
6	Reef Knoll	60
7	Crag Stones	62
8	Craig Y Longridge	66
9	Longridge Fell	76
	▶ Cardwell	76
	▶ Crowshaw	78
	▶ Finlandia	78
	▶ Kemple End	79
10	Nick Of Pendle	80

The chapter numbers match the crag numbers on the map, so that chapters are grouped alongside nearby locations.

THE QUARRIES

Chapter		Page
11	Duxon Hill	86
12	Hoghton	88
13	Denham	92
	▶ Baby Denham	98
14	Stanworth	100
15	Knowle Heights	106
16	Stronstrey Bank	110
17	Healey Nab	118
18	Anglezarke	122
	▶ Lester Mill	125
19	Cadshaw	128
20	Roundbarn	138
21	Lower Montcliffe	142
22	Brownstones	146
23	The Wiltons	160
	▶ Wilton 1	162
	▶ Wilton 2	177
	▶ Wilton 3	182
	▶ Wilton 4	188
24	Egerton	190
25	Ousel's Nest	194
26	Jumbles	196
27	Parbold	200

EAST LANCS MOORS

Chapter		Page
28	Troy	204
29	Holcombe Moor	210
30	Harcles Hill	216
31	Pinfold	220
32	Ashworth Moor	222
33	Deeply Vale	228
34	Birtle	230
35	Lee	232
36	Orchan Stones	238
37	Lobb Mill	240
38	Holder Stones	244
39	The Hammerhead	248
40	Stony Edge	250
41	Dove Lowe	262
42	Sladen Roof	266
43	Cow's Mouth	268
	▶ Wicken Lowe	276
44	Higher Chelburn	278
45	White House Quarry	284
46	Blackstone Edge	286
47	Withens Buckstones	314

This page: Project - Reef Knoll p61
Front Cover: Magic Beans, 7C - Troy p209
Back Cover: Private Press, 7B+ - Thorn Crag p36

Peter Würth enjoying a day of Porth Ysgo classics such as Jawbreaker (V5).
Photograph: Ray Wood

CUSHION THE FALL
Soft, strong and gentle - a pad you can fall back on

Highball

The hinged style Highball is an extremely popular pad with a great landing area, weighing in at a mere 5.4kgs, making it easy to carry between boulders and fit into car boots.

The extra thickness pad is also reassuring if you're venturing onto higher problems - this is definitely the pad to land on.

Like all of our bouldering pads, the Highball is very tough and durable. It has Ballistic Cordura on the base, 1000d Cordura on the top and Plastel on the closure flaps. The heart of the mat is a thick layer of open cell foam sandwiched between two high density foam layers which give a good even distribution, even when falling on uneven or rocky ground.

FEATURES

› A hinged style bouldering pad
› 3 layers of top quality dual density foam
› Extremely tough and durable
› Removable rucksack/shoulder strap
› Starter carpet for cleaning rock shoes
› Lowe Alpine Load Locker buckles
› Rubber moulded carrying handles
› Rounded corners to increase durability
› Extra straps for carrying bag, shoes, etc.

WWW.DMMWALES.COM

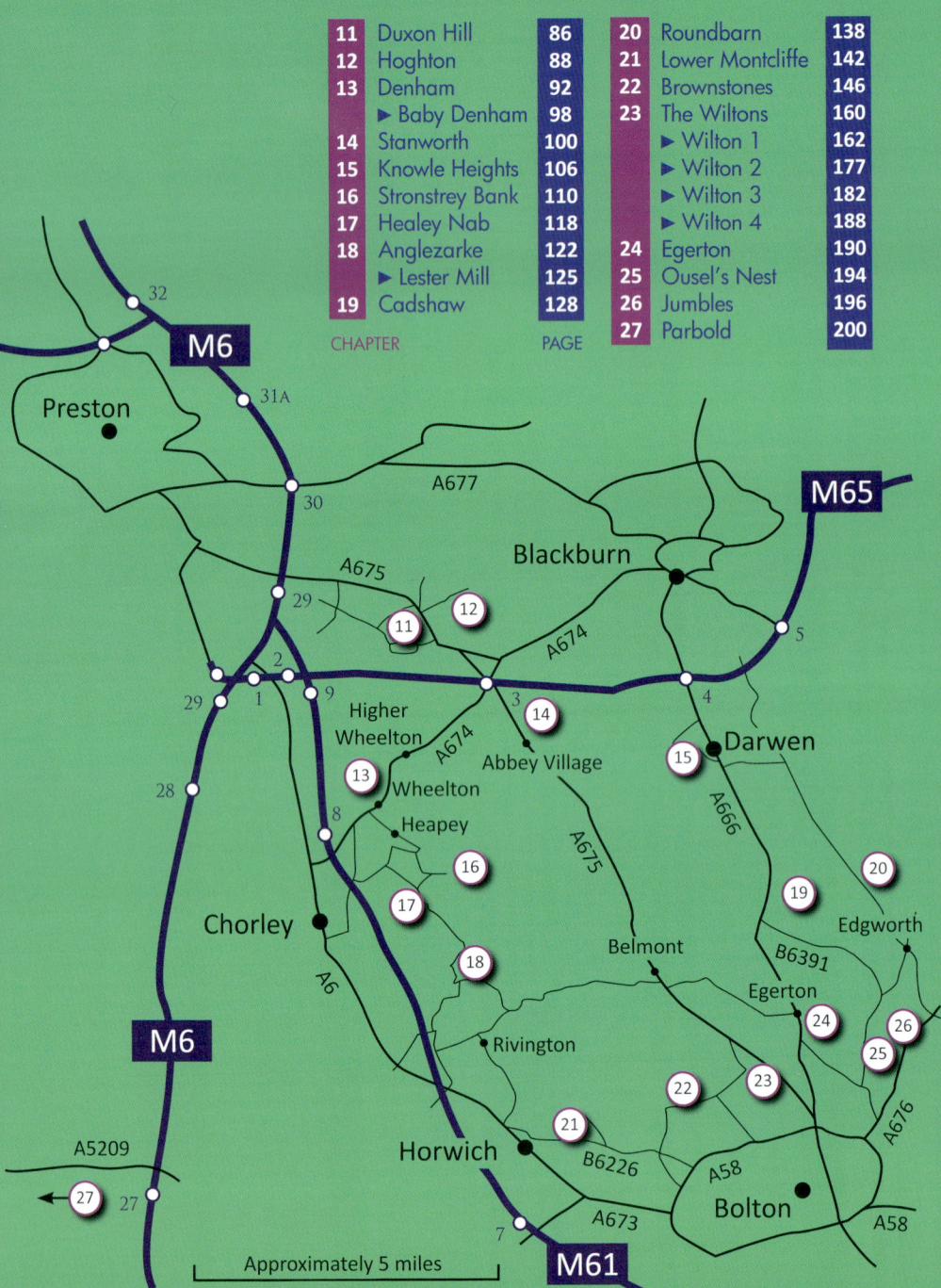

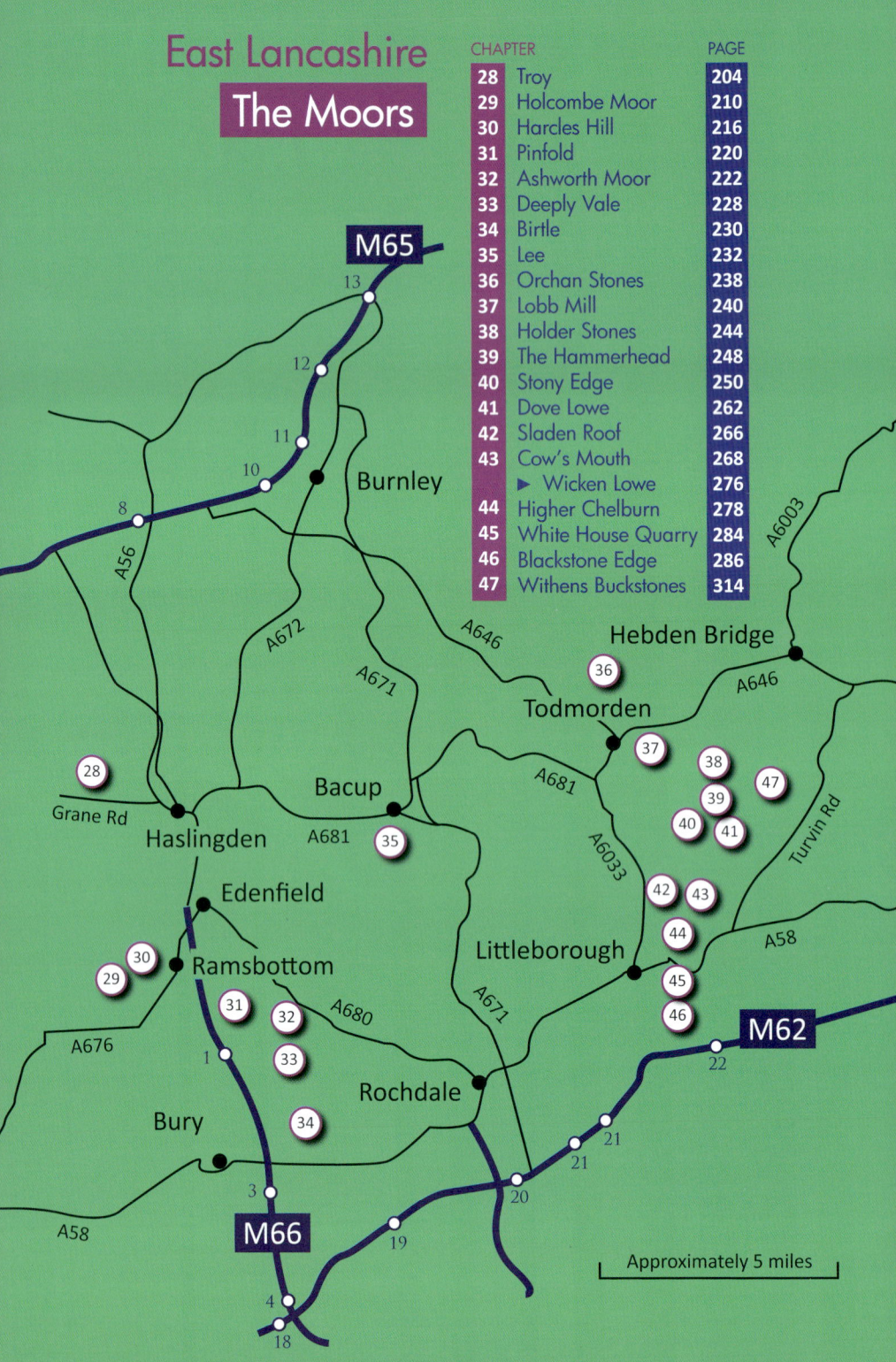

FOREWORD

This is the first book dedicated to Lancashire bouldering. To many people, its existence may come as a surprise. Once upon a time, everybody knew there was no bouldering in Lancashire. In a large county with so much rock and so many climbers, this always seemed like a strange and unfortunate situation. But things have changed. The boulderers have been exploring.

We've scoured the moors for the rocks that the trad climbers ignored. We've developed the quarries that the trad climbers neglected. And the result of all this zeal is quite amazing. Enough bouldering to fill up a book.

Even if you know Brownstones, Longridge and Thorn Crag inside out, there is a whole lot more on offer. There are moorland venues that have never been documented before - problems and locations that rival anything in Peakshire or Yorkland. And for the quarry afficionados, this book brings together all those secretive spots that you've heard muttered about in darkly lit pubs.

Lancashire is large and its gems are varied. I've climbed surrounded by dancing cottongrass. I've climbed above a cool summer lake. I've climbed on a moorland beach, in a hilltop wood, in a moonlit quarry, on a snowy fell. This book will take you to these places.

I hope you enjoy them as much as I do.

Robin Müller
Bolton, May 2014

STOCKISTS:
betaclimbing.com

IMPORTANT THINGS TO READ

Safety Disclaimer
Climbing is a dangerous sport. The environment in which we play has many potential hazards. Please be careful. The information in this book is the author's best guess, but do not rely upon it to always be correct. Make your own judgement about the safety of any activity you undertake. The author cannot accept responsibility for any injury.

Access
Not all climbing is on public land. Many landowners allow climbing, but access priviliges are subject to change. Check the BMC RAD (Regional Access Database) for the latest info on any crag. www.bmc.co.uk/rad

This guide does not give you the right to climb at any venue. If you are approached by a landowner, be courteous and if asked to leave, do so politely.

We are lucky to have free and unchallenged access to many unique climbing venues. Try to behave responsibly wherever you are climbing, because bad behaviour can ruin access for everyone.

Dogs
Some areas are fine for climbers but not for dogs. Dogs are not allowed at any of the crags on the Bowland Fells.

Smash Patrol, 6C - Stony Edge p252

WHERE TO GO FIRST

There's a lot of bouldering in this guidebook. Some of it is amazing and well worth travelling to (see **Local Info** for places to stay). Other areas are better suited to a short session if you live nearby. Here's an overview of the different experiences on offer...

Bowland Magic
The vast expanse of Bowland is a great setting for wild grit bouldering. Thorn Crag has classics at all grades and The Bull Stones has tons of mileage on easy problems, plus a small number of fantastic low 7's.

The Mysterious East
If you've been to Widdop, Bridestones and Scout Hut, you've already been nearby, but you've missed the best! Blackstone Edge, Stony Edge, Dove Lowe and Cow's Mouth are the main crags to check out. If you love gritstone, you will love these.

The Quarry Quest
The quarries are for locals only. Keep out unless you want to get spanked! Some of the county's best problems lurk in the quarries, but you are probably better off sticking to natural grit. It's easier.

Hardcore Hit
Craig Y Longridge is the place to visit if you like steepness. Most of the biggest numbers live here. There's also Stanworth, with two steep walls and an 8B slab. In addtion, this guidebook describes projects all over the county. Check **lancashirebouldering.com** to see which ones have been done since the book's release.

GRADES

There are a few things you should know about grades...

Font Grades
Font grades are used in this guide for most problems. They are the most popular bouldering grade in Europe (V grades are used in America) and originated in the bouldering heaven of Fontainebleau, which is almost as good as Lancashire.

Traverses
For long traverses where stamina is the main difficulty, this guidebook uses French sport grades. These don't have capital letters. For instance, a 7a traverse is very different to a 7A boulder problem - it will have easier moves but lots more of them.

British Technical Grades
British technical grades (the two digits in the second half of route grades, like in HVS 5a or E2 5c) were derived from Fontainbleau grades, but had a somewhat stunted development and became very vague above 6a, which is why boulderers don't use them. You can use the grade table to convert if you are new to Font Grades.

Accuracy
Decades of collective cogitating has been devoted to the consideration of the grades contained within these pages. Even so, it's likely that a small percent of them will be wrong. It's also likely that small percent will include the problem you are trying. If you feel defeated or cheated by this guidebook's appraisal of difficulty, it may be best to heed that time-worn adage: *the best climber is the one having the moist bun.*

Font Grades	V Grades	British Tech Grades
3		
3+		4a
4	V0-	4b
4+	V0	4c
5	V1	5a
5+		5b
6A	V2	5c
6A+	V3	6a
6B	V4	
6B+		
6C	V5	6b
6C+		
7A	V6	
7A+	V7	6c
7B	V8	
7B+		
7C	V9	7a
7C+	V10	
8A	V11	
8A+	V12	7b
8B	V13	
8B+	V14	
8C	V15	

Big Wind, 6A - Holder Stones p246

HOW TO USE THE BOOK

Stars
Throughout the guide, stars have been sprinkled on the problems which the author thinks are the best. The best moves, the best lines, the best rock, or maybe just the best fun. They are there to guide you to the most enjoyable problems at each crag, but of course you will probably find some no star problems that you think are brilliant and some two stars problems that make you very very angry. There are two star ratings:

★   This is a very good problem.
★★ This is a super good problem.

Sitstarts
If a problem is meant to be done from sitting, the word SIT precedes the grade. Sometimes a grade is given for both the standing start and the sitting start, as with this example:

1 Problem Name 6B SIT **6B+**

Sometimes there are also low starts, where the grade is preceded by the word LOW. Remember, to do a sitstart properly, your bum should be the last thing that leaves the ground. If no special start is specified, it's a standing start, using whatever you can reach.

LH And RH
One way that bouldering has evolved to differ from route climbing is that many problems now have specified starting holds. These are often described by indicating which hand should start on which hold. To save space, "left hand" and "right hand" have been abbreviated in this guidebook:

LH   Left Hand
RH   Right Hand

If you get your left and right mixed up, I'm sorry, there's no help for you.

MAP KEY

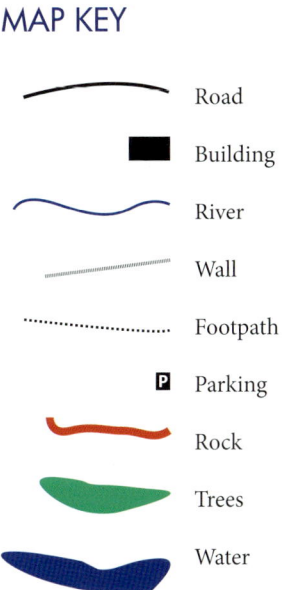

Finding A Crag
Find the chapter and page number of a crag in the contents page. If you have no idea where it is, look at the area overview maps, where the chapter numbers correspond to the crag numbers on the map.

Once you have a rough idea where you are going, turn to the appropriate chapter where approach directions and a more focussed map will get you to the rocks.

Finding A Problem
There's an index at the back, but you'll save time in the long run if you memorise the page number of every problem.

LOCAL INFORMATION

WEB STUFF

There is a lot of useful information on the internet. Because web sources are likely to change and sometimes eerily disappear, I'm not printing them here. Instead, go to lancashirebouldering.com to see links to all manner of useful things, such as...

- Video beta for problems
- BMC access details
- New problems
- Extra topos
- Web Cams
- Blogs

ACCOMMODATION

If you are travelling for a weekend hit, you will probably aim for Bowland or East Lancashire. The establishments listed below are near to climbing in those areas.

East Lancashire Moors

Stormer Hill Self Catering Apartment And Tea Garden
Bar House, Halifax Road, Littleborough, Lancashire, OL15 0LG
07872 112086

Fielden Farm
Blackstone Edge Road, Littleborough, Lancashire, OL15 0JN
01706 373760

Hollingworth Lake Caravan Camping Park
Roundhouse Farm, Hollingworth Lake, Littleborough, Gtr Manchester, OL15 0AT
01706 378661

Bowland near Thorn Crag

Greenbank Farmhouse B&B
Abbeystead, Lancaster, LA2 9BA
01524 792063

Bowland near The Bull Stones

YHA Hostel
King's House, Slaidburn, Clitheroe, Lancashire, BB7 3ER
0845 371 9343

Hark To Bounty Inn
Townend, Slaidburn, Clitheroe, Lancashire, BB7 3EP
01200 446246

Hydes Farm
Newton-in-Bowland, Clitheroe, BB7 3DY
01200 446353

PUBS

Lancashire isn't short of drinking holes. Here's a selection of the best.

Bowland
Pendle Inn - Barley.
Decent climber-friendly pub.

Blackburn and Burnley area
The Admiral Lord Rodney - Waterside Colne.
Good ales, food and regular bands.
The Royal Arms - Tockholes.
Welcomes dogs, climbers and walkers. Open fire, food and real ales.

Bolton area
Wilton Arms - Next to Wilton 1.
Upmarket but welcomes climbers. Great food, three real ales.
Black Dog - Belmont.
Traditional home of Lancashire Quarrymen and scene of the infamous Black Pudding Dinners.
Strawberry Duck - Turton.
Excellent food and ale.

Bury and Rossendale area
First Chop - Ramsbottom.
Excellent real ale, loyalty card and fine tapas.
Irwell Works Brewery - Ramsbottom.
Superb microbrewery in an old engineering works.
Lord Raglan - Nangreaves, near Pinfold.
Well established brewer with classics like Nanny Flyer, plus open fire.
Robin Hood - Helmshore, Near Troy.
Climber-friendly.
Shoulder Of Mutton - Holcombe.
Good food. Welcomes muddy people and dogs.

Rochdale and Littleborough area
White House - Littleborough.
Good for Blackstone Edge and nearby crags. A warm welcome for cold climbers.
The Baum - Rochdale.
Won CAMRA pub of the year and is excellent.

Todmorden and Hebden area
Cross Inn - Heptonstall.
Open fire, real ale and a good line in tea and biscuits.
Pack Horse Inn - near Widdop.
Open fires, great ale and food. You can even get a pheasant pie to take home or a brace of birds in the shooting season!

MOUNTAIN TRAINING COURSE PROVIDER

CWA Climbing Wall Award
SPA Singe Pitch Award
ML Mountain Leader Award
HMLA Hill & Moorland Leader Award
LLA Lowland Leader Award
Hill and Mountain Skills Scheme
National Navigation Award Scheme

 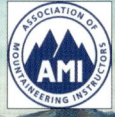

Stuart Igoe MIA WML
Alternative Adventure & Outdoor Activities Service
New Meadows Gap Cottage, Cranberry Lane,
Cranberry Fold, Darwen, Lancashire. BB3 2HZ

Tel 01254 704898 - altadv.co.uk - stuart-igoe.co.uk

WORLD CLASS INDOOR BOULDERING

YORKSHIRE'S ULTIMATE RANGE OF ROCK SHOES

AT THE DEPOT SHOP

The Depot Climbing Centre Leeds
173 Richardshaw Lane,
Pudsey, Leeds LS28 6AA

 0113 345 9295

 www.theclimbingdepot.co.uk
info@theclimbingdepot.co.uk

CLIMBING WALLS

CLASSIFIED LISTINGS. Where to get strong, where to hide from the rain, where to meet people. There are also several well appointed private training venues around the county, but if I told you where they are, I'd have to kill you.

North Lancashire
Lancaster University Climbing Wall
Lancaster University Sports Centre, Bailrigg,
Lancaster, LA1 4YW
01524 510 600

Lakeland Climbing Centre
Unit 27, Lake District Business Park, Mintbridge Rd, Kendal, LA9 6NH
01539 721 766 - www.kendalwall.co.uk

South Lancashire
Boulder UK
10a Heaton Street, Blackburn, BB2 2EF
01254 693056 - www.boulderuk.wix.com

West View Climbing and Leisure Centre
Ribbleton Lane, Preston, PR1 5EP
01772 796788

East Lancashire
Climb Rochdale
11-31 School Lane, Rochdale, OL16 1QP
01706 524 450 - www.climbrochdale.com

Greater Manchester
Awesome Walls Climbing Centre Stockport
The Engine House, Pear Mill, Stockport Rd West,
Lower Bredbury, Stockport, SK6 2BP
0161 494 9949 - www.awesomewalls.co.uk

Manchester Climbing Centre
St.Benedict's Church, Bennett Street, Ardwick,
Manchester, M12 5ND
0161 230 7006 - www.manchesterclimbingcentre.com

Vertical Chill Indoor Ice Wall
130 Deansgate Street, Manchester, M3 2QS
0161 837 6140 - www.vertical-chill.com

West Yorkshire
The Barn Climbing & Activity Centre
Unit 2, Ryshworth Works, Keighley Road,
Crossflatts, Bingley, BD16 2ER
01274 512990 - www.barnclimbingwall.co.uk

The Climbing Depot
173 Richardshaw Lane, Pudsey, Leeds, LS28 6AA
0113 345 9295 - www.theclimbingdepot.com

Merseyside
Awesome Walls Climbing Centre Liverpool
St Albans Church, Athol St, off Gt Howard St,
Liverpool, L5 9XT
0151 298 2422 - www.awesomewalls.co.uk

The Climbing Hangar
6 Birchall St, Liverpool, L208PD
01513 450587 - www.theclimbinghangar.com

BOWLAND

Within the sky above, one thought
Replies to you, O barren moors!
Between, I stand, a creature taught
To stand between two silent floors.

The Barren Moors - William Ellery Channing, 1800s

Shorter For The Tall, 6C

1 Great Stone Of Fourstones

Legend has it that the Devil dropped this stone on his way to build the Devil's Bridge in Kirkby Lonsdale. Ever since, it has idled on this bleak moor, waiting for its true purpose to be revealed. Now at last, boulderers have discovered the fiendish delights of this remote rock. There is not a great quantity of climbing, but a couple of the problems are very nice, and the walk is short. Be warned: wellies and a tarp can be useful after wet weather,

APPROACH 30 sec
This isolated boulder is located 2 miles south of High Bentham, on Slaidburn Road. It is visible from the car as you approach. Park in the obvious bay and follow the short path to the boulder.

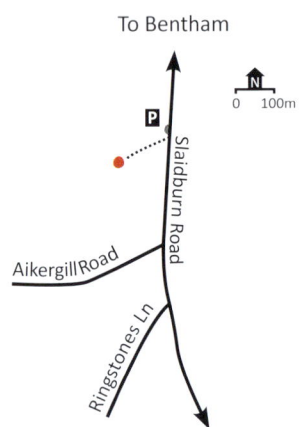

GREAT STONE OF FOURSTONES

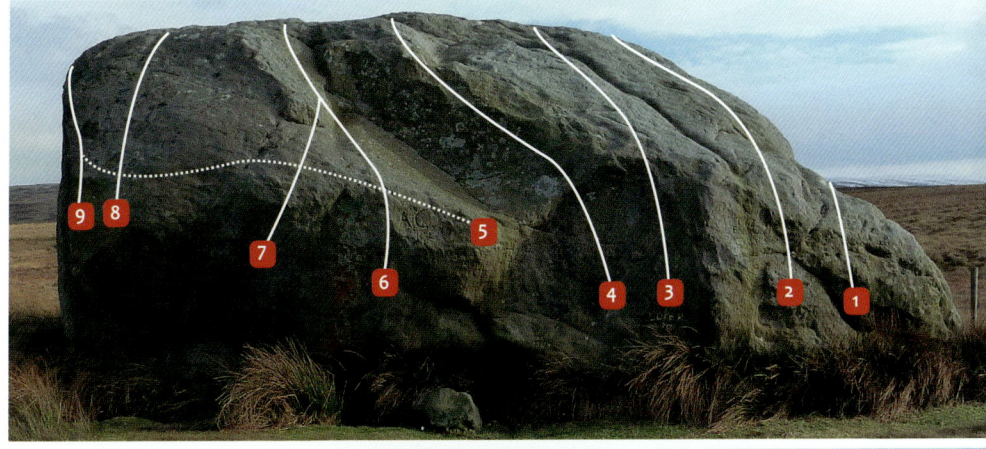

1 Surmountain 3

2 Old Music 4

3 Piper's Tune 5

4 Up Slide 3
The obvious groove.

5 Project
From big holds, traverse left to finish up the arete.

6 In Your Face 6B
Rockover and up.

7 Off Your Face 6A
Rock into the groove.

8 Treading The Eel ★ 7B
A fierce pull onto the slab. Stay off aretes.
Robin Müller 2014

9 Bleak House ★ 7A
The arete. Gaining the arete holds from sidepulls on the face to the left is **Road House ★ 7A+**.
Robin Müller 2013

10 Bogette ★ 6A
The arete on its right. Just right is **Bog Chic ★ 6B**.

11 Pretend Climbing 2
Big chipped footholds lead upwards. Look, no hands!

12 Clever Devil 2
You could use this as a descent after you've conquered the stairs.

13 Don't Stair 6A
From as low as you feel like, layback up to the break, traverse it left and top out at the end.

14 Shorter For The Tall 6C
Start crouching (or sitting if your arms are long enough) and crimp past small chipped holds.

The Drinking Man's Crumpet, 6B p31

Windy Clough 2

Although less extensive than the nearby Thorn Crag, Windy Clough's shorter walk-in and quick-drying aspect make it a popular local spot. When combined with the Far Side circuit, there's enough here for a pleasant day out. Expect easy highballs and hard lowballs - if that combination appeals, you might just have fun. Dogs are not allowed.

APPROACH   20 min

Leave the M6 at Junction 33. Take the first exit at the roundabout, then turn left immediately. Turn right at the T-junction, onto Chipping Road. Turn left at the crossroads, towards Quernmore. Continue for 3.5 miles. After passing through Quernmore Village Crossroads (signposted) the road bends left. After the bend, turn right onto Rigg Lane and continue for half a mile to a car park on the right.

From the parking, follow the obvious track uphill. Stay right when the path forks - continue along the boardwalk and through the woods. When you reach the ladder stiles, turn left uphill to the Main Sector. For the Far Side areas, cross the stile and continue on the right side of the stone wall towards the far hillside. When the wall turns right, follow it to a gate and turn left across the moorland to your chosen area. The Rigg Lane blocks are also marked on this map, but don't expect much if you decide to seek them out.

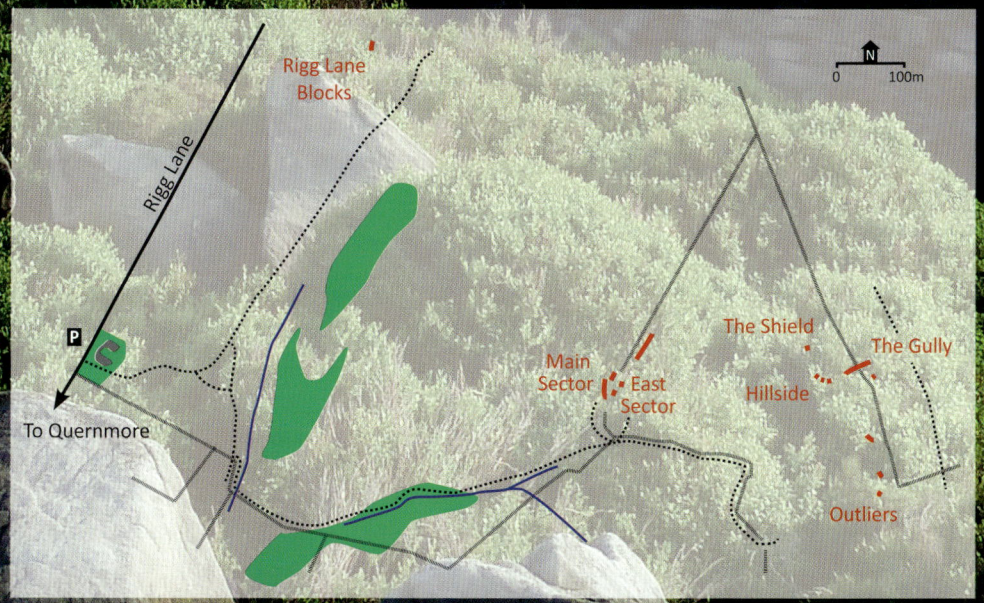

26 WINDY CLOUGH

Main Sector

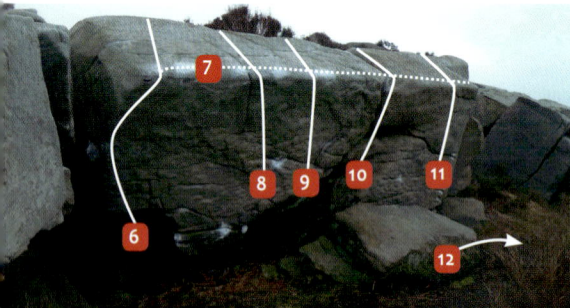

The Main Sector provides the meat of the crag's bouldering. It is on the left side of the ridge as you approach.

1 Sandy Crack 4+
The crack with the awful landing.

2 Windy Groove 6A+ sit 6C
A technical outing. Top out using the crack.

3 Two Mat Attack ★★ 6A+ sit 6C
Start sitting on the flat rock, then make a long reach from slots to the top. Stay off the flake to the right.

4 Windy Flake 4+ sit 5
Go straight up, via the flake.

5 Windy Traverse sit 6A+
From the obvious jug, head left across the face to top out at its end.

6 Live Evil ★ sit 6C+
From a slot below the roof, climb the arete to a slopey top.

7 Mr Owl Ate My Metal Worm ★ sit 7A
Start up *Live Evil* and traverse the lip to the end. No footblock.
Greg Chapman 2010

8 Central Wall sit 6B
Match the obvious crimp to start, then gain the lip and pull over.

9 Welcome To The Palindrome ★ sit 6C
Start from sitting on the ground (not the rock) and reach the lip via edges. Stay off the big crack.

10 The Gaping Crack sit 5+
Sitstart from a rock and feed yourself to the crack.

11 End Of The Palindrome sit 4
Sitstart from the rock and climb the wall right of the crack.

12 Old Man's Shuffle 6B
Follow the lip from left to right.

13 No Country For Old Men ★ SIT 7B+
Start with feet on the back ledge. Take a smaller grade if you can reach the top without moving your feet.
Greg Chapman 2010

14 Good Ol' Days SIT 7B
Link 13 into 15.

15 Country For Old Men 4 SIT 7A
Sitstart from a choice of poor holds and make a tough move.
Greg Chapman 2010

16 To Be Blunt SIT 6B
Sitstart from the ground, not the rocks.

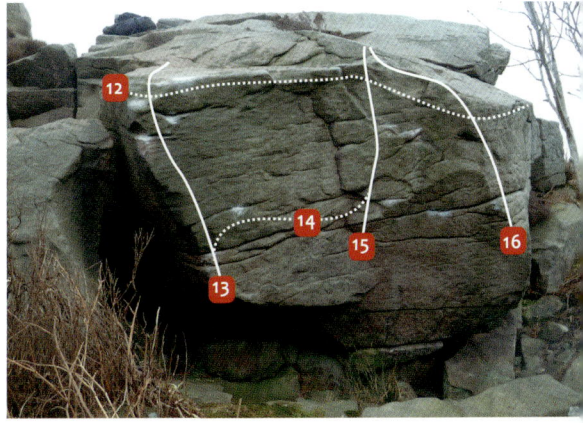

The East Sector has a little more to do. The first boulder is directly behind the Two Mat Attack boulder.

17 Cow Traverse 4+
Follow the top of the block into the finish of *Bully for Bugs*.

18 Bodacious SIT 7A
Start RH crimp and LH little sidepull. Now throw for the top.
Greg Chapman 2010

19 Bully For Bugs SIT 6C
Using sidepulls, climb the wall left of the arete.

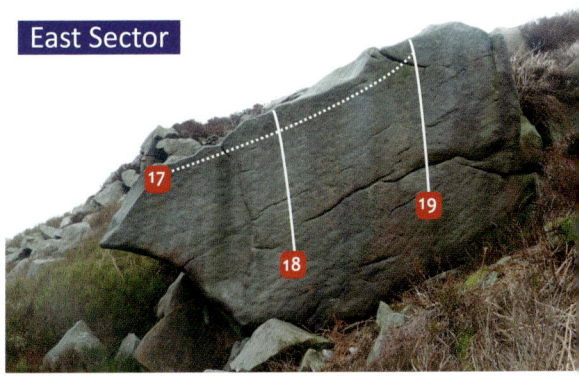

Nearby is a plate-like boulder with a large crack on one side. This has several grade **3** and **4** problems, with one exception being the wall left of the crack on the downhill face, which is a highball **5**. The climbing on this boulder is good but some of the landings are worrying.

Further along this ridge are several higher walls, which lend themselves more to soloing than bouldering.

WINDY CLOUGH

The Far Side Area is 10 minutes from the stile. The Shield is highball, Hill Top mostly lowball, and the Gully has a bit of everything.

1 Sword Song ★★ SIT **7A**
The centre of the side wall, to a big finish.
Greg Chapman 2013

2 Saxon ★ **5+**

3 Hoplite ★ **5+**
Exposed arete laybacking.

4 Ahem SIT **7B**
Sitstart from RH in the higher of two seams, LH on a choice of sidepulls. Starting RH on the face crimp is **6C**. Don't trek up here just for this.

5 Grabatron SIT **6C**
Start with a hand on each arete. Bump to the jug and up you go.

6 I Need Your Hands SIT **5+**
Climb the crack without using the block to the right.

7 Unnatural Selection SIT **5+**
The arete on its left.

8 Larsony SIT **6B**
The wall and arete, starting at the break.

9 The Curse Of Madame "C"rack SIT **4+**
Straight up the crack.

10 Wiener Dog Art SIT **5+**
Start from hands in the break.

11 The Far Side Observer SIT **4**
Sitstart and up the breaks.

12 Last Chapter And Worse SIT **5+**
Climb the steep side of the arete.

13 You're Sick Jessy! Sick, Sick, Sick! SIT **6A**
Sitstart, gain the break and wriggle up.

14 Cows Don't Have Opposable Thumbs SIT **6A**
The overlap on its right.

15 Crack Kids SIT **6A**
Pull up the crack and follow the ledge to its end.

16 Butch Pratchety And The Sun Dance Squid SIT **6C**
The arete from as low as you can sitstart.

17 There's A Hair In My Dirt SIT **5**
The right-most rippled wall, on its right. On its left is easier.

Midvale School For The gifted, 5+ p30

WINDY CLOUGH

The Gully boulders line the left side of the gully, 50m further on from the Hill Top boulders.

1 One Move Wonder SIT **6A**
20m to the left, sitstart a ledge to gain a pocket.

2 Crimp and Crack SIT **6B**
Go left and up. Poor landing.

3 Armscliff Wall ★ SIT **6B+**
From the big vertical slot, work up to the ledge then shuffle right to an entertaining finish up the groove. At least two mats and a spotter needed!

4 Armajesty ★ SIT **7A**
From the same slot, make a big span to the crack, then finish up the groove. Bring mats and spotter.

5 Gary's Arete ★ SIT **6A**
A great little arete.

6 Gary's Crack SIT **5+**
Sitstart the crack.

7 Beyond the Far Side 5
The arete.

8 Worthwhile SIT **4+**

9 Almost Famous SIT **6B+**
The centre of the wall, eliminating bigger holds near the crack.

10 Friction Slab 5

11 End Arete SIT **4+**
A little harder on its right.

12 Hound Of The Far Side 6A
Very highball climbing to scary a bulge.

13 August 1983 5+
The slab on the side of the big fin.

14 Project
Sitstart the fin. The landing is non-existent.

15 Totem Vole ★ SIT **6C**
The steep little pillar to an awkward top-out.

16 The Chickens Are Restless ★ **5**
A fine highball arete. HVS.

17 Midvale School For The Gifted ★★ **5+**
Splendid airy climbing up the centre.

18 The First Edition
Hardcover Box Set Weighs 8.8kg 5+
The wall on its right, with big reaches.

Gully

The last Gully boulder is on the opposite side of the gully. It's just a short scramble uphill, about 10m left of the dry-stone wall.

19 The Drinking Man's Crumpet 5 SIT **6B**
The end arete is short but good.

20 Dabbling In Laziness 4 SIT **5+**
Good holds lead up the wall just right of the arete.

21 The Fastest Slowcoach In The West 4
Up the middle.

22 Something And Nothing 3 SIT **5+**
You can just about sitstart the right arete.

The furthest of the Outliers can be reached from the path that crosses the end of the Gully. Turn right onto this and continue to a stile. Cross the stile and circle rightwards. This boulder is visible from the approach to the Far Side areas.

1 Project
Sitstart the wall, after you've moved the rock (a two-man job).

50m further back along the hillside towards the Gully area, just past another small gully, is a collection of mostly rubbish boulders holding up a roof with a bad landing.

2 Project
Sitstart from underclings.

View from the Outliers - more rock that way...

3 Thorn Crag

Bite-Size, 3 *p42*

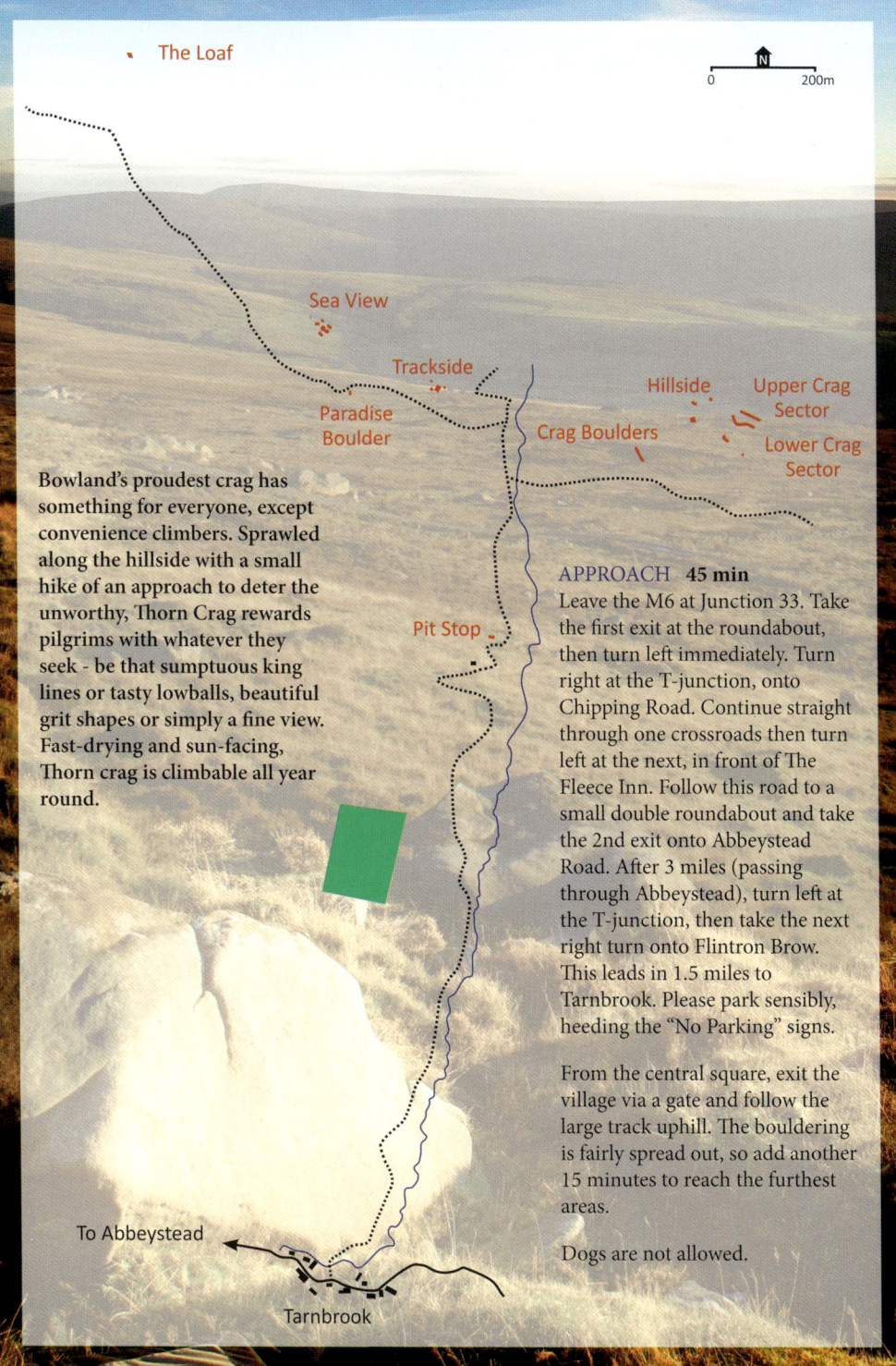

Bowland's proudest crag has something for everyone, except convenience climbers. Sprawled along the hillside with a small hike of an approach to deter the unworthy, Thorn Crag rewards pilgrims with whatever they seek - be that sumptuous king lines or tasty lowballs, beautiful grit shapes or simply a fine view. Fast-drying and sun-facing, Thorn crag is climbable all year round.

APPROACH 45 min
Leave the M6 at Junction 33. Take the first exit at the roundabout, then turn left immediately. Turn right at the T-junction, onto Chipping Road. Continue straight through one crossroads then turn left at the next, in front of The Fleece Inn. Follow this road to a small double roundabout and take the 2nd exit onto Abbeystead Road. After 3 miles (passing through Abbeystead), turn left at the T-junction, then take the next right turn onto Flintron Brow. This leads in 1.5 miles to Tarnbrook. Please park sensibly, heeding the "No Parking" signs.

From the central square, exit the village via a gate and follow the large track uphill. The bouldering is fairly spread out, so add another 15 minutes to reach the furthest areas.

Dogs are not allowed.

THORN CRAG

Pit Stop Boulder

Crag Boulders

The Pit Stop Boulder is the first decent rock reached en route to everywhere else.

1 Pit Bull SIT **4**
Start down on the left and pull up the arete.

2 Pit Fight SIT **7A+**
From the back of the roof, gain the lip and slap the break.
Greg Chapman 2007

3 Pit Stop 5
Traverse left along the break.

For the Crag Boulders, turn right to cross the bridge and head east. They are the obvious boulders on your left, shortly before reaching the crag itself.

4 The Slab 3

5 Dimple Dance 6B
On the back of the slab boulder is an obvious mantel problem.

6 Perfect 6B+
Traverse the Dimple Dance wall from left to right.

7 Jubilee Tower ★ 5
First hard, then exhilarating.

8 Wiggling Crack ★ 5+
Another airy jaunt.

9 Rising Smoke 4+
Can you float up the chimney?

10 Perving Arete ★★ 5
Start up the arete on its left, then rock round and finish on its right.

11 Slab Run 3
Race up the middle of the slab.

12 Score ★ 3
It's another win for gritstone.

13 Neil's Thorny Arete 5 SIT **6A**
The arete on its right.

14 Fire Wall ★ 7B+
Start RH pocket, then fire up and left.
Mick Adams 2005

15 Burnt Heather ★ 6B
The not-so-easy groove.

16 The Crack 4+
Stay away.

17 Grit Nose SIT **6A+**
From the shelf, climb the arete on its left.

18 Easy Karma 5+
Karmic laybacking.

19 The Plumbers Link SIT **7C**
Sitstart and traverse right to finish up *Fix My Sink*.
Mick Adams 2005

20 And For My Next Trick ★ 6B SIT **7A**
The central line, with powerful moves low down.
Greg Chapman 2001

21 Fix My Sink ★ SIT **7B**
Gain the incuts and spring for the arete. Follow this to the top.
Greg Chapman 2003

And For My Next Trick, 7A p34

THORN CRAG

Above the Crag Boulders is a good Hillside circuit, which leads nicely to the Crag Sector.

1 Cubic Zirconium ★ **6A**
The arete on its right.

2a Private Press ★★ **7B+**
Mount the slab just right of centre, then step left to attack the central line.
Tom Newberry 2011

2b Break Out Room 7A
Traverse left to finish up *Cubic Zirconium*.
Tom Newberry 2011

3 Here I Am Again ★ **6B**
Magic onto the slab, then teeter upwards via the crack.

4 Diamond Crack SIT **5**
The crack is taken on its left.

5 Strict Wall SIT **5**
The wall between the crack and slopers to the right.

6 Diamond Ribbing 3

7 Project
Super slabby. Is it possible?

8 Ouzel Thorn ★ **6B**
Highball and worth seeking out.

The boulder just right of Ouzel Slab isn't great, but feel free to climb it if you want.

9 This Was Left SIT **4+**
Sitstart left of the middle.

10 West Face, Best Face SIT **6B**
Pull to the arete, then follow this to the top. A harder start using RH arete and LH underneath is **6C+**.

11 Scrittly Slab 5

12 Monster Minds SIT **7A+**
From a clamping sitstart, thug upwards and swing round the arete to finish on its right.
Greg Chapman 2011

THORN CRAG 37

Crag Sector

The Upper Crag Sector hosts some classics, from easy to super hard. The first few problems are on neighbouring blocks on the left of the crag.

1 Mackerel Arete SIT **6A+**
Use holds on both sides of the arete, but not the block out left.

2 Sandy Crack 4

3 Crumple Stiltskin ★ SIT **6B**
Sidepulls lead out of the pit to a big move for better holds.

4 Cracker SIT **5**
Follow the diagonal crack.

The next problems are a little further right (see photo overleaf).

5 Moment of Clarity ★★ **8B**
The astounding arete is another Gaskins special. The hard bit is in the first half though the top is pretty high. You'd probably want a sea of mats (or some gear) to give this a serious go. The FA was practised on a top rope.
John Gaskins 2006

6 Return Of The Fly ★★ **7C+**
The best wall problem on grit? Top out via the gully.
John Gaskins 2003

7 The Bug SIT **3+**
The arete on its right.

8 The Bug Right SIT **6C+**
From sitting to the right, make a tough move to gain and finish up the arete.

38 THORN CRAG

Upper Crag Sector - Right

9 Warm Up Lip 5
Take care on the footholds, which are handholds for the other problems.

10 Fizzix Of Pop SIT **7A+**
Start LH mono, RH slanting edge. Hit the lip and follow this to the end.
Greg Chapman 2007

11 Vector ★ SIT **8A**
From poor crimps, vectorise.
Greg Chapman 2007

12 Patricky ★ SIT **7B**
The steep arete is a goodun.
Pat King

13 Blam The New Jam SIT **6B+**
Sitstart the arete from the slanting hold. Aim for a pocket and top out the niche.

14 Jazz Hands SIT **6A+**
An awkward start leads to the flake.

15 Diamond Ribbing SIT **6A**
The slim prow.

The last upper tier boulder is 50m further on.

16 Tong Po SIT **7A**
The central line. The rib to the left is a **6A** sitter.
Greg Chapman

The rest of the boulders in the Crag Sector are based around the lower tier. This starts with Banana Slab at the west end (see overview on previous page).

17 Bananamor 6C+
From sloper and slot, hit the top.

THORN CRAG 39

18 Banana Split SIT **6C+**
Climb left of the arete, starting from a pocket and sidepull. Finish leftwards.

19 Banana Boat 4

20 Look No Hands 3+
The crack. Use your hands if you like.

21 Lower Slab Direct ★ 4+
No crack, no arete. Brill.

22 Banana Land 3
The arete on its left.

23 Project
Sitstart the pinchy wall.

The Squirrel Blocks are 50m right of Banana Slab, looking uphill.

24 Galumphing Balderdash SIT **4**
Sitstart at the break.

25 Great Scot SIT **6A**
From the break, climb the arete on its left.

26 Project
This time, take the arete on its right.

27 Squirreling Dervishes ★ SIT **6C+**
Rising from a pit is an undercut arete. Climb this on its left.

28 The Man From Del Monte ★ SIT **7A+**
Tackle the centre of the prow, heading right to finish.
Greg Chapman 2006

The next boulders are slightly downhill.

29 The Short Side Of The Moon SIT **6B**
Pull on with the undercut and edge. Slap.

30 Bad Moon Rising ★★ SIT **7B+**
From underclings, beefy moves lead to a crux throw for the lunar hold.
Neil Kershaw 2003

31 Slice Of Life ★ SIT **7A+**
From the big flake, style up the face to a scary last move.
Neil Kershaw 2003

Jalapeno Arete, 6B p42

THORN CRAG   41

Trackside Boulders

1 Shield Bug 3+

2 Knights Of The Turntables ★ SIT **6C**
The left arete on its right.

3 Guns N' Ammo ★ SIT **6C+**
Climb into the right arete, with a hard last move.

4 Deadly Sins 3
The left arete of the slab.

5 Sins Sans Deadly Bits 3
The slab, no aretes.

6 Jacaranda 5
Start at the seperated block, then work up and over the protruding summit.

7 Emission is Purile 5
The rounded left arete.

8 Resistance Is Futile ★ **7A+** SIT **7C+**
From the sidepull flake, climb into the left arete then up. The sitter starts LH undercut, RH sidepull, and bum on the slabby boulder.
Greg Chapman 2002, SIT 2012

9 RIF Light 6A+
Start at the flake and rock onto the slab.

10 Elemental ★★ SIT **6C**
Follow the lip all the way to the end, then finish upwards.

11 2001 A Grit Odyssey ★ SIT **6C+**
From roof pockets, go for the lip then cruise to the top.

12 Gritasaurus 3
Wander up the dinosaur spine.

There are a few lines on the broken wall 20m to the right. The middle arete is 5+ from sitting and the wall to the left is 3+.

Paradise Boulder

150m further on, the Paradise Boulder is to the left of the track, just before the Sea View Boulders. Not as bad as it looks.

13 Red Rose Addict ★ SIT **6C+**
Journey along the lip to finish up the groove.

14 Snap, Crackle and Top SIT **5+**
Start from the damaged hold,

15 Visions of Paradise SIT **6B**
The arete on its left.

16 Paradise Found SIT **6B**
The groove.

THORN CRAG

Sea View Boulders

1 One Eye Willie SIT **6A**
Start from sloper and pocket.

2 The Goonie SIT **5**
The obvious runnels.

3 Snot Right 3
Scrape rightwards along the uphill lip.

4 Fresno SIT **6A**
The cheeky nose, taken on its right.

5 What? 5+
Rock onto the ledge, then reach for the top left point of the arete. Eliminate.

6 Really? SIT **3+**
From the lip, swing up arete. Really.

7 Apprentice Edge 3+
The left arete. Welcome, novice.

8 Bite-size 3
Smear upwards, left of middle.

9 Revision 3
More smearing, right of middle.

10 Beginner's Slab Award 3
Now the right arete. You've earned a badge. Affix it wherever you please.

11 Jalapeno Arete ★★ 6A SIT **6A+**
The fine arete on either side, with a sitstart on its right.

12 Yatsufusa 6A SIT **6B**
Slopey holds lead over the bulge. Finish rightwards via the flakes.

THORN CRAG 43

13 Endangered Species ★ SIT **8A+**
Sitstart in a depression and pull on using a poor dish and opposing nothing hold. Suck it up and lurch to a decent LH edge. Continue more easily and finish via the flakes.
John Gaskins 2003

14 Chilica SIT **5+**
The scary arete on its right.

15a Mothership Reconnection ★★ SIT **7A+**
The crag classic. Hug up the fat arete from a start on the low sidepulls. Finish on its left.
Greg Chapman 2002

15b Mothership Right Hand ★ SIT **7B**
Climb *Mothership* to the sloper below the top, then rock right via a poor sloper to gain a rail and finish up the groove.

16 Small Things 4+
The short slab.

17 Neil's Slab 4+
Climb the slab just right of the chockstones.

18 Flakey Back 3

19 Poblano ★ **5+** SIT **7A**
The subtle slab, staying left of the arete. The sitter is super thin.

20 Red Dusk 3
Climb the wall from a low start.

21 Serrano 3
Layback the huge flake.

22 Slender Days SIT **3**
Slight features lead up and left.

23 Chilli Billy 3+
Follow a thin seam up the slab.

24 Yule Jewel SIT **7B**
On a higher level, fight the ungenerous arete on its right. Possibly more duel than jewel.
Greg Chapman 2006

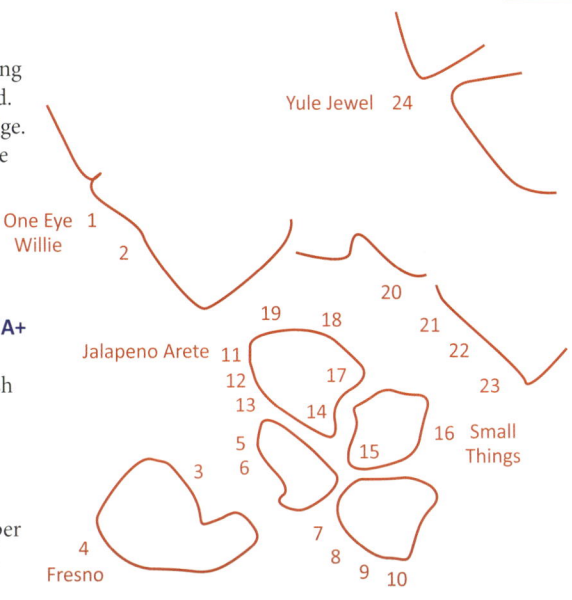

THORN CRAG

The next boulder is 5 minutes further down the path. It is easy to spot on the next ridge, about 100m off the track.

1 Positions Of Strength ★ SIT **7B**
Start at a sidepull and bust a move to gain a slot, then a slopey rail. Follow this leftwards to finish.
Greg Chapman 2009

2 Budmunk SIT **7A+**
Pull hard to get started, then mantel over the top.
Greg Chapman 2007

3 Outer Reach ★ SIT **8A**
Swing left to gain a line of slopers, then a positive undercut. Next comes the crux throw to a faraway dish, followed by a very fluffable finish.
Greg Chapman 2006

Ouzel Thorn, 6B

Mothership Reconnection, 7A+ p43

4 Wolfhole Crag

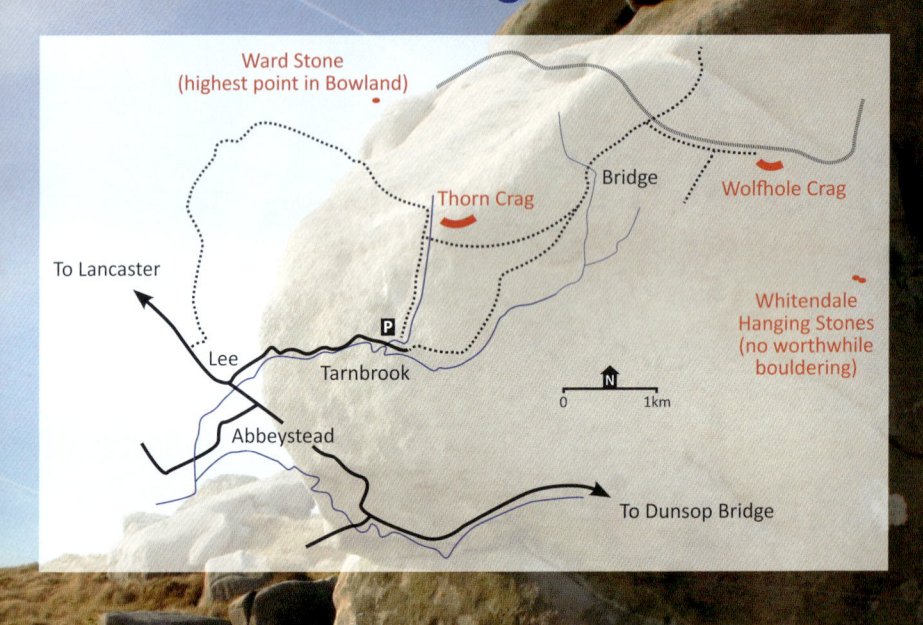

Ward Stone
(highest point in Bowland)

Thorn Crag

Bridge

Wolfhole Crag

To Lancaster

Lee

Tarnbrook

Abbeystead

Whitendale
Hanging Stones
(no worthwhile
bouldering)

0   1km

To Dunsop Bridge

Afterlife, 7B+

WOLFHOLE CRAG

Situated in the vast expanse of Bowland, few crags are lonelier than this. For those intrepid souls who embrace the challenge, the rewards are obvious: fine and testing moves in a wild location. Remember, mobile phone coverage may not be reliable and you are a long way from the road, so be extra careful. Bring sherpas if you have them.

APPROACH 1.5 hours
Park in Tarnbrook (see directions for Thorn Crag). Walk to the end of the hamlet and onto the large bridleway which leads uphill. Follow this for 3km to a fork in the path, ignoring the left turn shortly before. Take the left fork which leads steeply uphill, then drops down to a bridge. Cross the bridge and continue on the main path to the open gateway at the top of the hill. At this point, turn right off the bridleway and follow the path alongside the fence (which later becomes a wall) until the crag is reached after another 1km. Keep your eyes peeled for a white trig point by a fence and stile - the crag is just behind. No dogs are allowed.

200m before the main crag there are some boulders down to the right, which hold a few problems. The best problem is the obvious groove, **Freakeasy** SIT **7A+**. The slopey arete to its left is **Boss Drum 7A**.

1 Mind Storm ★ 7B+
Use a LH pinch to pull to the lip, then follow this rightwards to top out past the ledge.
Greg Chapman 2014

2 Lone Wolf ★★ SIT 8A
From sitting at a sloper on the left end of the wall, traverse right to finish up *Limbo*.
Greg Chapman 2013

3 Teen Wolf ★ 7B
Just right of the centre, dyno from head-height holds to the jug. Finish up and left.
Greg Chapman 2014

4 Limbo ★ 6B+ SIT 7B+
The prow on its left, with a sitstart from RH pinch, LH low hold. Gain a sloper at the lip, then move left and top out.
Greg Chapman 2013

5 Afterlife ★★ 7A+ SIT 7B+
Clamp up the prow, then head left along slopers to a good hold. Top out up and left.
Greg Chapman 2013

6 Afterlife Direct ★★ SIT 7C
Climb *Afterlife* to the lip, then move right to gain a crack and an easy but scrittly finish.
Greg Chapman 2013

7 Fifty Flyers ★ 5 SIT 6C+
Climb to the top via the crack. The sitter eliminates the black flake to the right.

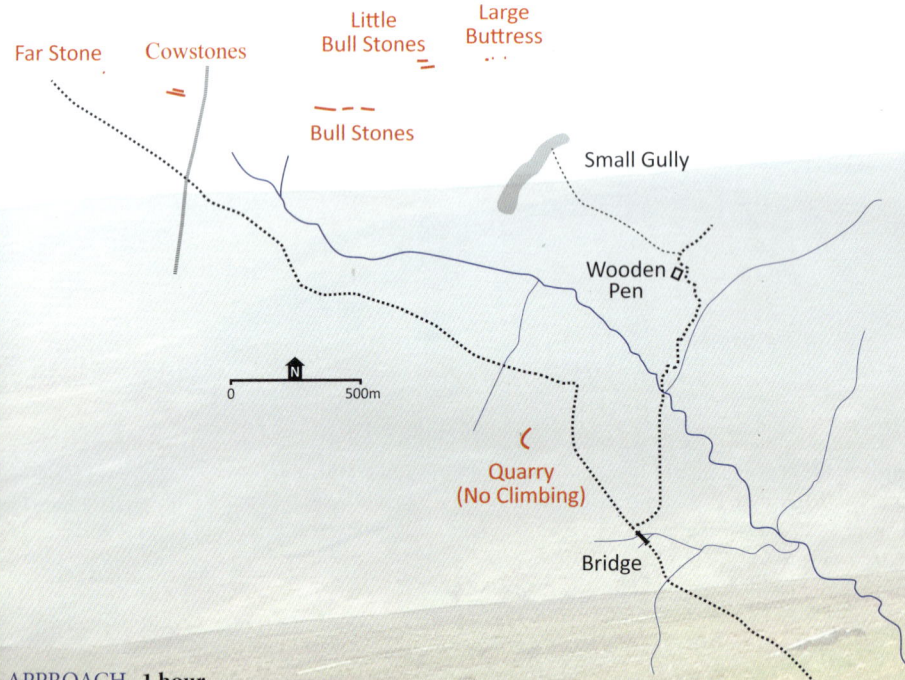

Far Stone   Cowstones   Little Bull Stones   Large Buttress

Bull Stones

Small Gully

Wooden Pen

N
0   500m

Quarry
(No Climbing)

Bridge

Woodhouse Lane

APPROACH 1 hour
From Slaidburn, follow the road between the Hark To Bounty Inn and the General Stores/Post Office building. After 1 mile, turn right down Woodhouse Lane (signposted to Mytions Farm Crafts). Follow this for 1.5 miles to parking on the left, shortly before the end of the the road. Be careful not to block the gate. Now choose one of two approaches, both of which can be reversed if you want to do the circuit.

Route 1
Take the rough road at the end of Woodhouse Lane, which leads after 4km to a gate in a fence. Continue through the gate, then turn uphill to either the Cowstones or the Far Stone a little fiurther on. The other areas can be reached from here by following the line of the edge back down the valley. This route is by far the easiest, and would be fairly straightforward on a mountain bike.

Route 2
Take the rough road at the end of Woodhouse Lane. Follow this to a tarmacked bridge. Turn right onto the landrover track, follow this over a stream (hop the rocks) and then steeply uphill. Look out for a small wooden pen on your left. After this comes a right bend in the track. Just after the bend, several small sheep trails turn off the main track - take the one just after a jumble of rocks and a little way before a wooden post. This trail leads across the valley side, aiming roughly for the shoulder of the ridge. Where the trail splits, take the higher path each time, to gradually rise up the hill. When the path disappears, head directly across the moor to the rocks.

The Bull Stones 5

The Bull Stones comprise a stretch of small buttresses and boulders lining a kilometre-long moorland ridge. Located one hour's walk from the road and 450 metres above sea level, the bouldering here is perfect for big summer days. The ample scattering of lower grade problems will appeal to free-spirited boulderers (more are documented by John Proud's online topo), while there are also harder gems to satisfy those who take a more focussed approach.

No dogs are allowed.

If you desire mileage on easier problems, take Route 1 to the Cowstones and Bull Stones. If you seek sterner challenges on steeper rock, take Route 1, but once at the crag, head back along the ridge to the Large Buttress and Little Bull Stones: most keen boulderers will find these latter areas more rewarding. The super keen can take Route 2, which is faster but strenuous. Reversing Route 2 is a good option for the return leg.

Gaucho, 4 p50

BULL STONES

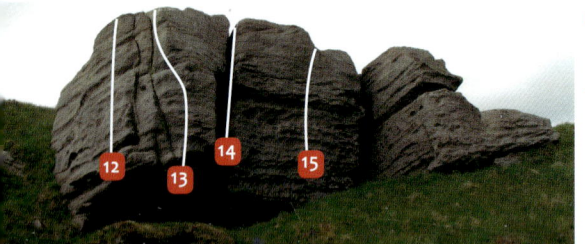

Far Stone

The Far Stone is the obvious large boulder visible on the far left end of the edge. Follow the main path through a gate and head uphill when you get close.

1 On Your Marks SIT **5+**
The arete right of the vertical crack.

2 Cross SIT **4+**
The cracks.

3 Breakfast SIT **6A**
Use underclings to get stood up.

4 Four John SIT **6C**
The arete on its right, without the crack out left (the pinch at the arete end of the crack is allowed).

5 Grupple SIT **6B**
The arete on its left, started from the crack sidepulls.

6 Witch Way SIT **6B**
The wall left of the arete, using the crack.

Lower Cowstones

Now walk back towards the fence along the line of the edge. After 200m, the Cowstones are reached. These are on two tiers and feature some lovely climbs in the lower grades.

1 Cowark 5
An awkward mantel.

2 Cower 4+

3 Cowheel 2
The fun slab.

4 Sacred Crow SIT **6A**
The short arete is worthwhile.

5 Gaucho ★ 4
A gentle slab, but hardest at the end.

6 Cowslip ★ 5
The left side of the fin.

7 Guernsey 5+
The right side of the fin.

Upper Cowstones

BULL STONES

8 Cowbell ★ 4+
Positive flakes lead to the top.

9 Madcows ★ 5+
The front wall is a little steeper.

10 C.J.D. SIT 6B
The wall right of the arete, via thin holds.

11 Tiny Cow Dance SIT 6A+
The small undercut boulder is strangely easier without the arete.

12 Mouth 4
The sidewall.

13 And ★ 4 SIT 6A+
Clamp up the prow, finishing leftwards at the top.

14 Foot 5
The big cleft.

15 Cowpox Right SIT 4+
Sitstart the short wall.

Taurus Boulders

Cross the fence and continue along the line of small boulders until larger rocks are reached. These are the Taurus Boulders.

16 Simon's Starter ★ 6B
The attractive left arete on its right, without using the right arete.

17 Mealtime 6C
Start on the footledge of *Simon's Starter*, then swing round the arete to finish it on its left.

18 All Or Nothing ★ 4+
The right arete.

19 Bullshit 4
The little slab.

20 Munchies ★ 6B+
The steep wall, with a powerful move from a pinch. Footblocks are not allowed. Don't underestimate the top-out!

21 Gruel 6A
This time, use the right arete.

22 Snow Bunting SIT 5+
Good holds lead upwards to a finish around the left arete.

23 Taurus 4
The slim slab just left of the main block.

24 Just Stand On It! 4+
The left side of the slabby boulder.

25 I'm Not Going ★ 5+
The centre of the boulder. Various fun eliminates can be contrived.

26 Rod's Way 4
The right-hand crack, on its left.

27 Giraffe In The Wind SIT 7A
The right arete, using a series of awkward layaways to get stood up. The wedged rock under the roof is out of bounds.

Robin Müller 2013

52 BULL STONES

100m further right are a few isolated walls. This is The Corral area.

1 The Ranch ★ **4**
The centre of the slab.

2 Toreador ★ **5+**
The high central crack.

50m right is the final wall in this group.

3 Bullneck 5+
Climb the scoop on the sidewall.

4 Project

5 Take The Bull By The Horns ★★ **5**
Climb up the slab on the right, then step onto the arete and finish up this.
Mark Gaddes 2003

6 The Cattle Truck 3

Four John, 6C p50

BULL STONES

The Pinnacles

70m right is The Pinnacles area, with a fine cluster of easier problems. Some of these are fairly high.

1 Bull Market 4
The arete.

2 John Bull 4

3 Bull Pen 4
The chimney.

4 One Pebble Slab ★ 5+

5 Bull In A China Shop 4+
The slanting crack.

6 Gold Bullion ★★ 4+
The thin pillar.
John Proud 2002

7 Brash Slab ★ 5+
The middle of the slab.

8 Red Bull 4+
The slab and arete.

9 Bulimia 4+
The slender slabby corner.

10 Hark To Bounty 4+

11 Bounty Hunter ★ 5+
The slight scoop in the centre.

12 Mutiny On The Bounty 4
From hands in the slot, climb the right arete.

13 Alan's Acme ★ 4+
The front left arete is incredibly bold!

14 Project
The side wall of the tower, using the aretes.

15 Bullish 4+
Climb the overhanging tower to jugs.

16 Bullworker 5+
Another steep tower, finishing via a flake.

There are more low grade problems on the scattered walls and boulders which extend 200m to the right of The Pinnacles - these are left for you to explore.

54 BULL STONES

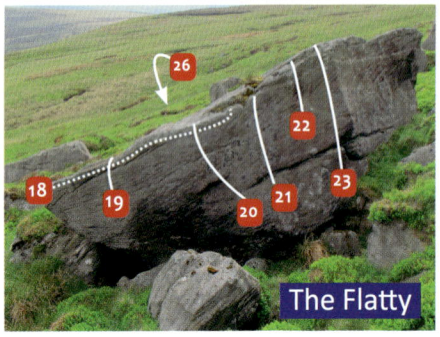

The next concentrated area is the Little Bull Stones on the next ridge line. This is 5min walk from The Pinnacles - continue to the clough and stream at the end of this edge, then head uphill to the obvious boulder jumble.

1 Picos 4+
The left wall.

2 Pamplona Run 4
Just right of the arete.

3 Olé! 4
The centre.

4 Beware Of The Bull ★ 6C
The undercut rounded arete on its right, with a classic pop to the top from a tenuous position.
Nigel Hodson 2004

5 Baron Of Beef 4+
The slabby pillar, above a dodgy landing.

BULL STONES

6 Suction ★★ **7A**
Suction onto the low bulge, then climb the face above to a slopey finish. Great moves, if a little scrittly.
Robin Müller 2013

7 Future Light Cone ★★ SIT **6C+**
The arete on its left, starting with LH in the crack. A tough move leads to the break, then a slopey top.
Robin Müller 2013

8 Shaken Not Stirred 5 SIT **6B**
The face right of the arete.

9 Cool Handle 5+
The arete on its right.

10 Rock Melt SIT **6A**
The steep little wall has positive holds.

11 Backwards Ballet SIT **6A**
The arete on its right.

The Top Tier is just over the crest of the hill.

12 Bulldog 4 SIT **5+**
Sitstart the arete on its right, then swing round to finish up the front.

13 Bull Terrier 3
The arete on its left.

14 Pit Bull ★ **6A**
The hanging arete is good value climbed on its right, though the landing is a bit sketchy.

The next three problems are on the undercut slabby boulder at the other end of the Little Bull Stones.

15 Rough Diamond ★ **3**
The left side of the slab, via the grooves.

16 Ace Of Diamonds ★ **4+**
Straight up the centre of the slab.

17 Cut Diamond ★ **4** SIT **7A**
Start RH slanting undercling, LH on the lip. Work rightwards until it's possible to rock back left onto the slab.

The Flatty holds the final cluster of problems.

18 Traverso Grande ★ **6B** SIT **6C**
A thuggy left-to-right lip crossing, with a standing start matching hands just right of the arete, or a sitting start from off the rock. Top out once you are stood on the break.

19 Just Do It 4+
An easy mantel.

20 Project
Sitstart the steep bit with RH on the end of the break and LH on a low sidepull.

21 Breaking News SIT **5+**
Sitstart from the left end of the break.

22 The Slanting One 6A
Start with both hands on the slanting sloper, then get the top.

23 Little Miss Crouch LOW **4+**
Start crouching from the right end of the break.

24 Yes SIT **4+**
The little arete.

25 Bull In The Field 6A SIT **6B** LOW **6C**
Using the top of the boulder, traverse leftwards from the short front-left arete, to finish around the next arete (or keep going if you feel like it). The low start is from RH in the crack right of the starting arete.

26 Return Of The Clangers SIT **6C**
Grind over the lip, using the LH crack.

27 Squeaky Bum Time SIT **7A**
A pretty hard mantel.
Robin Müller 2013

56 BULL STONES

Stirk Slabs

250m right of the Little Bull Stones are the Stirk Slabs.

1 Project
The sidewall of the boulder.

2 Bully Beef ★ SIT 7B
The arete on its left.
Greg Chapman 2013

3 Bull Run ★★ 5+
The slabby arete.
Alan Bates 2003

4 Bull Ring ★ 4+
Climb the slab from an undercut.

5a Don't Go Yet ★★ 6B+
Climb the left side of the very slopey wall above the roof.
John Proud 2003

5b Cascadia ★★ SIT 7A+
Start from the back of the roof for a bigger grade and a different name.
Greg Chapman 2013

6 Midsummer Nights ★ 5
The small groove.

7 Man Alive SIT 6A
Big holds lead to an easy finish.

8 Breathe In 4+
Direct through the roof. Needs a sitstart.

9 Vermicious Knid SIT 6A
Clamp up the rib and step into the groove.

10 Bulletin 4+ SIT 6B
The groove.

11 Stirk Slab 4+

12 Bullet Proof ★ 4+
The arete on its left.

13 Bulleted 4+ SIT 6A
The arete on its right.

BULL STONES 57

The next buttress to the right is Large Buttress. This is accompanied by Two Tier Buttress, which a little further right.

1 Nigel's Dream 4+ SIT 6A
The arete, from low holds.

2 Dreammaker 4+
The friendly wall, to a giant jug.

3 Dreamcatcher ★ 4+
Start on the lower level and follow the fun arete all the way up.

4 Illusion 5

5 Counting Sheep 4

6 Dreamboat 4

7 Dreamworks 4

8 Daydream 4+

9 Castle In The Air SIT 4+

10 Pipe Dream ★★ 5 SIT 6A
The scoop is a classic.
John Proud 2003

11 Toro Loco ★★ 6A SIT 6B
Another beauty - sustained rib romping to a tricky rockover back into the scoop.
Greg Chapman 2013

12 Project
A desperate sitter.

13 Wet Dream 5 SIT 6B
The slab, using the LH seam, but not the right arete.

14 Dream On 4+ SIT 6C
The arete on its left, with strange moves to get established from sitting.

15 Dream Up 4+ SIT 6A+
The arete on its right.

BULL STONES

16 Stinger SIT **7B**
Tackle the wall, with an awkward start from low edges.
Greg Chapman 2013

17 The Unknown 4+ SIT **5+**
Sitstart from undercuts and work up the sidewall.

18 Project

19 Project

20 Black Hole ★ 5+ SIT **6B**
Climb the face via a rounded undercling.

21 Thug On A Lug 4+ SIT **6C**
The arete on its left, with a hard move to the long sidepull.

22 Mug Without A Jug SIT **6C**
The arete on its right has sharp holds.

Two Tier Buttress

Toro Loco, 6B p57

Traverso Grande, 6B

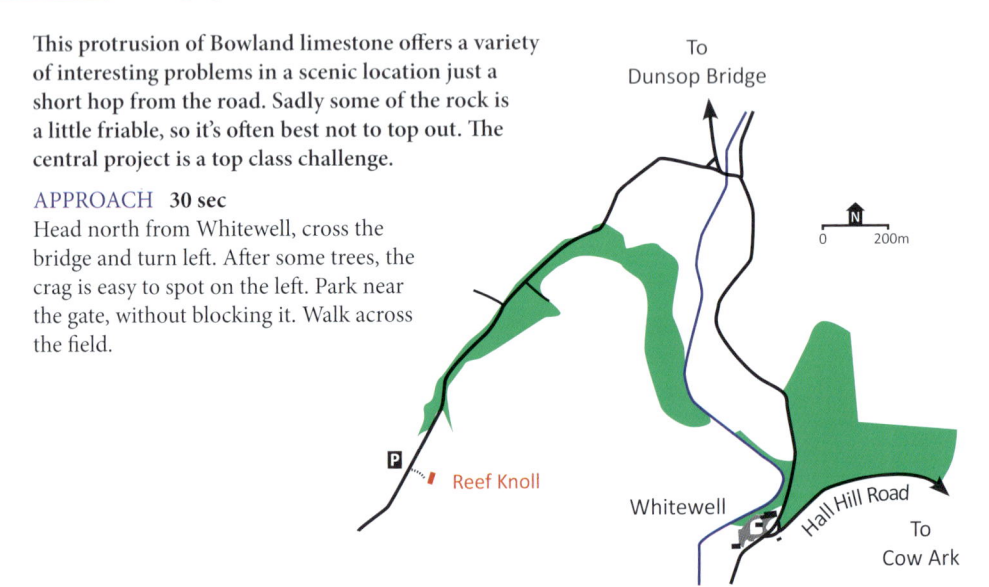

6 Reef Knoll

This protrusion of Bowland limestone offers a variety of interesting problems in a scenic location just a short hop from the road. Sadly some of the rock is a little friable, so it's often best not to top out. The central project is a top class challenge.

APPROACH   30 sec
Head north from Whitewell, cross the bridge and turn left. After some trees, the crag is easy to spot on the left. Park near the gate, without blocking it. Walk across the field.

REEF KNOLL

Some of the rock is a bit loose, especially at the top. On the central problems it's probably best to jump off or reverse once the difficulties are over. Take care on any problems you do top out.

1 Truckin' Easy 4
The groove.

2 Truckulent 5
The arete, on its left.

3 Project
An eliminate line between arete and crack.

4 Truckin' Hell 5+
The crumbly crack. Be careful!

5 Kebab House 7A
From good holds below the crack, climb the arete of the cave, without handholds in the crack (feet anywhere). Pull into a fingery slot, then head up and right to finish hanging big rounded holds above the lip.

6 Project
Traverse right from the start of *Kebab House*.

7 Project
Attack the roof via the crack pinch and a higher slot. Awesome.

8 Flying Truck ★ 6A+
From jugs, follow big dusty pockets into the next problem.

9 Sons Of Pioneers ★ 6A
The big crack, to a rounded finishing hold.

10 Finger Pie 6A+
Climb the thinner crack, using holds on the face. Move past a pocket to finish on the rounded hold.

11 Truck Of The Light 6B
The blankest section of rock is climbed via small holds, with a worrying landing. Once at the good ledge, it's best to reverse and drop off.

12 The Bulge 6A
Climb up to finish just right of the tree.

13 Maxi 5
Straight up from the undercling.

14 Midi 4+
Head past a letterbox-like slot.

15 Dru 5+
The pockety wall.

16 Lem 4+
The groove.

17 Obscene 5
The wall to the left of the tree.

18 Publication 4+
Start right of the corner and climb up to the arete.

19 Truckers Arse 5
From the hole, climb the arete.

20 A Road 4
The wall.

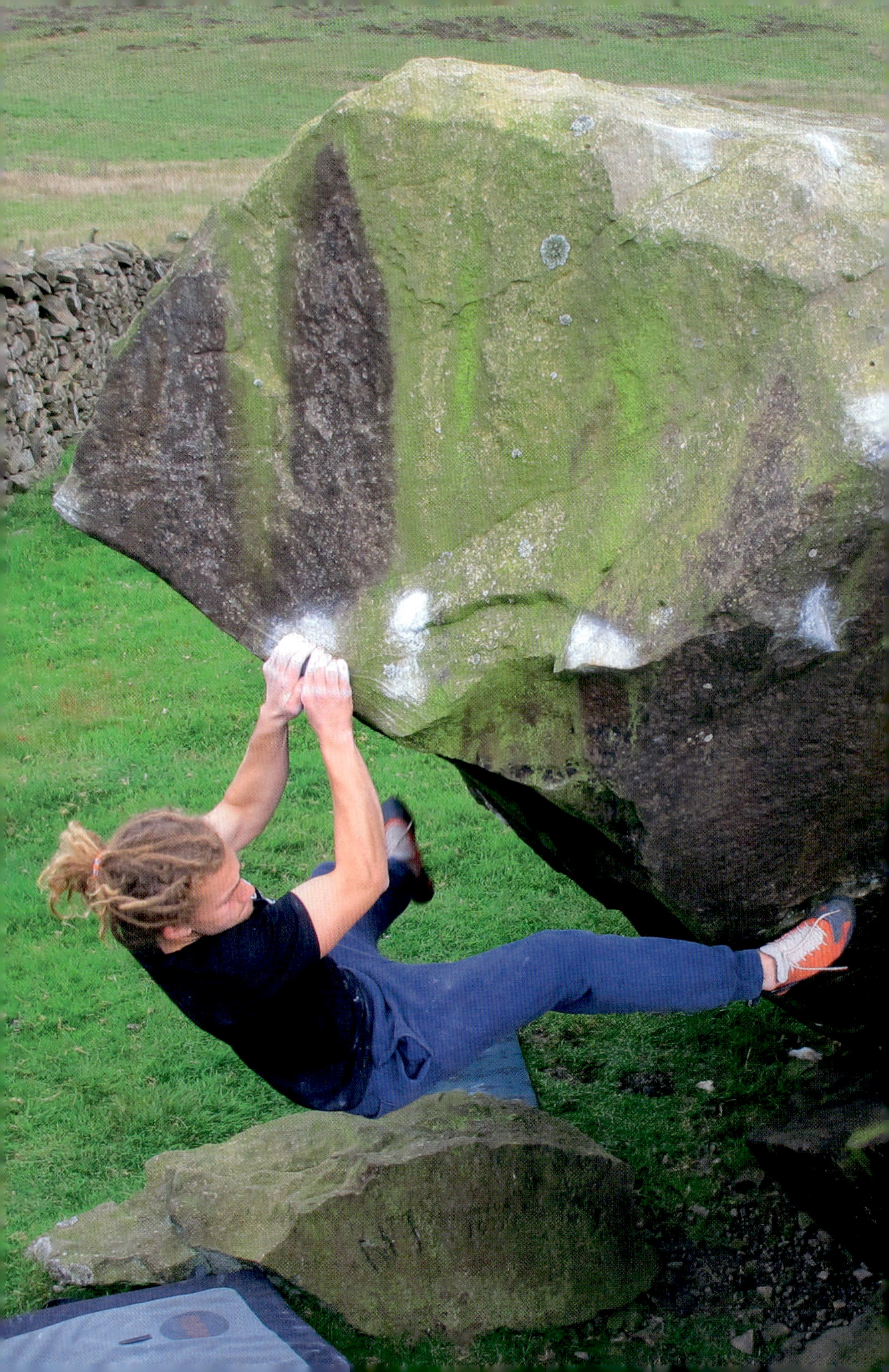

Crag Stones 7

Perched scenically atop a windswept moor in the Forest of Bowland, Crag Stones offers good sport in an excellent setting. Its four gritstone boulders are short but attractive lumps with decent landings. There are a few steep challenges and one obvious woody-style project. Sitstarts are the order of the day. The boulders are exposed on all sides and dry fast.

APPROACH 40 min

From the north or east, turn off the B6478 at the sign to Cow Ark. From the south, once at Cow Ark, turn at the phonebox and postbox, signposted towards Whitewell (not Whitewell and Lancaster), then take the next right, signposted towards Newton.

Once on this road, continue to a stile over a stone wall, next to some trees and opposite a lane leading to Crimpton Farm. Park sensibly, away from the lane. Cross the stile and take the unmarked permissive footpath over the Moor, which crosses a stile and later a bridge, until a final stile allows you to cross the wall and turn towards the rocks.

Follow the wall to Crag Stones, crossing one more stile. The rocks are about 1.5km from the road. The way is not marked and the terrain can be very boggy unless you visit in a dry spell.

An alternative approach is possible from the north. The route is online, hosted by DEFRA - google "crag stones permissive path".

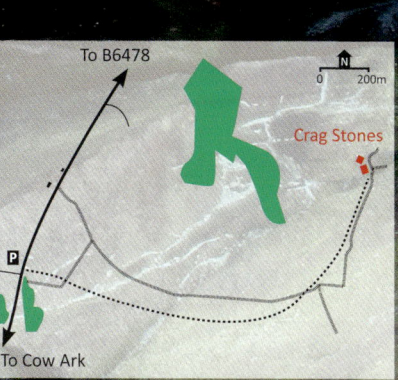

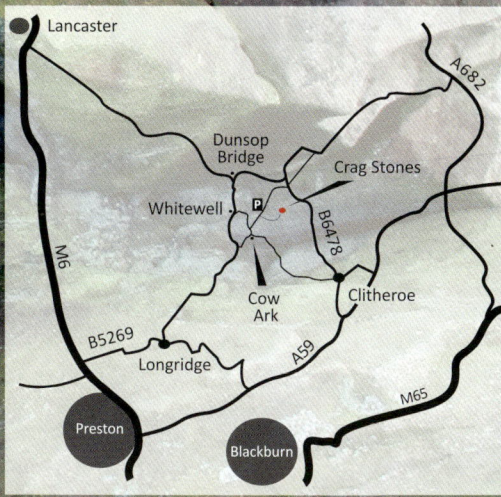

Moor Beast, 7B p64

64 CRAG STONES

Upper Boulders

1 Holey Cow 5+
Pull up the end face.

2 Wrap Speed SIT **6B+**
The arete on its left, from a low RH guppy.

3 Common Law SIT **6A+**
The arete on its right, from low holds.

4 Face of the Moor SIT **6A**
Sitstart the face from the flatty.

5 Underthing SIT **7A**
Start LH lowest sidepull, RH undercling and pull onto the face. No footblock.
Robin Müller 2012

6 Black Whirlwind ★ SIT **7A**
Sitstart from the rock, slap up the arete to a jug rail. The low undercling start is a hard project.
Robin Müller 2012

7 Moor Beast ★★ SIT **7B**
Start up *Underthing* then traverse the lip rightwards, past the arete. Gain big sidepulls and top out.
Robin Müller 2014

8 Hole In One 6B
Hang the lip and pull to the arete.

9 Glasses SIT **6A**
The tiny arete, starting from as low as you can.

10 No Mono No Cry SIT **7B+**
Start from LH sloper, RH anything. Gnarl onto the slab, with or without the vicious mono.
Robin Müller 2012

CRAG STONES

Lower Boulders

11 Cop A Feel SIT 6C+
Sitstart and pull from arete slopers onto the slab.

12 Gritstick SIT 7A
Climb the arete on its right.
Robin Müller 2012

13 Green Angle ★ 4 SIT 5+
Sitstart the arete.

14 Wrinkle 4 SIT 5
Sitstart the arete on its left.

15 Creased Up ★ 4+ SIT 6B
Slap up the arete on its right, until the right arete is accesible. Top out over this.

16 Origami ★ 4
Pleasant slabbing. A direct finish is no harder.

17 Thin Slice SIT 6C
LH arete, RH break. No footblocks!

18 Regal Patina SIT 6A
Start at the sidepull.

19 Un-Something SIT 6A
Start LH arete jug, RH big hold in the roof.

A few more easyish sitstarts are probably possible on this boulder.

Bend Of The Rainbow, 7A p71

8 Craig Y Longridge

Now owned by the BMC, here is an endless sidewards stretch of leaning gritstone, though the pleasant field that once played backdrop to mighty bouldering victories has been replaced by the equally uninterested entity of a new housing estate. Consequently, there are rules to climbing here: Don't climb after sunset or before 10am. No dogs. No music. No toileting anywhere. Read the sign at the entrance for more details.

The climbing here is, without exception, steep. Many of Lancashire's harder problems live on these looming walls, co-existing alongside arm-blowing traverses. If you love pulling down, you'll love this. The crag stays dry during showers, but parts are prone to seepage, so it can be risky after a lot of rain. Grey numbers refer to numbers painted on the rock.

APPROACH 30 sec
From the B5269 King Street which runs through Longridge, turn left onto Higher Road at the White Bull pub (signposted to Jeffrey Hill). At the fork, keep right (signposted to the Beacon Fell). After 500m, park at a layby on the left, just after the reservoir wall. Cross the road to enter the crag via a gate.

TRAVERSES
Traverse problems are numbered with black squares on the photos and black numbers in the text. Yellow arrows indicate the start and finish. Extra long traverses are given French sport grades at the end of the chapter.

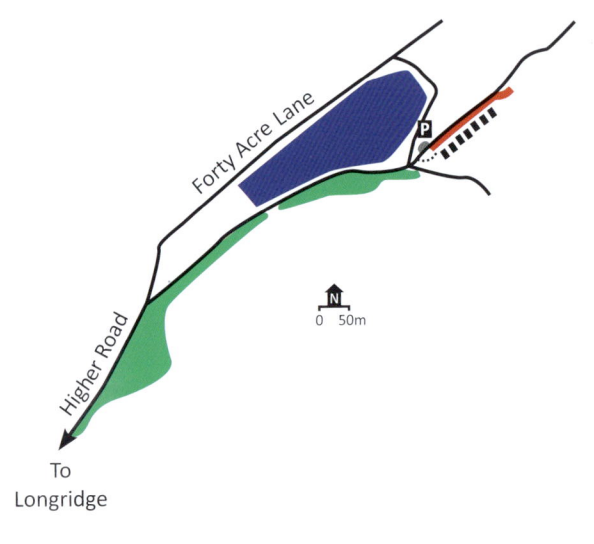

CRAIG Y LONGRIDGE

Late Pickings

1 1 Sessions End 5
From the very far left (start not shown above) traverse to *The Race*.

1 4 Pudding 4
Climb past the left side of the small cave.

2 5 Pie 4
Climb past the right side of the cave.

3 6 Gorse Bush 4
The wall a metre right of the cave.

4 7 Absolute Beginners 4
A metre right again, starting at a drill mark.

5 8 Bramble Ramble 4
Start to the left of the low fissure.

6 9 The Race 4+
Start just right of the low fissure.

7 10 Escalator 4
Start by a drill mark.

8 11 Snail Trail 4+
A metre to the right of the drill mark.

9 12 Paul Pritchard's Jacket 5
Follow small cracks upwards.

10 13 Stoning A Leper 5+
The left side of the sandy cave.

2 Kiss The Razor's Edge ★ 7A
Stay low, with feet just above the ground and finish at *Central Ice Fall*. Holds on the traverse line of *Tarot Plane* are off limits.

11 14 Pay The Witch 6A
The right side of the sandy cave.

12 14a Late Pickings 6A
Climb into the right arete of the upper wall.

13 16 Rifted Victiom 5+
Follow the little groove to the top.

14 17 Naked Lunch 4+
The wall right of the groove.

15 18 Black Jake 5+
The wall, past a slot.

Grow Wings

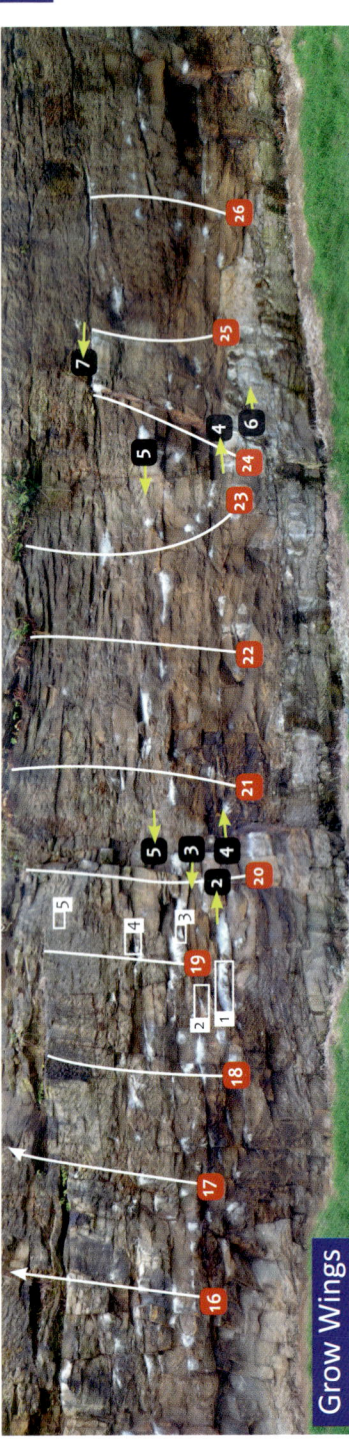

16 19 Timothy's Route ★ 6A
Climb a metre left of *Wobble Bottom*. Top out.

17 20 Wobble Bottom ★ 6A
Climb to the arete above the break and finish up this.

18 21 Seven A ★ 6B
Use the undercut to gain the break, or find a different way if you are feeling contrary.

19a Bomb Squad 6B
Gain the sloper in the hole, then make a bid for the top - usually done dynamically.

19b Vickers' Eliminate ★ 7B+
A classic eliminate. Follow the marked holds: Start low slopey ledge (1), LH press (2), RH slopey hold (3), LH to sloper in the hole (4), RH high crimp (5), LH top.
Ian Vickers

3 22 Tarot Plane ★ 6B+
Go left to the end of the crag.

20 23 Central Icefall Direct 5
The blocky line of weakness.

4 24 Hitting The Wall 6B+
Stay low and finish at *Pump 'Til You Jump*.

21 25 Babylon Blitz 5+
Climb the wall just right of the rib, using some footholds on *Central Icefall Direct*.

22 26 Thirty Feet Of Pain 6C SIT 6C+
A crimpy wall.

23 27 Haardvark 6B SIT 6B+
The wall left of the right-leaning weakness. The sitstart links into this from low on the right.

5 28 Cruel Country ★ 6C
From *Pump* to *Central Icefall*, along the higher line.

24 29 Pump 'Til You Jump ★ 6A
The right-leaning weakness.

6 30 Twelve Dreams 7A
A low line from *Pump* to *Mad Aardvark*.
Rob Smitton 1986-7

25 31 Still Raining, Still Dreaming 6C SIT 7A
The wall right of *Pump 'Til You Jump*, with a sitstart from an edge low on the right.

26 32 Grow Wings ★★ 6C+ SIT 7B
A lovely crimp ladder leads to a great finishing jug. The standing start begins on the second pair of crimps down from the jug. The sitter goes from a low slick hold.

CRAIG Y LONGRIDGE

Mr Skin

27 33 Imitation Arapiles 6B
Climb from one cave to the next. A highball continuation to the top break is 6C+.

7 34 Going Deaf For A Living 6B+
Left from *Mad Aardvark* to *Pump*, moving up to the high break.

28 35 Mad Aardvark's Tea Party 6B
Juggy climbing up the slanting crack.

8 36 Gruts ★ 6B
Right from *Mad Aardvark* to *Muddy Wobble Block*.

29 37 Pop Tart 6B+
From the good hold, climb straight up.

30 38 Like A Slug But Sucks 6B
A line 1m to the right of *Pop Tart*.

31 40 Slug The Thug 6A
Climb between two slim cracks.

32 41 Added Incentive 5+ SIT 6A
The sitstart is from down and right.

33 42 Muddy Wobble Block 4+
Follow big holds from the obvious jug, which no longer wobbles.

9 43 Mr. Skin ★ 7A+
Right from *Muddy Wobble Block* to *Semen Scream*.
Rob Smitton 1987

34 44 Waiting In The Wings 6A+ SIT 6B+
Crimps lead up the wall.

35 45 Muscles In Their Imagination ★ 6A+ SIT 7A+
Climb via the left side of the cave. The sitstart is from an undercut and small slot. Stay direct, or the grade drops to 7A.

36 46 Weir Aardvark 6A
Climb through the right side of the cave.

37 47 Blatantly Slimey Slug 5
The crack.

38 48 Company Of Wolves ★ 5+
The wall right of the crack.

39 49 The Howling 6A
The wall left of the next problem.

40 50 Dyno Bucket 5+ SIT 6B+
Make a big move for the big hold in the crack.

CRAIG Y LONGRIDGE

Big Marine

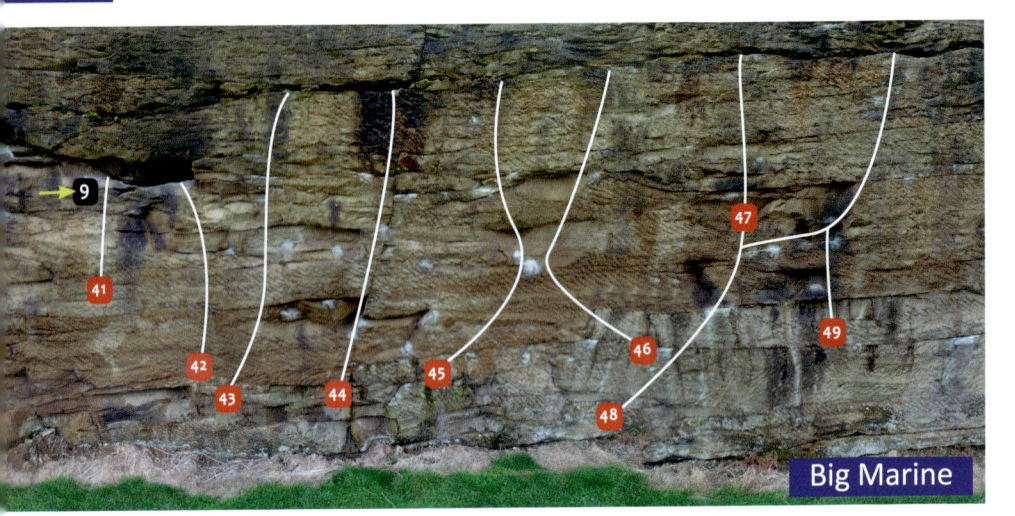

41a 51 Semen Scream 6A
Jump to the crimp, then gain the cave.

41b Seaman Stain 7B+
The standing start to *Semen Scream*, using a pinch.

42 Project
Start LH low undercut, RH crimp.

43a 52 Smeg City 6B+
Jump to start and climb straight up. Deviating drops the grade.

43b Smeg City Plus ★ 7A+
The standing start. Don't use the cave to the left. The sitstart is an obvious project.

44a 53 The Gauntlet ★ 6C+ SIT 7B
Follow the crackline - the sitter goes from a little slot and low sidepull.

44b The Gauntlet - Big Marine Link ★ 7B SIT 7B+
Link the two problems.

44c Gauntlet Failure ★ 7C SIT 7C+
Link *The Gauntlet* into *Renal Failure*.

45a 54 Big Marine ★★ 7A+
Jump to decent holds, then big moves lead upwards to a gaston finish. This used to be a standing start when the ground was higher.
Mick Lovatt 1986

45b Submarine ★ 7C+
The standing start goes from LH slopey sidepull and RH undercut.
Ryan Pasquill 2005

45c Super Submarine ★ SIT 8A+
A sitstart from crimps adds a bit. Formerly a crouching start, and probably a bit easier now the sequence isn't so bunched.
Gaz Parry 2007

46 55 Renal Failure ★ 7B+ LOW 8A
From the *Big Marine* start, head up and right via a pocket. The low start dynos into this from an edge down and right.
Paul Pritchard 1987 (stand)

47 56 Push To Prolapse ★★ 6C
Classy steep climbing using the big undercut. Eliminate the undercut for *The Motion Vector* 7A+.

48 The Priory ★★ 7C SIT 7C+
From *Push To Prolapse*, head right and use a crimp to finish a little left of *Colon Power*. The sitter goes from a crimp and small sidepull down on the left.
Paul Robins 2002, SIT Greg Chapman 2012

49 The Priory Direct 7C+
The direct start uses a gaston and crimp, but is pretty morpho.
Sam Davenhall 2009

Fertile Delta

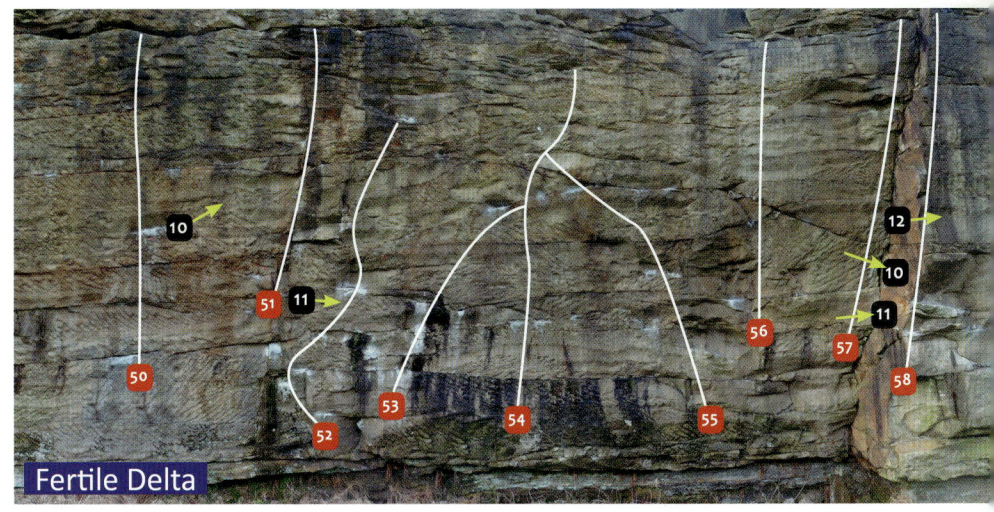

50a Colon Power ★ 7C
Start from the high jug - use the ladder, or get a leg up to reach it. Follow crimps up and slightly left to the break.
Paul Robins 2002

50b Pot Of Gold ★ 8A
Finger-jam the slot and make a big move to gain the jug, then finish up *Colon Power*.
Ryan Pasquill 2008

50c Baby Go Down 8A
Start from the high jug (ladder or leg up allowed) and link into *Push To Prolapse*.

10a 57 Bend Of The Rainbow ★ 7A
Start from the high jug (ladder or leg up) and arc magnificently across the wall to finish in the corner crack of *New Stone Age*.
Rob Smitton 1986

10b Bend Of The Rainbow Free 7B+
Start from the *Pot of Gold* slot.

51 58 Rug Thug 6B+
Climb the crack.

11a Gaz's Traverse ★ 7B
A low traverse from *Rug Thug* to the corner.
Gaz Parry

11b Excess Gaz SIT 7C+
Start as per *In Excess Sitstart* and link into the traverse.

11c Gaz's Traverse Sitstart SIT 7B
Start as per *Delta Force LH* and link into the traverse.

52a 59 In Excess ★ 6B+ SIT 7B+
Sitstart using crimps, gain a LH pinch, then pull up and right to a jug and the start of the standup, which climbs via a large sidepull.
SIT Rupert Davies 2008

52b Smiling Colon Sitstart SIT 7C+
Sitstart as per *In Excess*, then head for the *Colon Power* starting jug and finish up this. Eliminating the *In Excess* jug is **8A**.
Tom Newberry 2012

52c Excess Force ★ SIT 7C
Sitstart as per *In Excess*, then from the jug swing right and finish up *Fertile Delta*.
Sam Dewhurst 2010

53 60a Fertile Delta ★★ 7A+ SIT 7B
Sitstart at a jug, then make a rose move to gain the pocket. From here (standing start), get the jug, then gaston a sika'd hold.
Mark Leach 1986 (stand)

54 Delta Force SIT 7C
Start beneath the pocket and use tiny crimps. Eliminate good holds to the left - using these is *Delta Force LH*, **7A+**. Rarely dry.
Chris Davies 2008

55 60 Porridge Gun 6B SIT 6B+
Crimps lead into the finish of *Fertile Delta*.

56 62 Scorched August ★ 6B
The wall left of the corner

57 63 New Stone Age 6A
The corner.

58 64 Unknown Arete 5+
The arete.

CRAIG Y LONGRIDGE

Ascent Of Man

12 Unnatural Selection ★ **6C**
From *New Stone Age* corner (see previous page), follow a thin mid-height line right to *Jacob's Ladder*, above the line of *Low Life*.
Andrew Gridley 1986

59 Ping ★ **7B+**
From the small cave, head up and left. Dyno or crimp - the choice is yours.
Paul Robins 2001

60 66 Missing Link 7B
From the edge above the cave, leap for a big hold up and right.
Pete Black 1986-7

61 Chocolate Popsicle ★ **7A+**
The good holds soon run out, leaving just one very small crimp.
Andrew Griffith 1991

62 67 Moschops 6B
The wall a little left of the cracks.

13 68 Ascent Of Man 6A+
Follow the high line left from *Jacob's Ladder* to *New Stone Age*.

63 69 Jacob's Ladder 6A+
Follow the pair of cracks. Or Jacob, if he's up there.

64 71 Orifice Of Faeces 7A+
This wall used to be easier, but the ground got lower. That's how faeces evolve.
Adam Lincoln, Ryan Pasquill 2008

65 72 Neolithic Technology 6C
Climb past two hairline cracks. Formerly easier.

66 73 From Ape To Aardvark ★★ **6B**
Climb past the rectangular slot.

14 74 Descent Of Man 6A
Head left along the high handholds to reach the beginning of *Ascent Of Man*.

67 75 Runaway 5
Jugs lead upwards.

15 Low Life ★ **7A**
Follow the lowest break left from *Runaway*, to finish at the small cave (the start of *Ping*). **6C** if you stop halfway at *Jacob's Ladder*.

There are a few more problems on the wall to the right. They are all highball and about **5**. On the furthest right section of wall, there are three traverses which need a spell of dry weather to be in condition.

16 From Here To There To You 6A
From the crack, traverse right along the main slopey break.

17 Seeping With The Enemy 6A
From the crack, traverse right along the fingery lower break.

18 Let Seeping Dogs Dry 6A
From the crack, traverse right below *Seeping With The Enemy*.

Grow Wings, 7B p68

Gruts, 6B p69

CRAIG Y LONGRIDGE 75

More Traverses

Oh yes, many more... if this is your favourite page, please phone our helpline.

0800-ADDICTED-TO-PUMP

First, a couple of short ones that most people still use bouldering grades to describe.

19 Gaz's Colon 8A
From the *New Stone Age* crack, reverse *Gaz's Traverse* and finish up *Colon Power*.

20 Blackpool Car Jack 8A+
From the New Stone Age crack, traverse beneath the line of *Gaz's Traverse* to finish up *In Excess*.

And now for the traverses that swallow up lives. This is stamina-junky territory, so French sport grades are used.

21 The Traverse Of The Gods ★★ 8b+
Traverse the full length of the crag, normally done left to right. Use the high break from *Smeg City* to *Thug Rug*. Divine.
Dave Kenyon 1985-89

22 Going Down ★★ 8c+
From the right end, traverse left to the far end without using the high break. Oof.
Neil Carson 1995-96

The above can of course be broken into more eaily digestible segments. These are:

23 First Bit ★ 7b+
From left to *Central Icefall Direct*.

24 Halfway ★ 7c+
From left to the start of *Pop Tart*.

25 Middle Bit ★ 7c
From the start of *Pop Tart* to the high break above *Smeg City*.

26 Middle Bit Plus ★ 7c+
Reverse *Going Deaf For A Living* all the way to *Pop Tart*, then climb *Middle Bit*.

27 Bend To The End ★ 7b+
Link *Bend Of The Rainbow* into a reverse of *Ascent Of Man* and *Descent Of Man*.

28 Bend To The End Low ★ 7c
Link *Bend Of The Rainbow* into a reverse of *Low Life*.

29 Bend Of The Rainbow Free + Low Life 8a
The hard start adds a couple of grades.

30 Start To High Break ★ 8a+
Start at the left end and finish at the high break over Smeg City.

31 Second Fifth ★ 7b
From *Central Ice Fall Direct,* traverse to the start of *Pop Tart*.

32 Middle Third ★ 8a
From *Central Ice Fall Direct,* traverse to the high break above *Smeg City*.

33 Full Circle 8a
Climb *Gaz's Traverse* to the finish of *Bend Of The Rainbow,* then reverse this to finish on the good hold at the beginning of *Gaz's Traverse*.

Cordless Power, 7A

9 Cardwell - Longridge Fell West

This is a one-problem venue, but just around the corner from Longridge. It's well worth a visit if Longridge is in bad nick and you fancy a) something a little more technical or b) a view. This crag is currently banned, but hopefully the situation will change. Check the BMC RAD for updates.

APPROACH 2 min
See Longridge Fell map on opposite page.
Follow Forty Acre Lane to a gate located between the top of the hill and the triangle junction. Park sensibly, but don't block the gate. Hop into the field of reeds and follow a vague path downhill to the quarry.

Head to the right side of the quarry. The high pocket on this problem can fill with rainwater, so a rag is useful.

1 Cordless Power ★ LOW 7A
The arete on its left, starting matched on the break. The footblock marked "30" is out.
Robin Müller 2012

2 Project
It might be possible to climb the arete on its right, but a few pads and spotters are probably required.

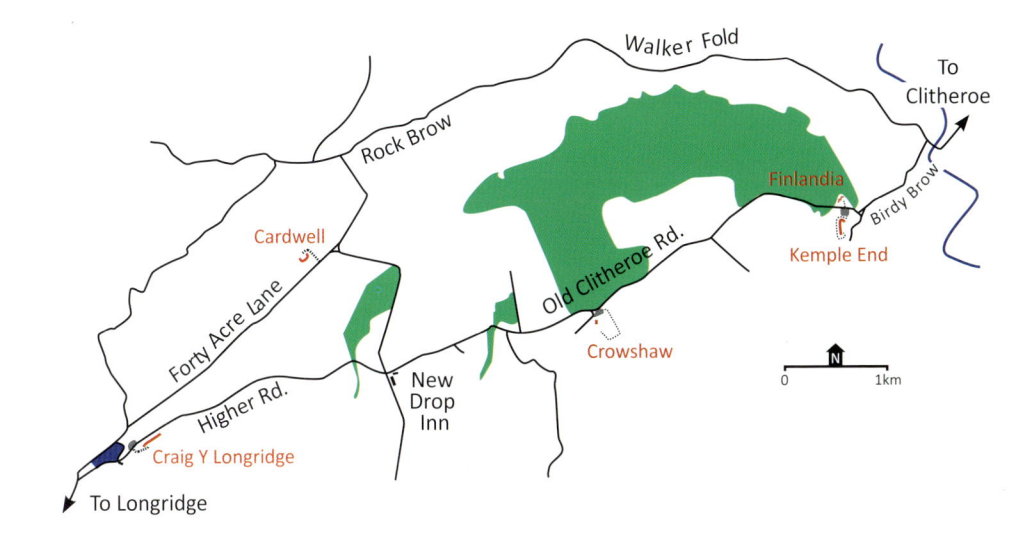

Longridge Fell East 9

A cluster of minor quarries populates the east end of Longridge fell. These are great for a quick hit of easy mileage, and each have their reclusive charms. They can be combined with Cardwell and Craig Y Longridge for a good pub-crawl style tour of the moor.

Crowshaw Quarry is the smallest of the three, but its limited climbing is also the most unique. Finlandia is a suntrap until the afternoon, with almost no walk in and short solo type problems. Kemple End has a small amount of low level bouldering, though one highball slab calls out to be padded out and padded up. All three are sheltered and mostly fast-drying.

Crowshaw Quarry
APPROACH   4 min
From Craig Y Longridge, follow Higher Road for just over 3 miles. Look for the big gated footpath on the left, which leads into trees. Park after this in the obvious bay just down the road. Follow a track that exits from the east end of the bay and heads downhill. Once at the bottom, enter the 2nd bay on the right and walk into the trees.

Finlandia
APPROACH   30 sec
From Craig Y Longridge, follow Higher Road for just over 4 miles. Look for a second big gated footpath on the left, which leads into trees. Park 100m after this, in the obvious bay on the right. Cross the road to enter the quarry.

Kemple End
APPROACH   3 min
Park as per Finlandia. The quarry is below the parking, and is gained by a path through the vegetation which leads from the car park and along the top of the crag. Follow this path to a descent next to a tree.

CROWSHAW & FINLANDIA

Crowshaw Quarry's main buttress has some unusual large features. Don't use the footledge near the ground. The descent is via a thin foot-ramp that can be carefully traversed to the right.

1 Waspeze 4+
Climb the corner.

2 Tumble 5
Pull over the ledge, then top out via the arete.

3 Supermarket Training 5+
Hand-traverse the shelf right to the arete and step off to the right.

4 Stiff Under Lip LOW **6C**
Start at the slot and traverse right below the lip. Rock round the arete to finish.

5 Low Cunning SIT **7A**
Eliminate the arete and gain the low traverse. Reverse to finish on the slot.

6 Rustication ★ 6A SIT **6B**
The arete on its left, with an awkward move to pass the shelf. Walk off left or continue upwards.

7 Zaggin' ★ 5+
The slabby side, with or without arete.

Finlandia's cleanest wall has some nice climbing, though the sloping landing makes it hard to pad, so it may feel like soloing.

1 Third Fin 5
The arete on its left.

2 Earth Wind and Fire 5+
The wall right of the arete.

3 Suomi 5
The slight rib.

4 Kalevala 5

5 Helsinki 5

Kemple End Traversing

KEMPLE END

The left end of Kemple End's main wall has a few short problems. These can all be topped out, but it's probably best to traverse off once the difficulties are over.

1 Fall Back 3
The left end of the wall.

2 Spring Forward 4+
An awkward move using the big flake.

3 Evening 5+
Use the LH sidepull at the bottom of the thin crack.

4 Midnight 6C
Dyno from the break to the ledge.

5 Morning 5
A RH sidepull aids a tricky step up.

6 Creaking 4+
Twin flakes. Using just the left flake is a little harder.

The right side of the same wall hosts some fun traverses.

7 Middle Earth 4
Traverse the break rightwards from *Spring Forward*, then drop down at the end and return on the lower break.

8 Learning To Wave ★ 5
Follow the wave of handholds between breaks and finish on good pockets.

9 Lower Earth 4+
The lowest break traverse.

10 Lowest Earth 6B
Traverse rightwards below the bottom break, with a fingery finish to match on the slanting edge at the far right.

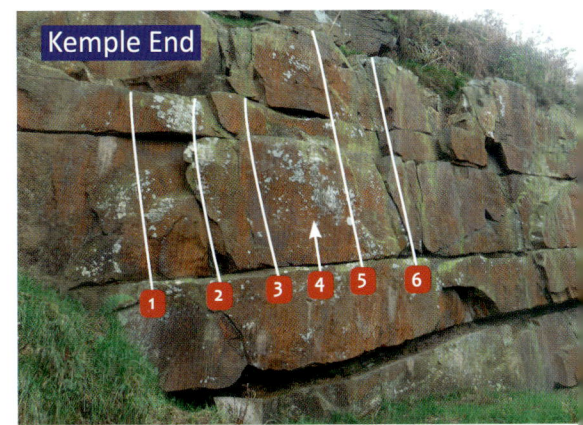

The star attraction here is this highball slab and arete, which is 40m right of the main wall. The landing is flat-ish but several pads are still desirable.

11 Project
The arete on its right. Has been climbed on its left, but the landing makes that version more suited to trad.

12 Ribblesdale High ★★ 6B
Up the centre to a high crux. E3.

13 Project

Toffee Nut Ice Cream, 6C p82

Nick Of Pendle 10

This is one of those local's venues with some surprisingly good problems, which make the most of a small amount of decent rock. Don't travel miles to boulder here, but do stop in if you are passing, or if you live nearby. The quarry is interestingly featured and usefully roadside, so it's ideal for a quick hit.

APPROACH   **30 sec**
Clitheroe Road runs between the A59 and the village of Sabden. Follow Clitheroe Road to the crest of the hill, where there is parking on both sides near a few obvious scrappy bits of rock. The bouldering is in the main quarry 30m from the road. This is accessed by any of several small paths.

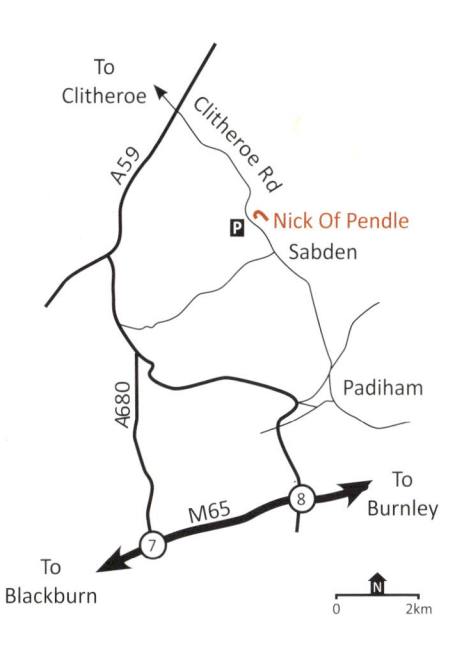

82 NICK OF PENDLE

The main wall is the obvious clean section in the centre of the quarry.

1 Onto The Slide SIT **4+**
Big layaways lead to an amusing top-out.

2 Shots All Round 5 SIT **6A**
A hard pull from shotholes leads to easier climbing.

3 Toffee Nut Ice-Cream ★ 6B+ SIT **6C**
Reach from the crack sidepull to the high slot. Sitstart from the shotholes down and right.

4 Scream ★ 7A SIT **7A+**
Gain the sharp LH crimp, then crank on it to get the slot. The sitstart is from the shotholes.
Robin Müller 2013

5 Gotcha 5+
The big ledges aren't as big as they look.

6 Shothole Wall Traverse SIT **6C**
From the shotholes, traverse into *Gotcha*.

There's a slab to the left.

7 Nock Of Pendle 3
The arete, with a dirty top - or just traverse off. Eliminate the arete at **5+**.

8 Knack Of Pendle 4
The centre of the slab, trending left to a good jug. Step off to the left.

Opposite the slab is a small, slopey boulder.

9 Exsqueeze Me 5 SIT **6B**
Pull up slopers to the arete, then the top.

10 Thugosity ★ **6A+** SIT **6C**
Beefy climbing up the centre.

11 Modicum 6A SIT **6B**
The left arete yields to a modicum of technique.

Extra value is added by linking these problems via the slopey traverse.

12 The Righteous Laugh SIT **7A**
Start as per *Exsqueeze Me* and traverse left to finish using the far arete.
Robin Müller, James Williamson 2013

13 Slope-Em-Up ★ SIT **7A+**
Start up the left arete, then follow the lip and pull round the right arete to a pumpy finish up *Exsqueeze Me*.
Robin Müller 2013

Finally, head back past the main wall to a little leaning arete at the far end of the quarry.

14 Keep Straining 5+ SIT **6B+**
A big first move leads to a jug in the crack, then an easier top. Eliminate the crack holds at **6C+**. For both versions, don't use any of the footledge.

15 Keep Training SIT **6C**
From matched on the small block to the left, traverse rightwards below the top, to finish via jugs on the sidewall. You can put your feet on the small left-hand sidewall, but not the block in the corner.

Keep Straining, 6B+ p83

THE QUARRIES

The stone was dropped by the quarry-side,
And the idle derrick swung,
While each man talked of the aims of art,
And each in an alien tongue.

The Conundrum of the Workshops - Rudyard Kipling, 1865

Shed Seven, 6B

It doesn't get much more esoteric! The bouldering here takes place on a small wall with a nice flat landing. There aren't many problems, but if you live nearby, why not? There is some potential in the pond quarry, but only for the very keen.

APPROACH 1 min
From Junction 3 of the M65, exit onto the A675 towards Walton Le Dale. At the T-junction, turn left and continue on the A675. Take the 2nd turn on the left, down Dover Lane. Then turn right and follow the road to a small layby with a view across a pond to the quarry.

Park here (not opposite the house) and follow the track uphill to the right. For the Small Quarry, turn right at the concrete structure and thread through the trees for 50m (there is no path) until you reach a grassy clearing containing the quarry.

When leaving the crag, it is easiest to follow the road in a loop (keep turning left), rather than trying to turn the car.

11 Duxon Hill

DUXON HILL 87

Small Quarry

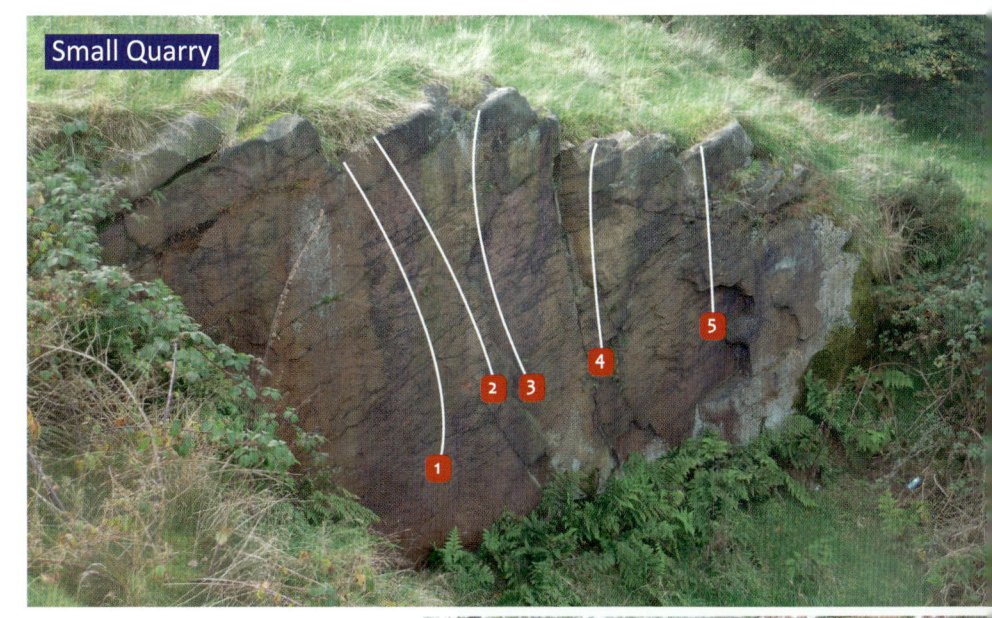

The Small Quarry is 50m through the trees from the concrete structure, in a clearing. Fast-drying.

1 Shed Seven ★ 6B SIT 7A
Sitstart and crimp up edges to the top. Good value.
Robin Müller 2012

2 The Monstrous Left Hand 6A
Use the rib feature for hands, but for feet use only the little edges and smears to its left. Finish up and left.

3 Feature Creature 5
Climb the juggy rib feature.

4 Small Shakes 4
Up the crack.

5 Umpulations 3

There are some super easy slabs just left. They are a bit grassy, but not bad for kids. There is also an eliminate sitstart problem which starts on the slopey ledge on the very short wall left of the arete. Go straight to the top from here - this is **6A**.

Pond Quarry

The Pond Quarry is reached from the car by following the uphill track, then turning left to hop over the second broken section of stone wall. Pick your way down the slope and head rightwards following the edge of the quarry around the pond. There are some highball possibilities, but the only problem with a decent landing is on the right side of the left side wall.

6 Project
The wall and rounded arete, using the good high footholds on the right. Technical.

12 Hoghton

Beneath the majestic quarried architecture skulks a scruffy but stimulating set of problems. All are conveniently clustered in a small area. The crag is best visited on a breezy day, as humidity can be an issue. Climbing at the crag is allowed only during summer, after the peregrines have fledged. Dates vary so check the BMC RAD for details - July and August are the usual months. On days when climbing is permitted, access is allowed on Sun-Tues between 8.30am and 5.30pm, and on Wed-Sat between 8.30am and 9pm. Music is not allowed.

APPROACH 10 min

From Junction 3 of the M65, take the A675 towards Walton Le Dale, signposted to Hoghton Tower. Turn left at the T junction and continue for 1 mile to the Boar's Head pub. Turn right in front of this, onto Chapel Lane. After half a mile, cross the railway bridge and park next to the chapel graveyard (without obstructing the road). Walk back over the bridge and turn left onto the footpath which leads to the crag. You can walk along the left bank towards the end, which avoids some of the mud. Bring wellies!

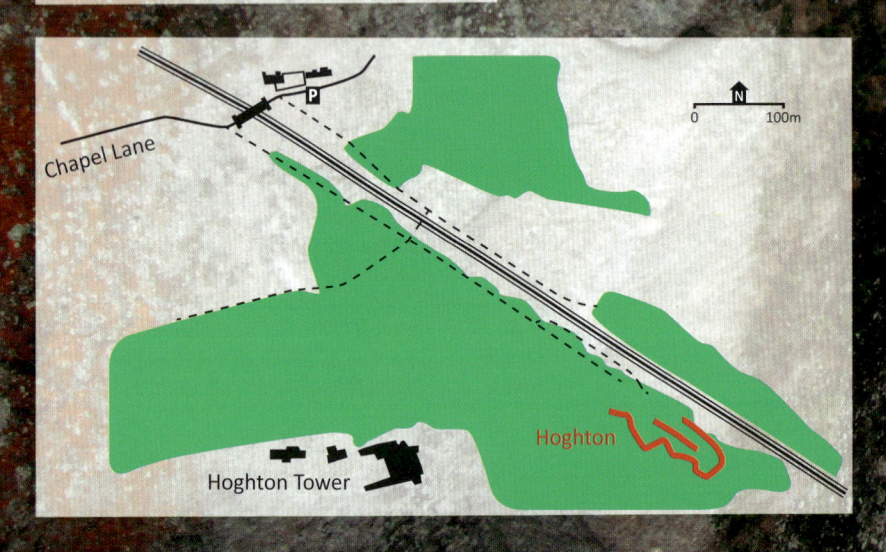

Monochimp, 7B p91

HOGHTON

Glue Wave is on a featured side wall, not far into the quarry. **Eldritch Sigh** is further left, at the back of the same bay. Mono Wall is just left again.

There is also some easy bouldering on the small lower tier.

1 Glue Wave ★ **7A+**
Work up sidepulls and underclings to a big finishing pocket.
Robin Müller 2012

2 Eldritch Sigh ★★ **7A+**
The slopey arete on its left. Classic.
Robin Müller 2012

Chimp & Chips, 7A p91

HOGHTON

Mono Wall

3 Arete 5+
The arete on its left.

4 Fingertip Traverse Start 4
Pull up the crack. Stop.

5 Slab For It 7A
Undercling to top.
Robin Müller 2012

6 Project
Sitstart and swing left on drilled monos, with a dearth of footholds. Bring out the wads.

7 Project
The LH is good but the RH holds are all poor monos. Pulling on is half the battle.

8 Chimp & Chips 7A
One big move, with the good chip for LH.
Robin Müller 2012

9 Monochimp ★ LOW 7B
A crouching start, matched on the twin monos.
Robin Müller 2012

10 Chump & Chips 7A
Another big move, with the good chip for RH.
Robin Müller 2012

11 Pandora's Boxed 7A
Start as for *Chump & Chips*. Swing leftwards to gain *Pandora's Box Left Hand*.
Robin Müller 2012

12 Pandora's Box 6A
From the jug, head to the ledge.

13 Pandora's Box Left Hand ★ 6A+
Layback the groove and rockover rightwards to the ledge.

14 Speech Impediment 6A
Big pulls up the crack to the good ledge.

15 Full Sail ★ SIT 6C
Sitstart the unfurled arete, with a couple of tricky moves low down.

16 Project
You might want spotters on adjacent blocks.

17 The Miggity Mac Daddy ★ 6B
An undercling leads onto a giant footledge. The next hold is the top. Lower grades for taller people, higher grades for people who remember Kris Kross.

21 Denham

Fast-drying verticalities, clean rock, no walk in. The quarry is annoyingly popular with local youths, so litter and graffiti are prevalent. That said, when evening sun slants upon the crag, Denham is not a bad place to be. A fair smattering of worthwhile problems will test even the fingeriest fingers.

APPROACH 1 min
Several approaches are possible, but the most straightforward is from the M61. Exit at Junction 8, taking the A674 towards Chorley. At the next roundabout follow the A6 north towards Clayton-Le-Woods. Continue for almost 3 miles to the Clayton Green roundabout (just after The Pines Hotel on your right). Take the third exit, signposted to Blackburn. Continue to another roundabout and turn left. Drive past the houses and take the next right onto Holt Lane. Parking for the quarry is on the left after half a mile.

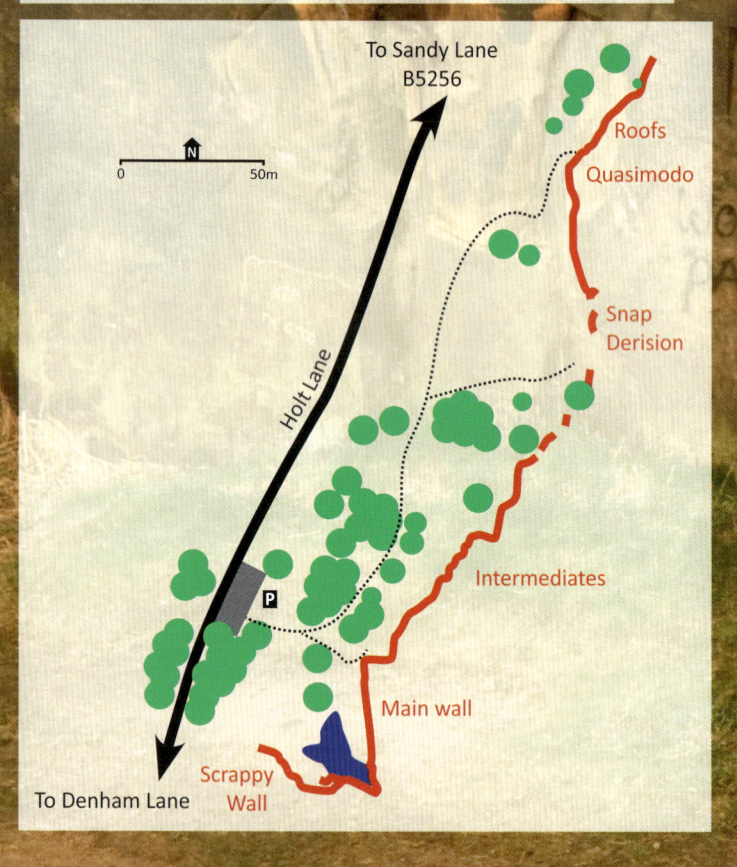

Pickpocket, 5+ p94

DENHAM

Main Wall Left

7 Crackpot ★ **6B+**
Finger your way up the thin crack.

The wall to the right used to give a good 7B, as well as the crux of a long traverse. Sadly, the rock has been ruined by fire.

8 Corner 4
The easy corner.

9 Groove 3
Useful as a descent.

10 Short Wall 5
Up the centre.

11 Short Wall Rightwards 7A
Crimp rightwards from good holds, staying beneath the top.

12 Short Wall Leftwards 7A
The reverse.

13 Project
From right, traverse using nothing higher than holds in the top seam.

14 Project
Somehow use that thin LH undercut sidepull thing.

15 Casio Feet sit **7A+**
Sitstart RH pocket, then push left to the good ledges.
Robin Müller 2012

16 Swatch Me sit **7B**
Sitstart LH pocket, gain the jug on *Undercut Problem*, then force a route leftwards.
Robin Müller 2012

17 Undercut Problem ★ **7B+** sit **7B+**
Pull up to a crux move for the undercut. Press on to match the high slopers. Then jump off. Only half a grade easier from standing, but less spiritually fulfilling.
Nik Jennings 2001, SIT Robin Müller 2012

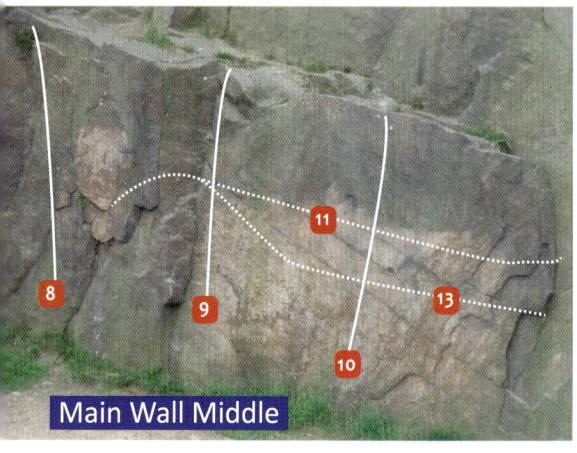

Main Wall Middle

The Main Wall is the first area encountered, right next to the pool.

1 The Arete 5+

2 Wall 5+

3 Sandy Cave 5+

4 Snatch ★★ **8A**
From the footledge, a sidepull sprag leads into mini nothings. Remember, this is a slab. Unrepeated.
Nik Jennings 2001

5 Pickpocket ★★ **5+**
From the flake, head for the big pocket.

6 Pickpocket Direct ★ **6A**
Crimp direct to the pocket, left of the crack.

18 Flick Of The Wrist Direct 6B
Climb the arete to the high slopers. Jump or dive to descend.

The rest of the problems in this area are accessed by walking round to the other side of the pool.

19 The Arete 5+
On its right.

20 Poolside Wall 6A
Without using the arete.

The Scrappy Wall is obvious just to the right.

21 Nik's Traverse 7A
From left, stay beneath the line of large holds.
Nik Jennings 2001

22 Rich In Rain 6A+ sit 6C
Sitstart from the slanting edge and climb upwards, staying off the big holds to the side.

23 Squall 5 sit 7A
Sitstart from the edge and sidepull.

24 Pocket Finder 4 sit 6B
Sitstart from the arete.

25 Infolding 4 sit 6A
A crunched up sitter into good holds and a top-out mantel.

26 Mars Attacks 4+
From right, follow the big holds all the way to Mars.

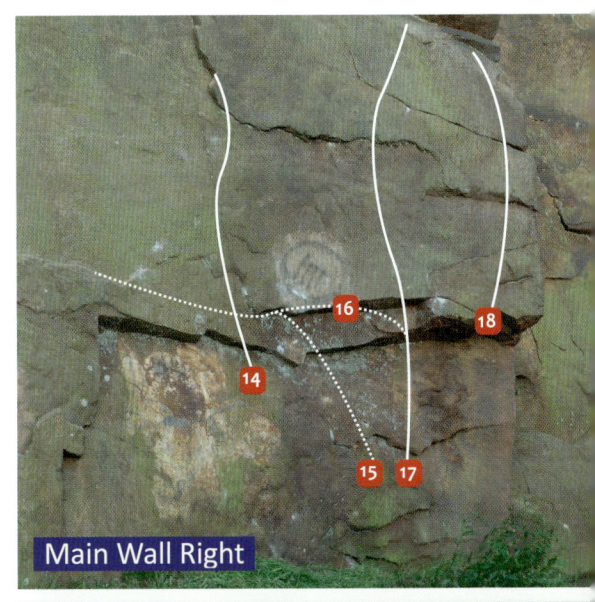

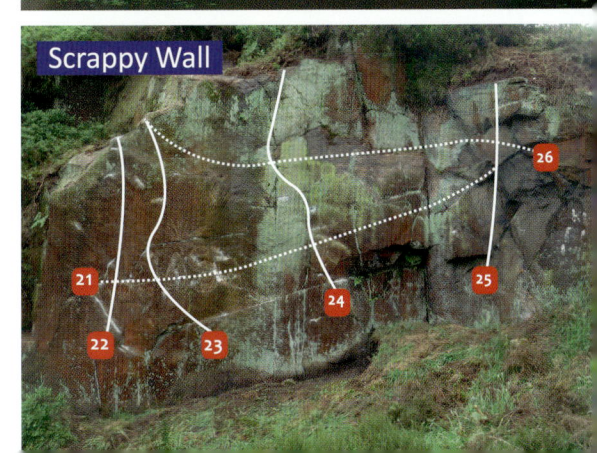

DENHAM

From the Main Wall, walk leftwards along the base of the crag to reach the Intermediates area: a long broken section containing a few decent problems.

1 The Clangers 5
Weee Wooo Wee Waaa Weeee Weeee Woooo. Or in English: climb the tall crack, whistling unintelligbly as you go.

2 Notions Of Disposability 5
The arete on its right feels high.

The next problem is left of the corner.

3 Rivet 4+

Some way left is the Hypno-Toad wall.

4 Drill Scar Wall 5

5 Thin Finger Crack 5
The arete on its right feels high.

6 Hypno-Toad 6C SIT 7A
The wall between the arete and the crack, finishing at the incut sloper.
SIT Gareth Wallis 2014

Continue on the path till a clearing. Snap Derision is here, on a short wall.

7a The Ceaseless Tide 6A
The arete leads to a highball slab.

7b Snap Derision LOW 7A
Start LH thin gaston, RH low sidepull. A tough move gains the obvious edge, then LH drillholes and a nose sloper lead upwards. Climb without the large foothold or cracks to the left. Finish at the break.
Gareth Wallis 2008

8 Fingerbore SIT 5
Climb the cracks into the groove.

Further left, above the descent to the lower tier, is a short, hard sitstart wall.

9 Project
Sitstart and crimp up the wall using the engraved symbol.

Continue leftwards and drop down to a lower level. The Quaisimodo problems are just past a couple of small boulders. One wall has sadly suffered chipping, and though it has been repaired, the marks are still visible.

10 From Ruins 5
The arete is good entertainment. **6A** without the starting footledges.

The next 4 problems all finish at a slopey top. Jump down or traverse off.

**11 There's A Ghost
In My Acid House ★ 6A+**
The wall on its right, with a French start to the LH sidepull (used as a gaston on the next problem). Swing into the middle to finish.
Goi Ashmore

12 Living Next Door To Acid 7A SIT **7B**
A crimpy sitter leads to a big crank for the RH gaston.
Robin Müller 2012

13 Quasimodo Right Hand 6A
The arete is less scary on its right side.

14 Quasimodo 5
The start of an E1 climbs the arete on its left.

The final problems are a bit further left.

15 Chronometer Eliminate 5+
Climb the wall to the roof, without the arete. With the arete it's **4+**.

16 Smearometer 5+
Climb the wall. Don't use the arete.

17 Project
The soaring lip is an obvious project. Mantel the jug to finish, then top out or reverse and jump off.

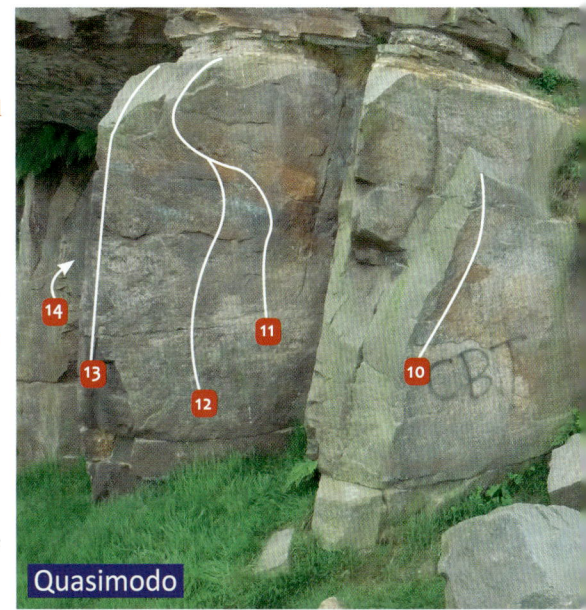

No Tome For Losers, 7C+

Baby Denham

With two leaning walls, Baby Denham throws a tiny bone to seekers of steepness. Climbing is accompanied by the sonorous hum of the M61, but there are a few decent problems and you won't need to queue. The right wall is almost perma-dry while the left wall needs a few dry days to stop seeping. Bring more than one crashpad. It also combines well with Denham, which is just round the corner.

APPROACH 5 min
Follow directions to Denham. Continue to the end of Holt Lane and turn right onto Denham Lane. Once at the motorway flyover, park on the pavement near the footpath sign. Cross the stile and walk uphill. Follow the wire fence on your left as it turns downhill. Cross carefully where it meets a wooden fence. Left Wall is immediately on your left. Right Wall is a little further on.

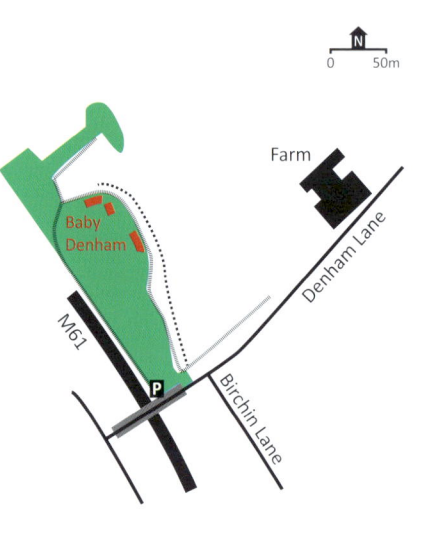

BABY DENHAM   99

Left Wall

1 Tree-Being ★ SIT **6B**
Sitstart the blocky arete from a clamping position. Don't use the obvious footblock.

2 Pinchetta SIT **6C**
Sitstart at LH slot and RH pinch.

3 Mucky Pup ★ SIT **7A+**
Sitstart from LH wide pinch, RH slot. Throw to the arete.
Robin Müller 2013

4 No Tome For Losers ★★ SIT **7C+**
Sitstart as before, then traverse left to gain the left arete jug. Rock onto the shelf.
Robin Müller 2013

5 Bumble Town **4+**
Traverse the face from the arete.

6 Project
Super-thin sitter.

7 Project
From a sitstart just in front of the tree, using LH undercut pinch and RH break, pull to the lip then traverse leftwards. Sadly, some of the rock is a bit friable. The moves are good though, with enough solid holds to make it worthwhile.

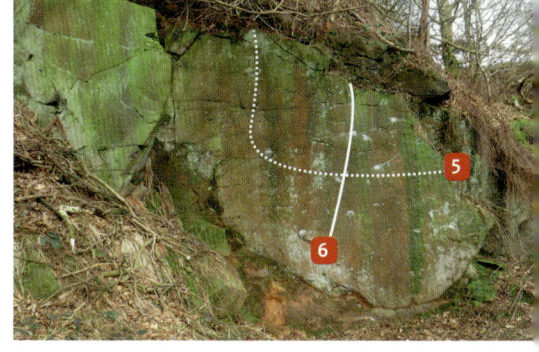

Right Wall

Another World, 7C+ p101

14 Stanworth

Landfill operations have long since ceased, and what was once a rather unsightly mess has now returned to nature. The overgrown top-outs of many routes tell of neglect, but thanks to recent efforts, bouldering areas are in good condition. The quality of problems is sure to attract a regular clientele. There are powerful steep problems on the undercut wall, fingery challenges on the red wall and even a world class slab.

ACCESS - Negotiations are ongoing, but the quarry and surrounding land is owned by BIFFA. It is possible that you will be asked to leave.

APPROACH 1 min
From Junction 3 of the M65, take the A675 exit towards Bolton. After the restaurant, take the first left turn, signposted to Stanworth Farm. Drive down the bumpy lane to a footpath sign on the right. Just past this, park considerately in the layby. Take the footpath to the stile, cross the lower level field and head uphill, staying left of the gate. Enter the quarry via the stile. Follow the edge of the quarry rightwards until it is possible to descend a steep grassy slope.

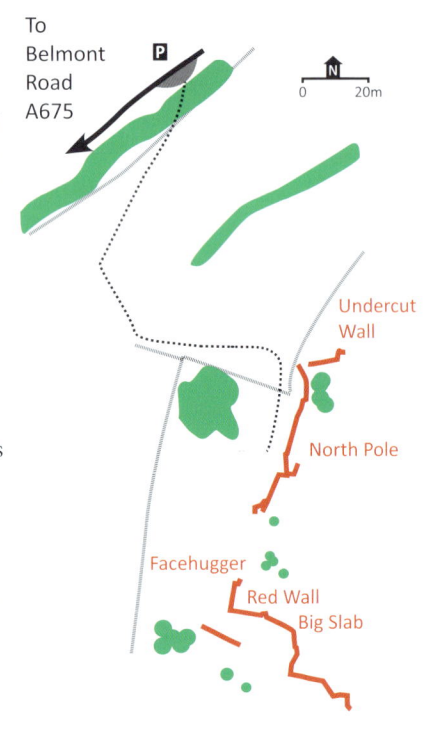

To Belmont Road A675

Undercut Wall
North Pole
Facehugger
Red Wall
Big Slab

STANWORTH 101

Undercut Wall

The furthest right buttress is home for the hardman. This is the place to come for a good old-fashioned spanking.

1 Shy Side SIT **6A+**
The wall and arete on the far left.

2 Project
The blank wall above a poor landing. It might be possible to climb into it from the right arete jug.

3 Toit Groove 5+
Climb the juggy groove.

4 Project
Pull to a slopey crimp and swing to the arete.

5 Project
Pull up to a slopey crimp and an airy throw to small but positive edges.

6 Project
The very vague arete.

7 Dynamo ★ 6A+
Hang the lowest hold and pull up via the pocket. Juggy but steep. No back wall.

8 Iddybits 7A
From matched in the break, crimp straight up. No holds on *Backslash*.
Robin Müller 2012

9 Shuffle Generation ★ SIT **7A+**
From a sitstart matched on the low arete crimp, stab leftwards into *Dynamo*. No back wall.
Robin Müller 2011

10 Backslash ★ 6B+ SIT **7A**
From matched on the low arete crimp, gain the slanting holds and the top. No back wall.

11 Fracking 7C+
Pull on to the two poor high holds and launch for the break. Stack pads if you can't reach, though it has been done from just one.
Dawid Skoczylas 2012

12 Project
Pull on with RH undercut and LH small face gaston used for RH by *Fracking*. Go for the top. The sitter is also possible.

13 Another World ★ 7C+
Starts from LH sidepull, RH undercut. No back wall or chossy pillar.
Robin Müller 2011

14 Skin Day SIT **6B**
The block just right, from sitting.

102 STANWORTH

North Pole Buttress

The North Pole buttress is the central section of the quarry, left of the Undercut Wall.

1 Rust Never Sleeps Direct 4+
The arete is fun on both sides. The slab is harder without using the arete - **5**.

2 Two For The Price Of One ★ 7A
Excellent arete climbing, without using the crack.
Robin Müller 2013

3 Sandman ★ SIT 7A
Sitstart the clean wall right of the corner to gain a slopey ledge. Make a brilliant grovel to stand on this. Use higher holds if you like, but they will probably come off!
Robin Müller 2011

4 Holier Than Thou 3
Use the hole within a hole. There is no spoon.

5 Somewhere On The Curve 5+
The arete on its right, staying away from the hole. A crimp aids matters, but watch the landing.

The next two problems are high, but a pile of pads might inspire confidence. Traverse off at the sandy break and downclimb a neighbouring route. The cracks to either side are **4+**.

6 Spitting Image E5 6a
Start up the right side of the slab and finish straight up the centre. The first ascent of this was a gearless solo, but you'll probably be thankful for a bit of foam.
Phil Garlick 1986

7 Subzero E6 6B
The left side of the slab, via the obvious hole.
Dave Kenyon, Greg Rimmer 1983

Just left the problems become shorter again, though the landings can be slopey.

8 Heeby-Jeeby 5
The right arete is a little scary. Drop off at the jug.

9 Project
Climb the left arete of the right-hand wall. Use face holds but not the right arete.

10 Bering Strait 4+
Bridge up the niche to finish at the jug.

11 When The Mountain Leans 6A SIT 6B+
The right side of the left arete, to a jug.

12 Baffin 5
Follow edges up the slab. Make sure you are happy to reverse or descend another route.

13 Barents Low Start 6B+
Start with the big RH pocket near the arete and something smaller for LH. Make a big move to the jug, then an easier finish. Reverse and drop off.

14 Treasure Style 4+ SIT 6A
Clamp up the rib to good jugs.

15 Face In The Crowd 3
An easy slab.

16 Scorched Earth ★★ 6B+
Fantastic climbing up the arete and sidepulls.

17 Blacky Woo Woo Bon Bon Pipkins ★ 6C
Start from poor pockets left of the big sidepull and make a hard move for the ramp. A big rockover to the bore hole follows. Using the big sidepull to gain the ramp drops the grade to **6B**.

18 Pack-Ice Strict 5
The big flake, without the left wall. Scary.

19 The Arctic Traverse 6B+
From the flake, follow the ramp across the wall to finish on the slabs past *Scorched Earth*.

Down to the left is a worthwhile groove.

20 Spitsbergen ★ 5
Bridge stylishly upwards to big holds at the top of the arete. Luckily, you don't need to use the overgrown crack.

Project p104

104 STANWORTH

Big Slab

3 Project
There are holds. Can anyone use them?

4 Endless Nameless ★★ **8B**
The hardest slab in the world? Use a LH pinch and climb to the undercling. Head right to a sidepull, then back left to good holds. Step left at the top to avoid the overhanging grass.
John Gaskins 2005

5 Project
Make a few moves to stand on the slot, then contemplate the final two metres. How hard can it be?

Here it is. *That* slab. A majestic sweep of desperation dotted with the smallest of friction points, all at a daunting height. Come ye aspirants, teeter and snatch...

1 Project
Up the slab to gain the thin crack and finish at the ledge, staying off the big crack to the left.

2 Stranded Passenger **E4 6C**
This old E4 might make a good highball.
Dave Kenyon 1985

6 Project
Traverse the slab.

7 Project
Layback the rib.

8 What's Occurin' SIT **7B**
Gain the fat sidepull and make a move to a finishing edge.
Robin Müller 2012

STANWORTH   105

Red Wall

Right of the big slab is a red wall with interesting rock.

1 Project
Thin holds lead into a high groove.

2 Edge Of Extinction 6C
Climb the crack to a tricky top.
Dave Cronshaw, Bob Macmillan 1985

3 Project
Sitstart just right of the crack.

4 Too Hard For Greg Rimmer ★ 6B
Climb the flake to a large jug just past the top break. Downclimb or garden upwards.

5 Too Low For Greg Rimmer 7A+
Sitstart the above, starting from a good RH edge and not much for the left.
Robin Müller 2011

6 Monsoon 7B
Given VS 5A as a route, but either this was originally done as a jump start or the ground level has changed. Use the flake and poor holds to gain the jug, then an easy move to the finishing break.

Further right is a good double arete feature.

7 Edge Game ★ 7A
The left arete is fingery. Doing it without the giant chipped starting hole is better, at 7A+.
Dave Kenyon 1987

8 Facehugger ★★ 7A+ SIT 7B
Clamp straight up the double arete, with a crux move to the good flat edge, then a fun top-out.
Robin Müller 2012

Race To Base, 7B p109

15 Knowle Heights

Despite a fairly large area, only a small amount of rock protrudes from the heathery cheeks of this scruffy old quarry. A short roof block makes the bouldering good value for locals. A few rain-resistant (but not rain-proof) vertical walls seal the deal.

APPROACH 10 min
From the A666 in Darwen, turn onto Borough Road. Take a sharp right in front of the park to turn uphill onto Inverness Road. Take the next right onto Westland Avenue and park sensibly near the end of the road.

Follow the lane that leads rightwards from the end of the road. Just after cottages, the lane forks. Keep left and continue until it is possible to turn right just after a wooden fence. Hop the stream and follow the path into the quarry.

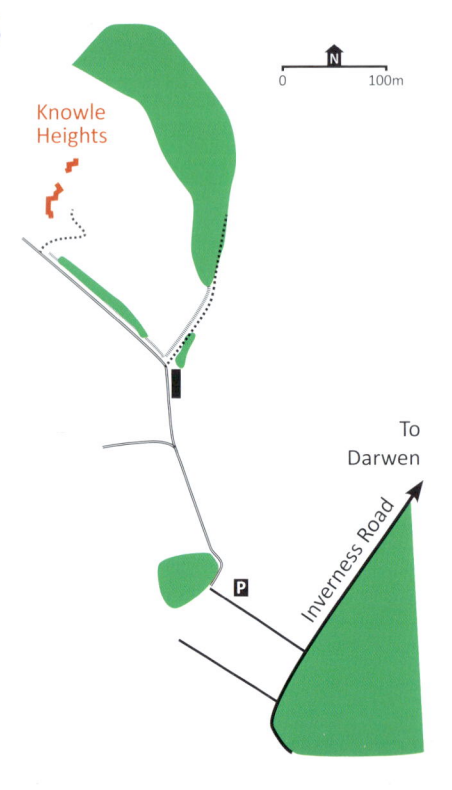

Mind Over Matter, 7B p109

108 KNOWLE HEIGHTS

Left Section

The Left Section of the quarry can sometimes stay dry during light rain.

1 Blue Moves 7A
The short arete from sitting.
Robin Müller 2012

2 Hash Lee ★ SIT 7A+
From the lower level, start with RH big sidepull/undercling and LH on a large painted edge. Work into the gastons up and left, then gain the big hole and finish at the break.
Robin Müller, Will Harris 2014

3 Project
Straight up the wall, staying left of the big hole.

4 The Wierdy Hole 7A
From the sandy hole, rock left and up to the break.
Robin Müller 2012

5 Project
The arete just right of the corner is a bit overgrown, but looks like it could be hardish.

For the meat of the bouldering, wander over to the quarry's Right Section. A fast-drying roof block offers good entertainment.

KNOWLE HEIGHTS 109

6 Project
The arete on its right.

7 Mind Over Matter ★ **7B**
A sandy start leads into a fine highball.
Robin Müller 2014

The obvious roof has rules. The back wall is divided by a vertical crack. Everything left of this is the Left Back Wall; everything to the right is the Right Back Wall. The foot-slab down and left is always off-limits.

8 Super Ted 5
The crack and ledgey upper arete.

9 Project
Sitstart and pull straight up the wall.

10 Easy, Tiger 4+ SIT **7A**
The arete on its left. No back walls.
Robin Müller 2012

11 The Knowle Edmunds Project
Sitstart (LH crimp, RH crack undercut) and climb the arete on its right, without the back walls. Use the roof crack but not the continuation vertical crack.

12 The Monk of Crunk 5 SIT **7A**
Sitstart from underclings and pull straight into the wall above. The right back wall is out - using this is **6C**.
Robin Müller 2012

13 Race To Base ★ SIT **7B**
Start at the break, then clamp through the crack and lip to pull up the far wall. The left back wall is out.
Robin Müller 2012

14 Kerfuffle 5+
The centre of the slab.

15 Project
The slab at its highest point.

16 Shakin A Donkey 6A
From a stance on the right, traverse the break to finish up the final arete. Also good in reverse, finishing up the slab.

17 Flash 6A
Esoteric offwidth heaven. Maybe.

Right Section

The Noisy Cricket, 7C p111

16 Stronstrey Bank

Several clusters of bouldering add up to a reasonable quantity of problems, some of which are excellent. The hillside aspect means Stronstrey has scenic views and good sunsets, as well as generally fast-drying rock.

APPROACH   **10 min**
From Junction 8 of the M61, take the A674 towards Wheelton. Go through the roundabout and take the next right turn at traffic lights, onto Blackburn Road. After a mile, take the last left turn before the motorway bridge, onto Knowley Brow. After 1.5 miles, turn right in front of The Railway pub, signposted to White Coppice. The village can also be reached from Anglezarke by heading north and following signs for White Coppice. Once at White Coppice, continue to a bumpy road which leads to parking by the cricket ground. On match days, please park on the bumpy road. The footpath starts from the bridge. The main area is reached by turning right, then following a path uphill when it becomes obvious.

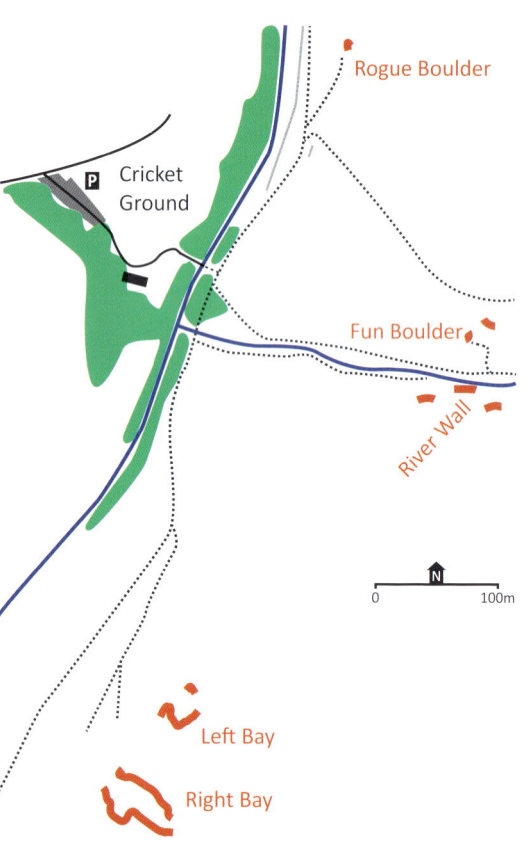

Rogue Boulder

Cricket Ground

Fun Boulder

River Wall

Left Bay

Right Bay

STRONSTREY BANK

The Rogue Boulder is visible from the parking, but soon hides itself when you head towards it. Turn left after the bridge, then where the path splits (after a small wall on the right), take a small path in between the two larger paths to head up the slope towards a small boulder. The Rogue Boulder is just 20m left of this.

1 Phil SIT **5+**
Start from high undercuts and pull round onto the front for a slopey finish.

2 The Noisy Cricket ★ SIT **7C**
From RH edge and LH lip pinch, make powerful pulls to match poor holds and gain the top. Long-armed folk might be able to gain the top with a stretch from the start, but this is missing the fun.
Robin Müller 2012

3 Project
An extension to *The Noisy Cricket*. From the low edge, crossover leftwards to gain the start holds of the standard problem. No footblocks.

4 Project
Sitstart at the low edge, with feet on the back wall. No footblocks. Desperate pulls on slopey fingerholds.

5 Grim Leaper SIT **6B**
Start at the low edge, then pull to the finish without the big hold out right. Footblocks are in.

6 Jim Reaper SIT **6A**
Start at the low edge and go to the top using the big RH hold.

7 Day Glo Man 5+
From right, cross the lip and mantel once round the arete. No footblocks.

The next area is by the brook and can be reached by following the water channel on its left, or a shortcut from where the path splits near the Rogue Boulder.

1 Fundango 4+
Traverse the wall from the ledge on the left.

2 Funhouse ★ SIT **7A+**
Dyno from the angled jug to the ledge. Feet on the right wall only. It's a real crazy throw, where anything can go.
Robin Müller 2009

3 Funrise SIT **5+**
Head up and left to the cutaway. The left back wall is out.

4 Funset SIT **5**
As before, but head up and right.

The lava-like slab to the right is **Funwalk**, and can be climbed without hands, and wearing anything on your feet (or indeed on the rest of your body).

STRONSTREY BANK

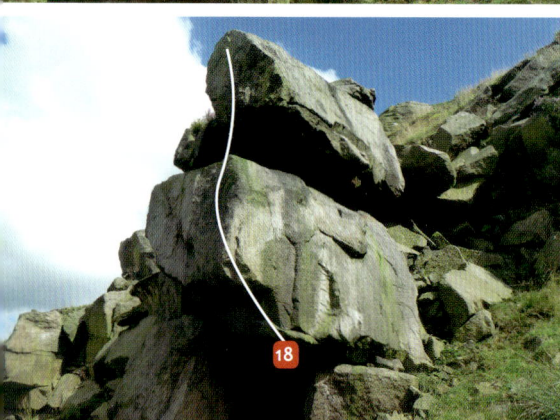

Left Bay

The Left Bay is reached by following the uphill track towards the main quarry, then heading up the steep grassy bank to the bay. The very left bay has nothing in it: continue up to the higher bay. Bouldering starts on the back wall.

1 The Bulge Traverse Project
Sitstart LH crack RH arete. Traverse right to finish up the crack. Super hard.

2 The Bulge Project
A short but very tricky bulging arete.

3 Make Like Brunel And Bridge It 5+
Engineer a solution to the crack.

4 The Drunken Crimp 6A
The wall on its left, using sidewards holds.

5 Project
The arete has a bad landing.

6 Hold Em And Fold Em ★ SIT 6B+
Climb the arete and stand on the lip to finish. Use nothing left of the crack.

7 One Giant Lip For Mankind LOW 6C
Dyno from the slanting hold to the lip. The continuation mantel is a project.

8 Squirm If You Wanna Go Faster 6A
Pull into the groove, then traverse left to finish matched on the left arete.

9 Ho-Humming LOW 5
The right side of the green wall, from the low ledge and without using the arete.

10 Featherback 4+
The dirty face.

11 Mucky Duck 3

12 Duckbill 3

13 Mirth Of The Ducks ★ 7A
Starting from crimps, climb the slender arete without using nearby blocks.
Robin Müller 2009

14 Hand Me Ups 5
The left arete.

15 Squint 6A
Use neither arete.

16 The Hoard 4+ SIT 5+
The right arete, on its left.

17 Bob On SIT 6C
Sitstart the arete, using the crack jug.

18 Howsat SIT 6B
Start from the lip jug, without using any lower blocks for feet.

Mirth Of The Ducks, 7A p112

Right Bay

The Right Bay is just a short walk further along the hillside. It can also be reached from the main path by continuing along the obvious uphill track to the quarry.

1 Wurzealous sit **6C+**
Staying left of the big hand and foot holds, sitstart from crimps and climb straight up. The block on the left is off limits.

2 Wurzel Gummidge ★ sit **5+**
Sitstart using the big holds and climb up to a rockover.

3 Mr Tumnus ★ **5**
From the ground (not the higher block) climb the wall and arete.

4 Entry Crack 3+
The one on the left.

5 Wam 4+
The one on the right.

6 Reunion Wilderness ★ **5**
The arete on its left. On its right it's **3+**, and **6C** if you eliminate the big jug.

7 Biteside sit **5**
From a sitstart on the block, climb the left arete and swing right to reach the scoop.

8 TREEEOH sit **6C**
Negotiate the trio of obstinate edges.

STRONSTREY BANK   115

Right Bay

9 Closing Time 6C
Undercling to good edges. Stay off the block on the left.

10 Project
The blank wall to the right of the good edges. Pull up the centre, then leftwards to a small crimp.

11 Lovehandle ★ LOW **4+**
Start hands matched in the break, then up the groove.

12 Sans Arete ★ LOW **7A**
Dyno from underclings to the top.
Gareth Wallis 2010

13 Phat Haendel LOW **6B**
From matched in the break, climb the wall using both aretes. Eliminating the left arete is **Haendel Direct 6C.**

Bouldering continues on the opposite side of the quarry.

14 Project
The scruffy arete from sitting.

15 David Vetter ★★ **7A+**
The blade-thin arete on its right, with the crux at the very top. Be careful of suspect top-out blocks.
Gareth Wallis 2010

16 Escaping Jam SIT **5**
Sitstart in the dip and pull past the steep crack to rockover leftwards.

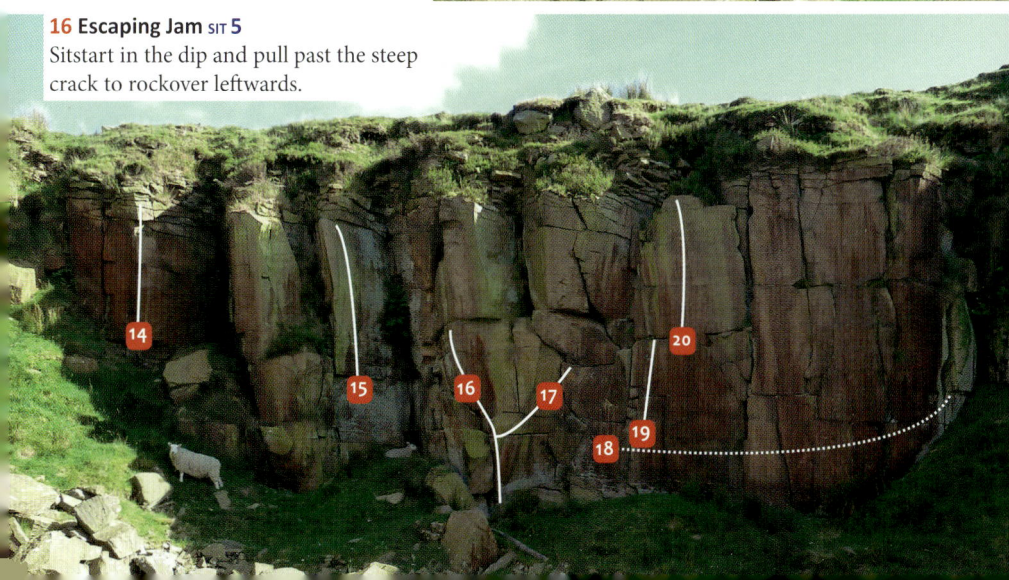

116 STRONSTREY BANK

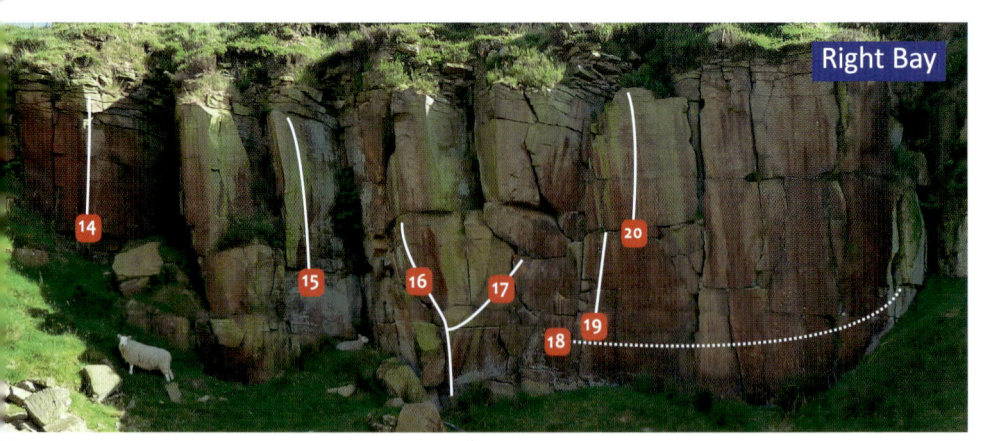

17 Cackhanded Compliment ★ SIT **6B+**
From the same sitstart at the steep crack, swing right along the break, then up the flake to a jug at its top.

18 Spanners 6B
From the slopey ledge, head right to finish round the slight arete.

19 Tony Bland 6A+
From the rail, dyno or mantel to the upper break, eliminating all other cracks.

20 Project
The highball upper wall.

21 Notch 5+
This wall was not named because it was first climbed by Edward Notch.

22 Tranquilo SIT **6B**
Sitstart the arete. Eliminating holds left of the arete is **6C**.

23 Holed Hold SIT **6C+**
Sitstart LH central layaway, RH small hold. Climb the arete via the big hole.

24 The Nerds And The Knees ★ SIT **7A+**
This time, stay away from the hole.
Robin Müller 2012

25 Hellebore ★★ **7B+** SIT **7C**
From the same start, climb the wall without deviating to the arete. Fantastic.
Robin Müller 2012

Hellebore, 7C p116

Double Dutch, 7B+ p120

17 Healey Nab

Sequestered in leafy surrounds, Healey is a great place to Nab some climbing in sun-baked summers, offering shady spots and a broad spectrum of hards and softs. It can be popular with mountain bikers and fire-building yoofs. Be preprared to do battle with a small amount of lichen, for which you will be rewarded with good landings, proper top-outs and even some steepness.

APPROACH   10 min
Follow driving directions to Anglezarke. Once at the triangular traffic island, turn left and continue on this road to a bridge at the north end of the reservoir. Continue for 600m and park well onto the verge just before the turn-off to White Coppice. Walk back down the road to a footpath between hedges. Follow this into a triangular field and cross to the stile leading into the trees. Follow the edge of the woods rightward, then take a left turn uphill on a small path that leads to the quarry.

There is also limited parking on the bend just north of Anglezarke reservoir. Follow the footpath uphill, through a field and over a stile. Once at the trees, head right in front of the fence. Turn left through the first gate and walk through the woods to the crag.

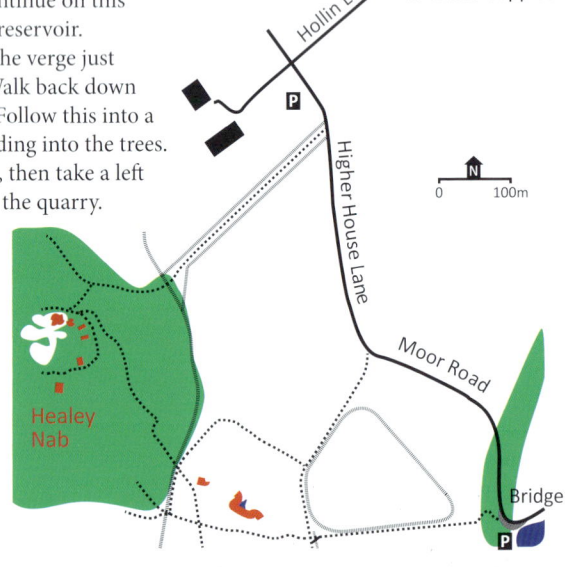

HEALEY NAB 119

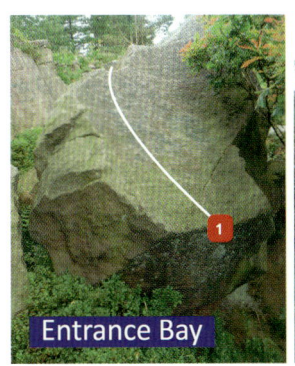

Entrance Bay

1 Quality Control SIT **7A**
Up and left of the other problems is a tiny boulder. From a sitter at the low end, mantel elegantly onto the slab.
Robin Müller 2012

2 Project
The wall using a gaston and assorted razor blades.

3 Grabadabadoo ★ **6B+**
The cheeky arete, from standing. No footledge.

4 Titanium Traverse 7A
Start up *Grabadabadoo*, then swing right, staying just below the top (the small edge is allowed) to finish up *Indium Traverse*.
Gareth Wallis 2006

5 Legs Not Included ★ SIT **7C**
From matched on the low arete hold, swing right along crimps, then stretch to jugs and swing on to the foot ramp.
Robin Müller 2012

6 Burgle SIT **6A**
Straight up the face from the low sitter.

7 Mantel Illness 4
Don't use the footramp.

8 Indium Traverse 5+
Follow the top, in either direction.

9 Heely Grab SIT **5+**
Using just the small crimp (no hands behind the ramp) pull straight to the top.

10 Chipped Slab 5+

11 Slime Pillar SIT **6A+**
Start using the good LH sidepull. The blocks to either side are out.

12 Slab 4

HEALEY NAB

13 Scrunch ★ SIT 6B+
A wierd and wonderful manoeuvre from the cavey niche to pull up to the lip and then the top. Possible with or without the crimp on the right arete.

14 Slaptasm SIT 5+
Sitstart the arete and slap along the lip to pull up at the end.

15 The Coolboy Slap SIT 5+
Match big underclings and go for the good hold.

16 Double Dutch ★ SIT 7B+
From matched on underclings, pull to a RH gaston, then uncoil to pounce on the arete jug. A beast of a move.
Robin Müller 2008

17 Project
Blast straight up the middle. You'll get a gold medal if you do this one.

18 Man Up ★ SIT 7A+
From underclings, dyno to good edges.
Robin Müller 2012

19 Sooty Corner SIT 4
A dark and deadly sitstart.

20 Hide The Medals 6C
Pull on and slap for the arete jug. Continue to the top.

21 Project
From Barmfingers, swing into the arete. A good line, but sadly a key hold is both often wet and eroding.

22 Project
The groove is hard.

23 Barmfingers SIT 6C
Sitstart using the good LH sidepull. The block to the right is off limits.

24 Encore SIT 7A
Head right to gain the arete, then the top. The slab to the right is out, as are jugs on Barmfingers.
Robin Müller 2012

HEALEY NAB

The Woods

Follow the path into the trees and The Woods will proffer several courses of lichen-coated finger food.

25 Pop SIT **5+**
The steep wall and arete.

26 Project
The graffitied slab is thin and needs cleaning.

27 Project
From sitting, pull into the centre.

28 Feed Me 5+
Escape the maw, if not the moss.

29 Trick or Feet 6B
The technical wall. **6C** without the arete or nearby sidepull.

30 Project

31 Dusty Usty 6A
The blunt arete, on its left.

There are several other minor possibilities in the woods, starting with the uncleaned slab just right. In the next-door quarry is a vertical wall with a bad landing. The overgrown crack on its left is **Calvin And Hobbes Crack 6A**. There are also a hard looking wall and a fingery traverse, beneath which the fallen tree trunks could be rearranged into a delightful decking area (as opposed to a decking-out area).

Ticketybang, 7A+ p124

18 Anglezarke & Lester Mill

Anglezarke is a big crag without much bouldering. The Grey Wall offers some amusement and can stay dry in light drizzle. Midges can be bad during summer. Lester Mill is a smaller crag without much bouldering, but it does have a couple of good lines, some fast-drying rock, and a novel DWS traverse.

ANGLEZARKE APPROACH 2 min
From Junction 6 of the M61, take the A6027 towards the Reebok stadium. After 1 mile, this road ends at a roundabout. Take the first exit onto the A673, signposted to Horwich and the West Pennine Moors. Continue through Horwich. Once past a reservoir on your right, take the next right turn, by The Millstone restaurant. Follow this road to a right turn just before a bridge over the motorway. Turn right here (signposted to Anglezarke). The road leads between reservoirs, then to a triangular traffic island. Turn right and park in front of the quarry entrance at a small bay just by the bend. Follow the track into the quarry. If this parking is full, use the alternative parking marked on the map.

LESTER MILL APPROACH 10 min
Follow the same road directions as for Anglezarke, but keep left at the traffic island, then turn left off the hairpin to enter the main car park (pay and display). From here, the obvious path leads to the quarry. Alternatively, follow the road round the hairpin and up the hill. Park on the left at a large bay and follow a footpath downhill from the north end of the bay. The footpath turns right past trees and leads along the top of the quarry to a steep left turn downhill and past The Pinnacle.

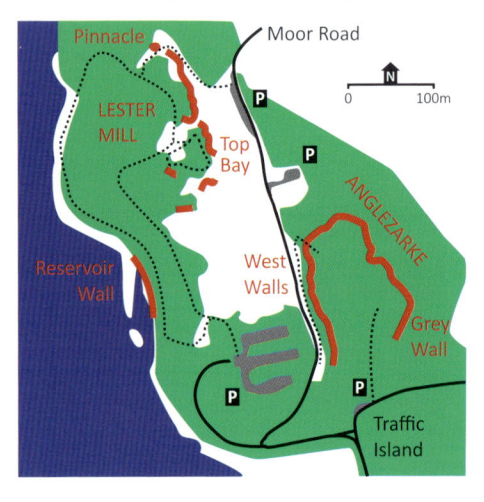

ANGLEZARKE 123

Grey Wall

Anglezarke's main bouldering wall is close to the small parking space to the south of the quarry. It is obvious on the right as you approach. Usefully, it stays dry during showers.

1 Prack 6B
Climb the tricky crack until you can stand in it. Don't use the arete.

2 Arete Sitstart 4

3 Finurgle SIT **6B**
Finurgle through the undercuts.

4 Anglezyno 7A
Dyno from the big edge to the top.

5 Bite Me SIT **7A**
Start LH in the break, RH on a sidepull. Climb up through the slight groove. No arete holds, but a foot next to the right hand is fine.

6 Layback Sitstart SIT **4**

7 Trev The Trav Chav ★ 6C
From the central jug, move left with a tough drop down between seams. Romp along the ledge to finish in the groove.

8 Easy Up 3

9 Lurch ★ SIT **7A**
From the low slopes, gain the ledge, then lurch to finishing holds.

10 Project
A big sidewards jump.

11 Project
Sitstart from LH sidepull and RH arete.

Just right of the Grey Wall, a short boulder lords over a small rock jumble. There is a nice patioed landing, so now it's very easy to sit beneath the boulder and curse.

12 Project
Sitstart the small hanging arete using mini crimps, poor pinches and feet in your ears. Sounds good for the sole?

50m to the left are some tall walls with various sitter possibilities, but these tend to drip after rain and have not yet been developed.

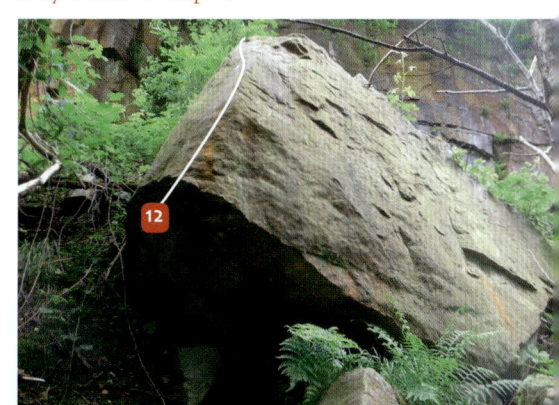

124 ANGLEZARKE

On the north walls (just right of the footpath that leads up the slope and out of the quarry) there is a small Leaning Face, at a right angle to the main wall.

1 Ticketyboo 7A
French start to the crimps, then head left to a good lip hold before finishing up and right on the higher jug. If you use the sidewall to gain the crimps it's **6B**.

2 Ticketybang ★ 7A+
French start to the crimps. Instead of heading to the jug out left, make a big move to the high jug.
Paul Robins 1995

Leaning Face

There is some scrappy bouldering on the West Walls of the quarry, for those who have done everything else.

1 Go Left SIT **6C+**
Pull left to match the ramp. That's it. Crap.

2 Go Up SIT **6B**
Straight up.

3 Go Right 7A+
Start on small edges, from a sitstart with a left heel on the big ledge to the left. Pull up through small holds.

West Walls

4 Bum and Grind 6C
Hang the face jug, swing to the lip, then up onto the slab, without using footholds beneath the lip. **6A** if you use them.

To the left are some clean walls that might tick the box for pleasant highballing. Expect a bit of polish.

Project p125

# Lester Mill

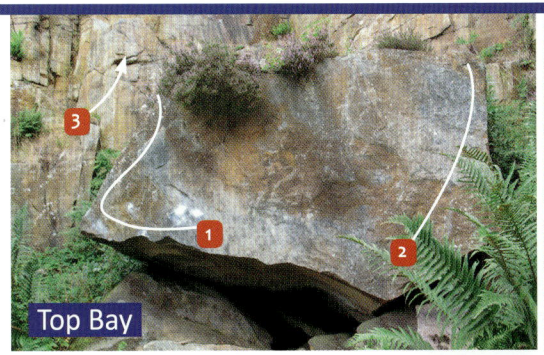

Top Bay

Anglezarke's little sister is Lester Mill. She's not as big, but she's a lot tougher.

On the right side of the quarry is the Top Bay, which is at a higher level. Follow the main path from the main Lester Mill car park. Just after the right bend that leads to the quarry, turn right uphill on a small track that leads past an obvious boulder perched at the top of the bank. Follow this track through trees to the left end of the Top Bay. The first problems are on the fast-drying undercut boulder.

1a Project
Pull on to RH sloper and LH undercut. Gain the arete and head for the top.

1b Paper Cut SIT **6B+**
Start matched low on the arete and pull rightwards to the top.

2 Blister ★ SIT **7C**
The right arete on its left, using the jammed footblock. Infuriating.
Robin Müller 2014

3 Project
Behind the boulder is a blank wall with a thin diagonal crack.

Off to the right is an impressive looking prow. Very fast-drying.

4 Laissez Faire Stare ★★ 7A
Climb the imposing arete. Highball.
John Gaskins 2006

The Pinnacle

At the far left side of Lester Mill, up the steep path is a Pinnacle. This can be also be accessed via the clifftop path leading from the top parking. Beware of potentially loose rock on the upper section. Two pads are useful.

5 Here Come the Midgets SIT **6C**
The arete and crack.

6 Rapunzel SIT **7B**
From sitting on the lower rock, with feet on the good foothold, climb the arete on its left. Keep off the slab jug.
Robin Müller 2012

7 The Enchanted Tower ★ 5+
Climb the arete and slab. **6A** without the arete.

LESTER MILL

Reservoir Wall

1 Judi Drench 5+
Pull off the bank to gain a juggy break line. Follow this to the first good ledge. The grade is the same in reverse.

2 Who Left The Tap On? ★ 6A
From the ledge, drop down to hand-traverse the shelf around the slight arete, then finish on the low hands-free ledge. Same difficulty in reverse.

3 Summer Rain ★ 6C+
From the low ledge, move along the break, to a crux entering the niche. From here, drop down past a protruding boss, then make technical moves to finish. A grade easier in reverse.

4a Project 7b
The full traverse from left to right is excellent, and has not yet been done in one.

4b Fishing For Compliments ★★ 7a+
The reverse is easier but still very good.

On the small island right of the traverse is an undercut wall which has some potential. A canoe is useful to transport the bouldering mats.

5 Project
A few lines are possible but the arete on its left looks the most interesting. Finishing at the ledge is probably wise.

To reach the Reservoir Wall from the main car park, drop down to the lower path and follow this to an information sign on the right. Shortly after this, hop over the wall to a small track which leads down the slope to the north end of the crag.

Lester Mill's summer destination features a fun traverse above the water. It is split by large resting ledges and the three sections are given seperate boulder problem grades, as well as a French sport grade for the whole lot. Water depth may vary, so be careful.

It is also worth noting that this problem was done during a long hot summer, with low water levels. When the water is higher it is likely that some of the line described will be submerged.

Fishing For Compliments, 7a+ p126

Great Wall Of France, 5+ p121

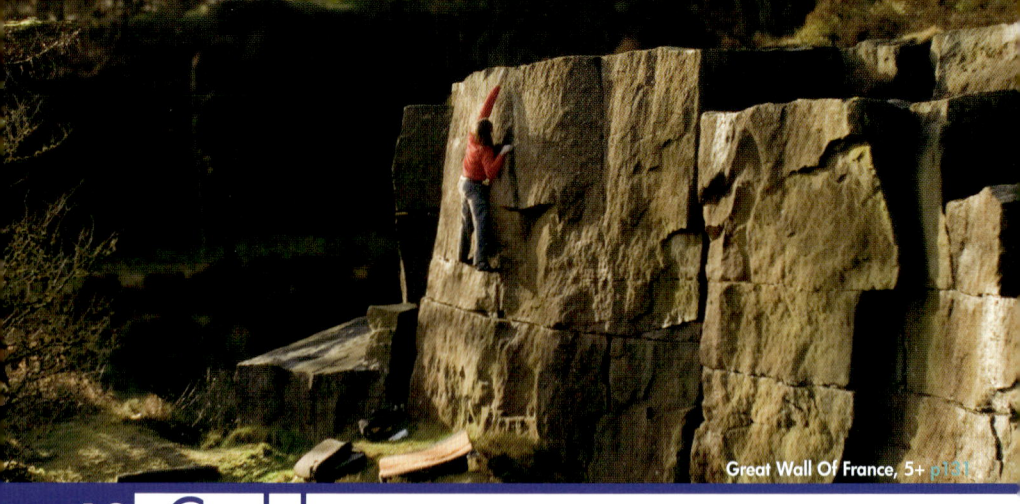

19 Cadshaw

Cadshaw hosts a suprisingly varied collection of bouldering, generally clustered into small areas which each offer several decent challenges. The beginner's circuit at the Small Quarry is friendly and well established, but in recent times the fingery tests of the leaning Red Wall and the summer cool River Blocks have begun to show their charms.

APPROACH 15 min
Turn off the A666 Blackburn Road and onto Green Arms Road. Park in the bay marked at the side of the road. Walk back to the junction and turn right onto the main road. After 80m, turn right at a gate and stile. Follow the large track until the Small Quarry is reached on the left. Continue along the main track for another 5 min to reach the Main Quarry.

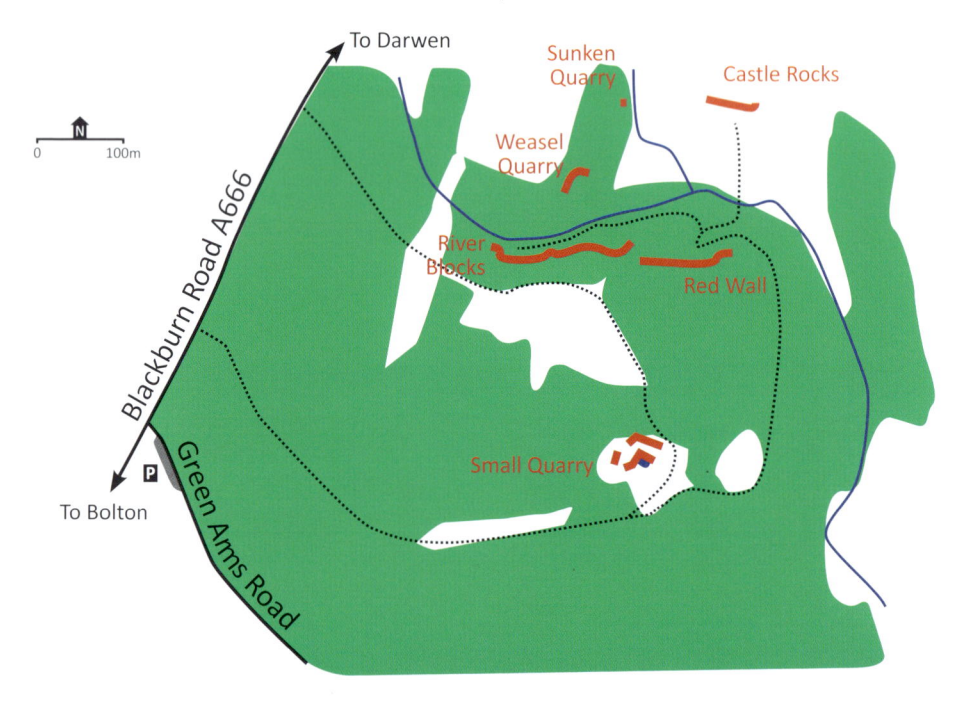

Hawkeye, 6C p133

CADSHAW

The Small Quarry is a popular, clean and open bay. It is obvious to the left of the path after an easy 10 minute walk.

The lower tier is densely packed with easier lines and one or two scary highballs. The upper tier bouldering has become overgrown and so some of these lines have been omitted from the guide (if you are undeterred, all of the undocumented lines are easier than **5**).

Small Quarry

Upper Tier

CADSHAW

1 Folklore 3
The left-most crack.

2 Myths 4+
The central crack.

3 Legend 4
The right-most crack.

4 Silver Falcon 5
The wall between arete and crack.

5 In Praise Of Idleness 4+
The arete on its left.

6 Life On Earth 3
The steps lead to a crack.

7 Willy Visits The Square World 5
Climb the wall using just the undercling.

8 The Visitors 3
The arete on its right.

9 This Game Of Golf 4
The wall right of the arete.

10 Success 2
The vague groove.

11 More Magic 4+
The arete on its right, from the ground.

12 Great Wall Of France 5+
The thin wall to the right of the arete.

13 The Proud Sheriff 4
Climb through the overlap on its left.

14 John Citizen And The Law 5+
Tackle the overlap on its right, finishing left of the small crack.

15 Living Embryos 5
Climb the slender crack.

16 The Atom Rush 6A+
Small crimps lead up the rather highball wall.

17 Wildlife In Britain 5
The arete.

18 Joy Of Nature 4
The corner.

19 In The Blood 4+
The arete right of the corner.

20 God, Genes and Destiny 6B
A worrying highball, straight up the big wall without using the ledge to the left.

21 The Rhesus Danger 4+
The flake.

22 Calculus Made Easy 4+
The wall right of the flake.

23 The Betrothed 5
Step off the ledges and traverse all the way to *Folklore*.

On the left end of the upper tier are a few reasonable problems.

24 Rainbow In The Sky 2
The arete.

25 Cut Flowers And Bulbs For Pleasure 2
The crack.

26 Leaf In The Storm 4+
The wall right of the crack, via a large hole.

27 Bird Of Paradise 5
The wall to the right of the hole.

28 Things A Boy Can Make 2
The green crack further right.

On the right side of the upper tier there are a few more problems that can nearly be topped out.

29 Intermediate Magnetism And Energy 2
The central crack.

30 Insurance 4+
The wall between crack and arete.

31 The Secret Country 4
The arete on its left.

CADSHAW

Red Wall

The Red Wall is the first section of rock on the left of the main quarry. It is slightly overhanging and can often be dry after rain. Other boulders are off to the right.

1 Mighty Mouse SIT **7A+**
Start matched on the long very low edge and crimp up the wall to better holds.
Robin Müller 2009

2 Readers Beware SIT **5+**
The corner crack. Finish on the jugs.

3 Outcast 6C+
From the arete, traverse right at a low level (using all footledges) to finish on a jug below the overlap.

4 Brian Jacques ★★ SIT **7A**
Slap into the arete and make good moves off tricky holds to finish on jugs.
Robin Müller 2006

5 Rivers Of Blood ★★ **7A** SIT **7C**
Climb straight up the wall without the arete. The standing start is only possible for tall people.
Gareth Wallis 2011

6 Jump Arete 6A SIT **7A+**
Start as before, but make a dynamic move to the jug on the right arete. Finish up and left. **6A** if you jump off the ground to start.
Gareth Wallis 2011

CADSHAW

7 The Crack SIT **6A**
Climb up the crack to jugs.

8a Hawkeye ★ SIT **6C**
Gain a RH crimp beneath the overlap and a lower LH crimp on the wall to the left. Make a long move to tiny edges on the seam, then finish on the juggy ledge up and left.

8b Project
From LH low sidepull and RH on the low rounded hold on the arete, go for the LH hold high on the face. Continue up *Hawkeye* to finish.

9 Large Type SIT **5**
Follow good holds up the arete to a big ledge above the overlap.

10 Rakkety Tam 6B+
Dyno from the groove jug to the ledge.

11 Cataplexy SIT **6B**
Get established on the ledge, then use tiny holds to reach good crimps.

12 Project
Match the bottom hold, then go up.

13 Project
The wall left of the obvious arete at the top of the slope. Stay off the arete and finish at the juggy edge.

The next problem is reached by climbing the slope right of problems 16 and 17.

14 Project
Climb the short boulder without rocking round the right arete.

15 Giganticus ★ SIT **7B**
The triangular block is small but steep and provides an excellent slopey battle, with a tricky finish on the right side of the arete. The proper start is from edges below the lip (try toe-hooking the bottom of the boulder and the arete). No footblocks are allowed.
Oliver Müller, Robin Müller 2013

16 Too Hot To Hurdle SIT **6A+** LOW **6C**
The low start is LH lowest sidepull, RH base of arete.

17 Too Manly To Be Healthy SIT **7A**
The wall on the right of the arete, using the arete.
Robin Müller 2014

Castle Rocks

On the opposite side of the valley is a natural grit outcrop known as Cadshaw Castle Rocks. There are two worthwhile fast-drying sitstarts.

18 Cadswallop SIT **6A+**
The arete on its right. Finish at good holds higher up.

19 Cadger ★ SIT **6B**
Sitstart the polished blobs and pull past these to finish on jugs.

20 Castle Traverse 5+
Traverse the crag at a low level. Yes, all the way.

Giganticus, 7B p133

River Blocks

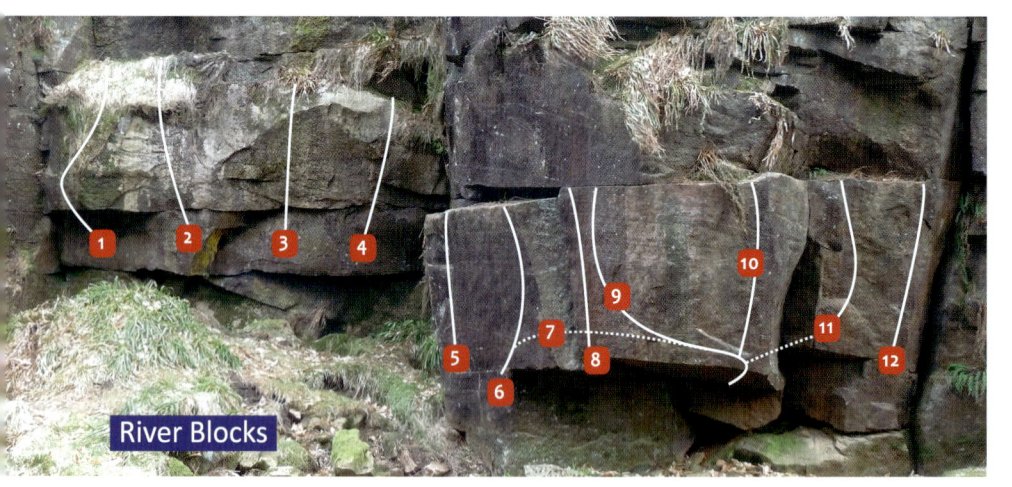

The River Blocks are a great option on hot days, especially with a south-easterly wind to keep the midges at bay. They are slow to dry. There are two approaches:

1. Continue upstream from the Red Wall (stay on the same side of the river and follow the low muddy path).
2. Turn off the main track onto the uphill track that leads past a gate and past the Small Quarry. Keep going until you pass a gate on your left, then turn right downhill where the trees thin. Negotiate the steep slope down to the river and head downstream.

1 The Chunklate Factory 4 SIT **6B**
Use undercuts to sitstart, then gain the arete and head right to good holds.

2 Stairway To Somewhere 3+ SIT **6A**
Follow chunky edges to the top.

3 Project
Right of centre is the hardest looking line.

4 Project

5 Stocking Thriller SIT **4**
Big jugs lead to the finishing ledge.

6 Runs On Beetroot SIT **6C+**
The arete sitter has a dynamic move. Stay off jugs to the left.

7 Twist And Shout ★ 7A+
Starting from the a jug on *Stocking Thriller*, traverse right via powerful moves to finish up *Twist*. The footblock below *Twist* is not in.
Robin Müller 2012

8 Wide Ride SIT **4+**
The big crack is over too fast.

9 Copernicus ★★ SIT **7C**
Sitstart the central block from hands clamped on the aretes.
Robin Müller 2013

10 Project
Filthy, nasty, ugly crimping.

11 Twist ★ LOW **5+** SIT **7A**
Without using the footblock, start low on the obvious hold and bridge upwards to glory. A sitstart from the big slanting rail on *Copernicus* bumps the grade up to **7A**.

12 Last SIT **5**
The wall just to the right. The footblock is in.

Just downstream from the River Blocks (back towards the quarry) are two boulders wedged in the river. Be prepared to clean and chalk.

13 River Man SIT **5+**
The left arete.

14 Time Has Told Me SIT **6B**
The right arete.

15 Naiad ★★ SIT **7B**
The steep side of the boulder, starting RH on the good incut hold. Make a big move to a LH gaston and use the arete to good effect.
Robin Müller 2013

16 Project
Sitstart with LH on the incut hold and RH on the arete.

17 Martin The Warrior 5 SIT **6B**
Start from the slanting ramp and use the arete to head up and left.

18 Magic Goods ★ 6B SIT **6C**
Start from the slanting ramp and head for the right arete. Harder than it looks.

Also downstream from the River Blocks, up a bank on the right side of the bay, is a highball undercut wall.

19 Project
The arete.

20 Project
The wall right of the arete.

Cross the river and climb the bank to access Weasel Quarry. The bouldering is on the left-most wall. This can also be reached from Red Wall area: cross the river towards Catle Rocks, then turn left before the fence to follow a small path leading to the quarry.

21 Project

22 Project
The obvious line up the red wall, finishing at a good ledge on the left.

There is one final area, known as Sunken Quarry. From Weasel Quarry, head towards Castle Rocks. At the edge of the trees is a small stream that feeds into the main river. Follow this upstream, staying on the wooded side. Sunken Quarry is reached shortly. Some bouldering has been done here but it probably isn't worth the walk.

Weasel Quarry

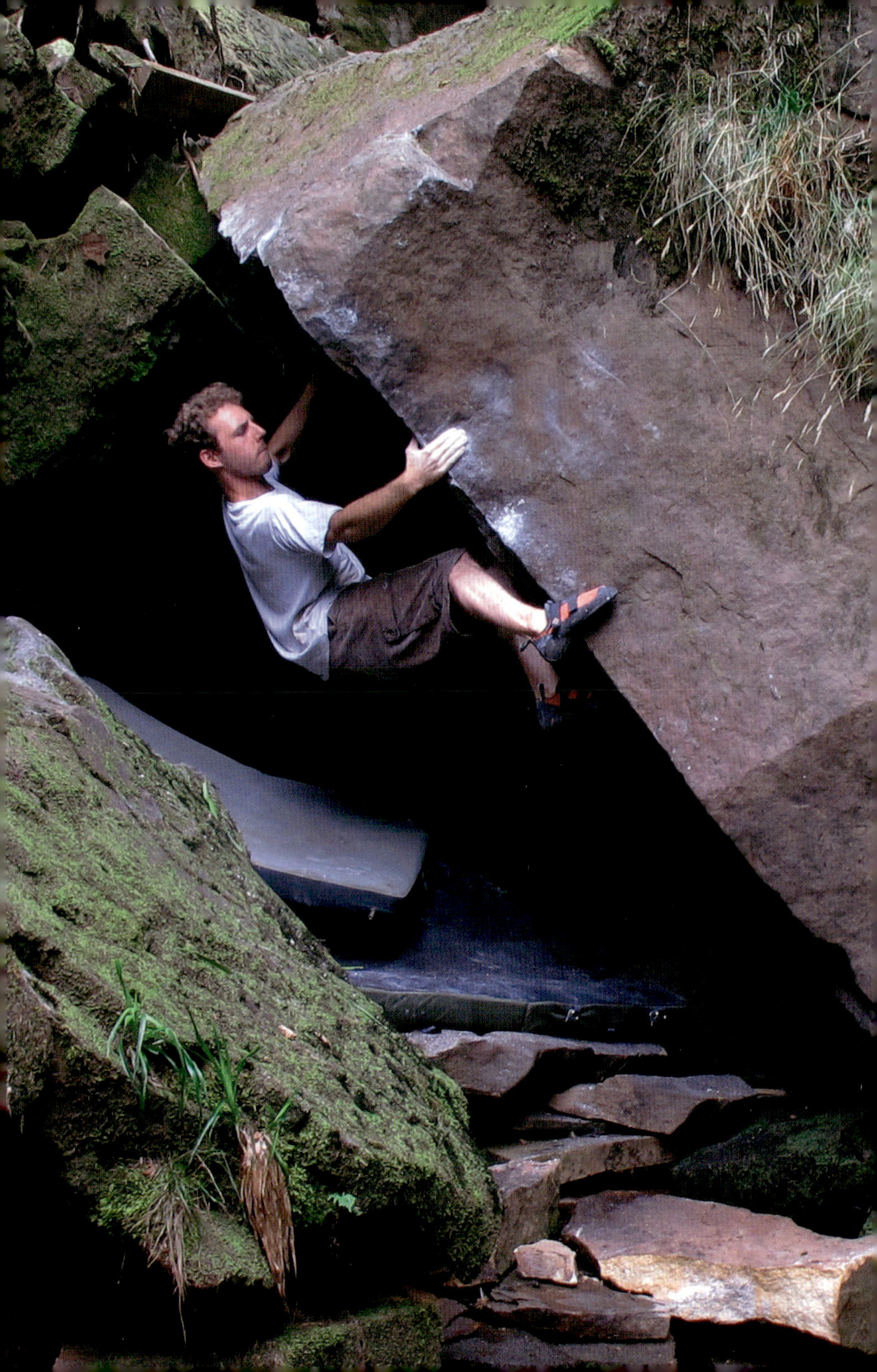

Naiad, 7B p135

Whisker, 7A p141

Roundbarn 20

One of Lancashire's (even) more esoteric venues, Roundbarn has a large amount of rock but very little bouldering. Nonetheless, there are one or two gems on south-west facing walls which dry fast and catch the sun.

APPROACH 3 min
From Edgworth, follow Blackburn Road north-west (past the famous Holden's Ice Cream parlour and the post-office). After roughly 2 miles there is a white house on the right, which bears street-signs reading "Blackburn Road" and "Roundbarn". Park sensibly uphill from the row of houses. Walk back to the footpath next to the white house and follow this to the quarry.

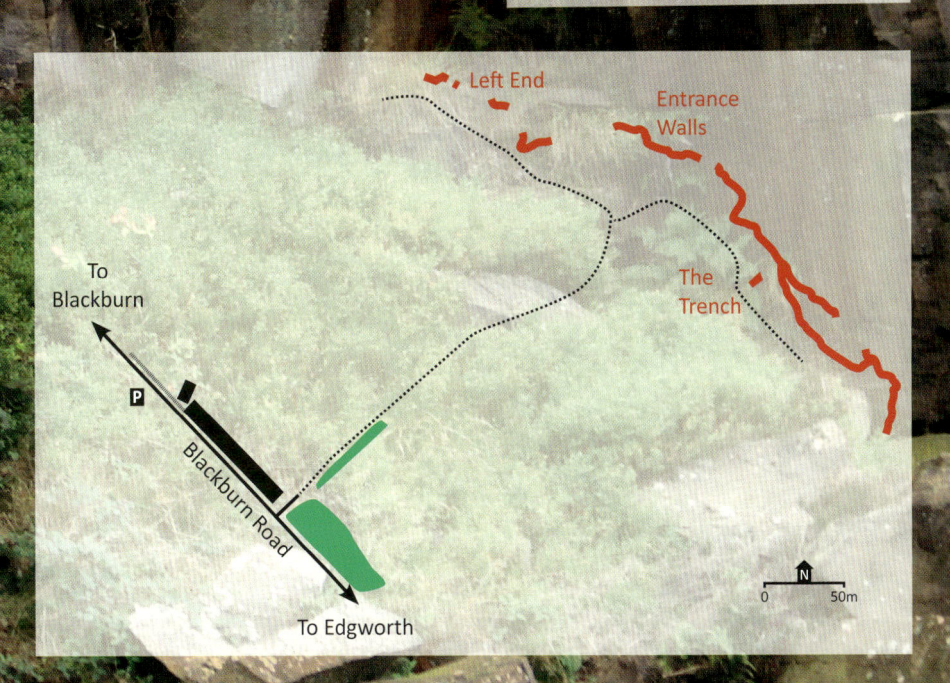

- Left End
- Entrance Walls
- The Trench

To Blackburn

Blackburn Road

To Edgworth

0   50m

ROUNDBARN

Left End

The most concentrated bouldering area is at the far left end of the quarry.

1 Leave Your Hat On 6B
A clever heel allows upward progress. Drop off at the break.

2 Burgess 5
Good holds lead up the wall. Go as high as you feel comfortable

3 The Back Of Beyond ★ 6C+
A technical dyno from crimps and a sidepull to the sloper.

4 Third Man 6B+
The wall left of the arete, finishing up the fiddly crack. Descending is tricky.

5 Left Maclean 5
The arete on its left, to stand on the jug.

6 Strict Maclean 4
The arete on its right.

The next slab can be slow to dry.

7 Quiver Upriver ★ 7A
Use the left crimp for RH.
Robin Müller 2012

8 Project
Up the middle, without the fisheye.

9 Fishface ★ 4

Further right is a daft lowball.

10 Ridicule At Roundbarn SIT 6A
In need of amusement? Persuade someone else to climb it.

ROUNDBARN 141

The Entrance Walls are roughly opposite the entrance to the quarry.

11 Whisker ★ 7A
Crimp up the left arete to a crux move into the high holds. Finish on the jug.
Robin Müller 2012

12 Catfoot ★ 6B SIT 6B+
From sitting, make a move to the break (look for an often overgrown foothold) and continue up the technical arete, staying off the crack out right.

The next few problems are a little further right.

13a Oli's Prow 6A+
Pull on using LH on the left arete crimp and RH on the right arete.

13b Oli's Prow LH 6A+
Pull on with RH on the left arete crimp.

14 The Waxing Hour 3
Up the easy face.

15 Licking The Barrel ★ 3 SIT 4+
Start matched on the low shelf.

16 Flake Out 3
A highball up the pocketed slab.

17 Crackling 3
Follow the crack.

Further right in the trench is a boulder jumble containing two slabby ripple-fronted boulders.

18 The Great Big Skip 3
The short front arete.

19 Novelty Wobble 4
The tall arete with a dodgy landing.

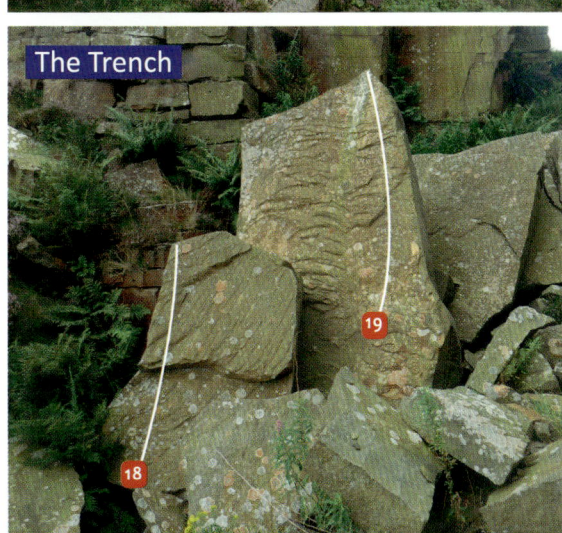

Information Highway Revisited, 7C+ p138

21 Lower Montcliffe

There are a few good problems here, but only a few. The fast-drying slab is worth an hour if you live nearby and seek lower grade stuff, while at the opposite end of the scale, one of Lancashire's best looking highballs still awaits a second ascent, though this one is slow to dry after rain. There is also some fun to be had in the End Bay, but you may need to battle some vegetation.

APPROACH 3 min
The B6226 Chorley Old Road runs between Horwich and Bolton. Turn off this onto George's Lane. After just over half a mile, park at any of the small sidings. Take the footpath on the left, just before the trees. Turn left at the bottom, then left again for the first bay.

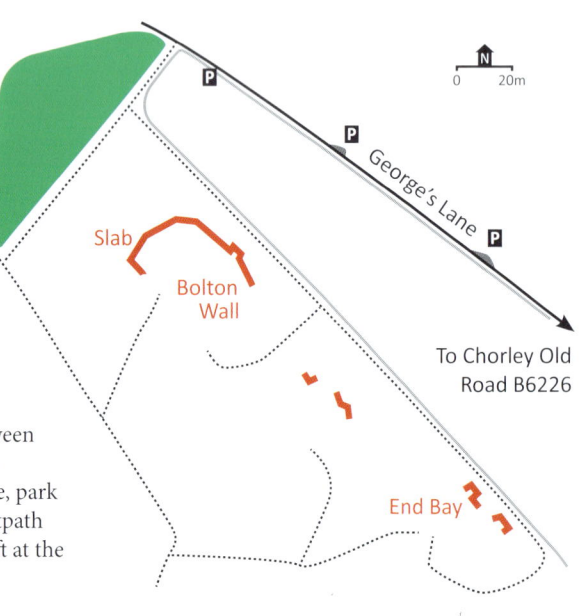

Slab
Bolton Wall
George's Lane
To Chorley Old Road B6226
End Bay

LOWER MONTCLIFFE 143

Bolton Wall

Bolton Wall is the back wall of the quarry. Many of the problems on this wall can be slow to dry. Some have poor landings.

1 Bolton Staircase 4
Gain the ledge via a large crack.

2 Bolton Ladder 5
The wall to the left.

3 Letter-box Wall 4+
Climb the blocky cracks to a good jug.

4 Astra 6A+
The black wall on slippery holds, to finish at a good edge.

5 Old Money 5
The thin crack, to a good hold.

6 New Money 6B
Climb the thin wall between cracks.

7 Naughty Crompton 4
The arete, from sitting. Top out.

8 Fling Somefing 6B SIT 7A+
Start from undercuts and pull up the tricky face to top out. The aretes (and the big notch low on the right arete) are off limits.
Robin Müller 2011

9 Information Highway Revisited ★★ 7C+
One of Lancashire's most impressive lines. Verging on route territory, but there is no gear so you'll want a decent pile of pads. Slow drying.
John Gaskins 2006

10 Intent ★ 7B
Pull up the corner, then make extremely crimpy moves right to gain better holds.
Robin Müller 2012

11 Undercutting the Market SIT 5
Climb the little arete on its right, to gain good holds higher up. No bridging.

12 Dicing With Doom LOW 6A
Start matched on the lowest edge. Make a couple of moves to good holds in the break, then traverse right to the arete. Watch that landing!

13 Rabbit Crossing SIT 5
From sitting on the right, bounce left along the fun jugs and hop over the ledge.

144 LOWER MONTCLIFFE

The next problems are on The Slab to the left of the quarry. These are fast-drying.

14 Bach 7A+
From the right arete, traverse leftwards beneath the line of pockets. Finish at the left arete.
Robin Müller 2007

15 Wanderer's Return 4
The right arete.

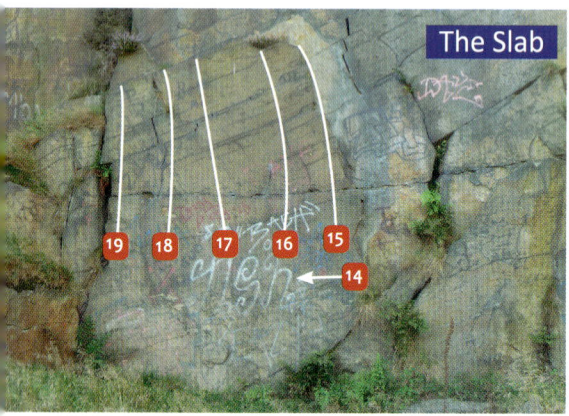

16 Horwich Haul ★ 6B+
The wall left of the arete, from the two large pockets. Tricksome.

17 Slower Montcliffe ★ 5+
The centre of the wall.

18 Raining Down, Warming Up 5
The zig-zag crack.

19 Dance For Breakfast 4
The left arete.

The final area is the End Bay of the quarry. The first problem is on the left.

20 Maid In Stone ★ SIT 7A
Slap up sidepulls and underclings. Finish matched on the top block.
Robin Müller 2008

There are more problems in the mini bay on the right.

21 Dinosaur Adventure 3D ★ SIT 6C+
From sitting (you may have to pull back the vegetation) gain the ramp and make a tricky move to the top.
Andrew Emery 2006

22 Flow Chart 4
The scoop.

23 Project

24 Indian Face ★ 6B+ SIT 7A
The bulging arete.

25 Project
A rightwards finish is possible.

Dinosaur Adventure 3D, 6C+ p144

22 Brownstones

Classic quarried bouldering, perfect for mileage in the lower grades, with some harder historical rites of passage and a few million eliminates. South facing and fast-drying, but can be midgey on still summer days. Whilst some eliminates have been described here, there is not space to cover the entire multitude, so head to the online Brownstones Wiki if you are eager for more.

APPROACH 3 min
From Bolton, turn off the A675 onto Scout Road, half a mile north of The Wilton Arms. Follow this for roughly 2 miles (it changes name to Colliers Row Road) and park on the verge on the left, shortly before a row of cottages on the right. Cross the road and follow the obvious footpath to the crag.

From Blackburn or Preston, take the M65 to Junction 3, then the A675 towards Bolton for 7 miles. Pass through Belmont and continue for just under 2 miles until the first road on the right. This is Scout Road. Continue as above.

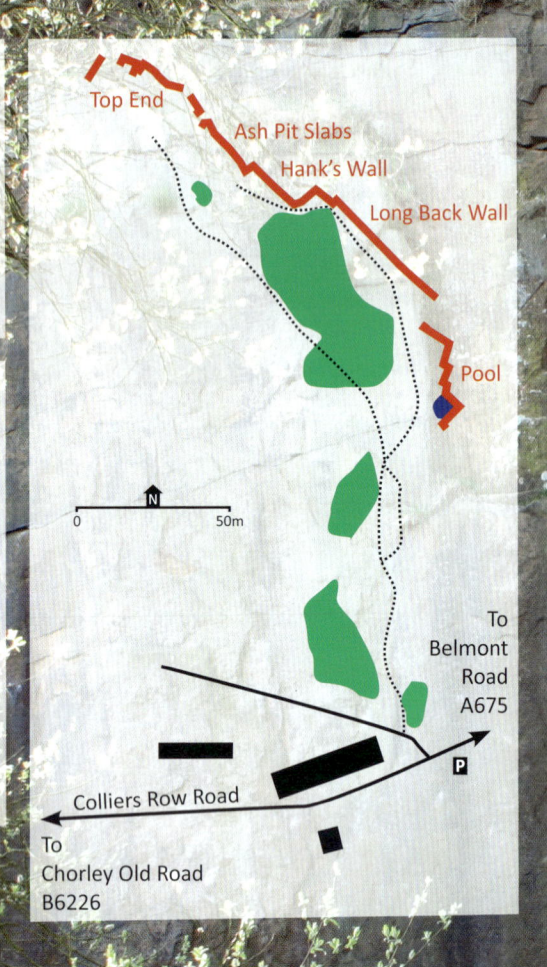

Top End
Ash Pit Slabs
Hank's Wall
Long Back Wall
Pool

0   50m

To Belmont Road A675
Colliers Row Road
To Chorley Old Road B6226

The Bignag, 7B p152

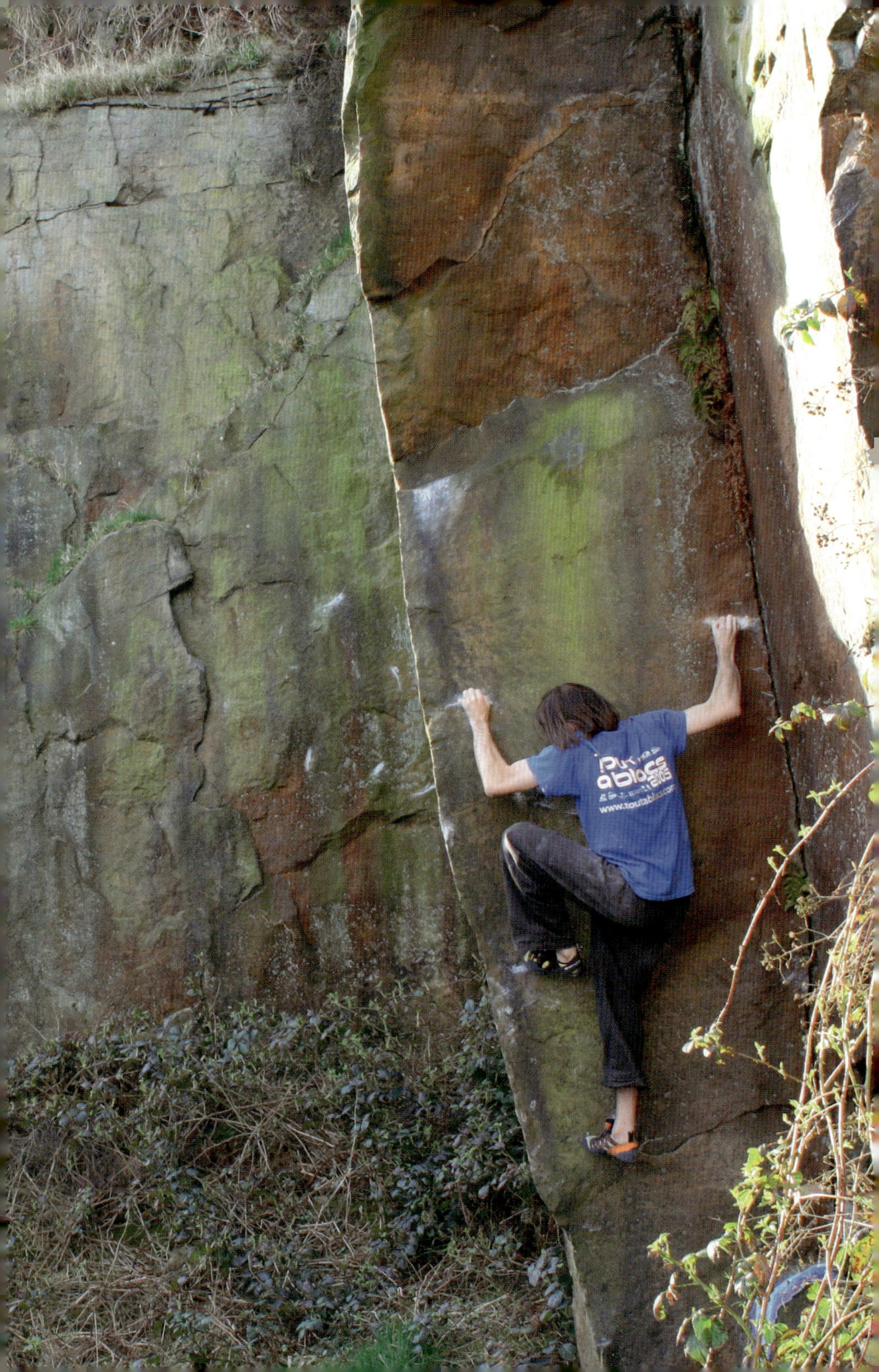
a blocs
2005

BROWNSTONES

The Pool

The Pool Walls have a great concentration of easier climbs with good landings. And a pool.

1 Pond Traverse ★★ **6C**
Traverse the whole wall from the ledges left of Hernia to a finish past the pond. Good in either direction.

2 Hernia ★ **5+**
The slippery slab right of the arete.

3 Lobotomy 5
The slab via a shallow groove.

4 Slimer 5+
Climb the slab left of the crack.

5 Brownstones Crack ★ **3**

6 Moss Wall ★ **5+**
The wall to the right of the crack.

7 Verdi Ramp 5
Start up the corner, then step left to follow the ramp up the slab. The direct start is **5+**.

8 Verdi Corner 4+

9 Verdi Wall 5
Start the short crack from an oblong pocket.

10 Two Step Left Hand 5+
Follow the good footholds left and up.

11 Two Step 4
Follow the good footholds right and up. Can be done hands-free at **5+**.

12 Mantelstrug 3
The arete on either side.

13 Chockerblock Corner 3

14 Muddy Wall 4+
Large holds lead the way.

15 Muddy Arete 5

16 Wet Corner 4+

17 Slab Variant 3
Start in the corner and head right to finish up the arete.

18 Watery Arete 4+

The climbs around the pool have dry landings in summer, but in winter they are more exciting.

19 Wet Foot 5
The first crack right of the arete, past the large hole.

20 Splash 6A
The second crack right of the arete.

21 Splish 5+
Twin cracks, roughly in the centre of the wall.

22 Splosh 6A
The crack to the left of the corner.

23 The Corner 5

24 Piddle 5+

25 Middle 6A+

26 Riddle 6A+

27 Ponder 5

28 Pondule 3

BROWNSTONES

There are also several classic eliminates in this area, mostly based around Two Step and Muddy Wall.

29 Low Break Traverse 6A
The centre of the wall, past an undercut.

30 Verdinand 6B
The groove right of the corner, staying off both the left wall and holds on *Verdigris*.

31 Verdigris 6A+
Launch up to the break and keep going, but stay off jugs on the arete.

32 No Step 6C
Using crimps a little to the right of Verdis Wall, get a foot up to the lower breakline and bid for the top. The good low footholds are not allowed.

33 Dynostrung 6A+
Dyno from the low arete jug to the top.

34 Little Wall SIT **5+**
The little wall is fun.

35 Niche Sitter 1 SIT **6B+**
Start matched on the big slippy sloper and crimp to the finish.

36 Niche Sitter 2 SIT **6A+**
Start from undercuts and crimp upwards. Stay off the jugs to the right.

37 Low Niche Traverse SIT **6C**
Start from undercuts and head left on the low crimp line.

38 The I.L.T. Dyno 6B
A 2nd-gen dyno between big holds (see start and end of arrow). It can be done as a rockover, but this is missing the point (and the grade).

150 BROWNSTONES

Long Back Wall

The Long Back Wall has some of Brownstones' best problems, though it is often overlooked.

On the left side of the wall, the landing drops away and the wall here is rarely climbed. However, there are a couple of worthy challenges.

1 Impo 6A+
The groove.

2 Dylan 7A
From the corner of the overlap, climb up and left to gain the groove.
Geoof Hibbert, Paul Robins 2001

A few metres to the right, the main bouldering section begins.

3 Knah 5+ SIT 7A
The forking crack is not too bad, but the sitstart is much trickier - it uses only crack holds for hands, and is called *Knahrl*.

4 Lifeline ★ 6C SIT 7B
The sitter starts matched on fat undercuts and leads into the wierd technicalities of the standup, which is perhaps a bit of a sandbag. Most people finish at the obvious good hold.
Unknown 1979-83, SIT Robin Müller 2006

5 Var 5+
Jump to the jug, then press on to the top.

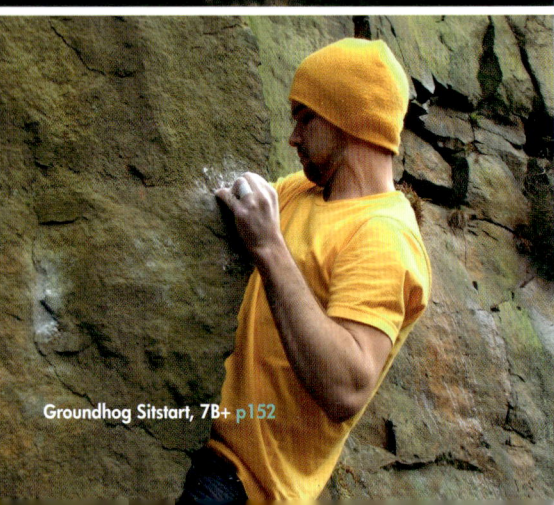

Groundhog Sitstart, 7B+ p152

Long Back Wall

6 Big Muff ★ SIT **7A**
From big undercuts, use small crack holds to pop for the jug that marks the start of *Var*. The end.
Robin Müller 2006

7 Hardline ★ **6A+**
Climb the right-slanting crack like Jerry. Now you're ready for *The Ace*.
Jerry Moffatt 1979-83

8 Project

9 Heartline 5+

10 Faintline ★ **6A**
The slanting crack can prove taxing.

11 Thunder ★ **7B**
A classic '80s highball that defeats most suitors.
Mark Leach, Paul Pritchard 1979-83

12 Ninja Fingers ★ **7A+**
A French start gets you to the jug, then thin climbing proceeds above.
Paul Robins 2006

13 The Slanter 4+

14 Project
The big slopey sidepulls have so far remained unclimbed. Just getting to the mid-height break would be a worthy achievement. Sadly, this wall often seeps in winter.

15 Dave's Other Route 6A+

16 Knep 6A
The left-hand fork.

17 Butt End 5+
The right-hand fork of the tall crack.

18 Big Butt ★ SIT **6B+**
From underclings, traverse right to gain the left-hand crack and finish up this. Sustained!

19 Stop Butt 4+
Two diverging crack lead upwards. Use them both.

20 Rusty Wall ★★ **6C+**
The thin crack is excellent.

21 Colt ★★ **7C+**
The superb wall between cracks. A crux move using poor shotholes gains a small slot and a fingery finish.
Paul Robins 2001

22 Black Wall 5+
Climb the slab left of the crack.

23 Unfinished Wall 6B
An interesting sequence leads up the wall. Jump off at decent edges.

24 Hank 5+
The corner.

25 Old Tricks 6B
A technical sequence on sidepulls. Rock left onto the ledge to finish.

The shady section left of the Long Back Wall is the Groundhog area. It can become overgrown - some lines have not been described because they aren't really worth the effort. However, the following all get regular traffic and are worth seeking out.

1 The Bignag ★ **7B**
Step off the rock and use spaced crimps to aid a throw to the slopey ledge. Match this to finish (there's a good bit near the arete).
Robin Müller 2012

2 Groundhog ★★ **7A** SIT **7B+**
Fingery climbing up the steep arete. Finish at the good hold on the ledge.
Geoff Hibbert 1993, SIT Jordan Buys 2005

3 Project
From the crack, somehow cross the mostly blank wall to gain the arete. Futuristic finger-strength needed.

4 Crackhorse 7A+
Growl up the right-hand fork of the crack. Proper gnarly finger-locking. This one is less frequently climbed, so you might need to pull out some weeds.
Calum Berry 2006

Left of the corner, the next few lines all finish on good holds as the top is rarely accessible.

5 Snatch 7A+
Just left of the corner crack, pull on to a thin LH sidepull and decent RH edge. From here, throw for a positive hold and continue for a few moves until the angle eases. Stay off holds on *Y Front*.

6 Y Front 4
Big flakes.

7 Satisfying Sloper Problem ★ **6B** SIT **6C**
Crimp to a slick sloper, then pull through to the jug.

8 Tom Slap 6A
Dyno from the low jug to the good higher hold (start and end of arrow). Without dynoing, it's **5**.

Right Hand Hank, 7B+ p154

BROWNSTONES

Hank's Wall

The Hank's Wall area is a densely packed history lesson in quarried bouldering. Here you can work your way through the testpieces of each decade, then move on to the eliminates...

1 Little Man 4
The crack to the left of the arete.

2 Crooked Crack 4
The distinctly devious fissure.

3 Gullible's Travels 6A
The wall between cracks, passing a low overlap.

4 Way Down 4
Climb over a smaller overlap, using cracks.

5 Vertigo 4+

6 Inferno 5

7 Traditional Mantel Problem 6C
Mantel onto the flat hold, using only the crimp near the end of the arrow to aid progress. Feet on smears and the handhold only.

8 Dragnet 4

9 The Pillar 6C
The very thin wall, staying off the cracks. Start RH pinching the overlap and LH on a sidepull lower down.

10 Haskit 5
Climb forked cracks, or just the left crack at **5+**.

11 Alana 6A
The thin wall between *Haskit* and *Layback*, starting from a low crack sidepull. The crux is gaining crimps high on the left arete. You can eliminate these and use holds on the left edge of the *Haskit* crack - this is *Playback*, **6C**.

12 Layback ★★ 5 SIT 5+
The classic polished crack. Can be done one-handed (called *Slayback*).
Pre 1948

13a Hank's Wall ★★ 7A+ SIT 7B
From the sidepull, reach a pinch on the arete, then crimps higher on the face. No crack holds allowed, including feet. The sitstart uses the back wall for feet and a notch on the lip for RH. It involves a wild throw from a bunched position, but you may need to de-grass the starting footholds.
Hank Pasquill 1979-83, SIT Dylan Fletcher pre 1999

13b Right Hand Hank ★ 7B+
A strict line eliminating the left side of the wall. Gain the small LH eye hold and RH ripple, then stand up on a poor foothold and snatch for a tiny RH crimp just left of the crack. Easier moves follow.
Andy Kay 2004

14 Parr's Crack ★★ 6A SIT 6A+
The crack eases with height, but it's quality all the way.
Eric Parr and friends 1948-49

15 Pigswill ★★ 6C+ SIT 7A
The wall between cracks. Most people use a sidepull just left of *Parr's Crack*, though of course it can be eliminated.
Hank Pasquill 1981-83, SIT Andy Kay 1983

16 Parabola ★ 5+
From big sidepulls, trend right to climb over the top of *Pigswill*.

17 Parabola Direct 6A+
Instead of heading right, continue straight up the small crack. Stay off the big crack to the left.

18 The Chimney 5
Not really a chimney.

BROWNSTONES 155

Nexus Wall

Nexus Wall is at a right-angle to Hank's Wall. Due to its leaning angle, it's a useful place to escape light drizzle. Many eliminates have been done here, but there is only space to describe the most popular - the dynos. If you are eager for the others, the internet will provide.

1 Nexus ★ 4
Climb the centre of the wall using whatever the heck you want, except the arete.

1 Cack Hand 6B+
Climb the arete using only your right hand. Finish on A. No, it's not a dyno, but it pleaded to be included and I couldn't say no.

2 Nexus Dyno 6C
LH G - RH H. Jump for A. Has got harder since the loss of the big corner flake.

2 GCW6a 6B
LH B (arete + dink for thumb) - RH C. Jump for A.

3 The Good 6C
LH D - RH E. Jump for A. Getting trickier as E erodes.

4 The Bad 7A
LH E - RH F. Jump for A.

5 The Ugly 7B
Both hands on F. Jump for A. Fierce!

7 Nightlife 7A+
Both hands on G. Jump for A.

8 The Witching Hour 7A+
LH F - RH G. Jump for A.

BROWNSTONES

Ash Pit Slabs

The Ash Pit Slab wall is home to some splendid lower grade highballs.

1 Ash Pit Slab ★★ **3**
Big ledges lead upwards. A variation climbs via the slanting seam at **4**.

2 Digitation ★★ **6A**
The centre of the slab is brilliant.
Hank Pasquil pre 1969

3 Fraud ★ **5+**
The left side of the slab, via chipped holds. Staying off the chips is tricky, at **6A+**.

4 Analogue 4+
The crack.

5 Directissima ★★ **6A**
The wall between cracks.
Hank Pasquil pre 1969

6 Degree Crack 4+

7 Hopper ★ **4**
The slab, using the obvious line of holds. Staying direct is **5**.

8 Corn Mantel ★ **5+**

9 Unjust ★ **6B**
Climb the bulge without the big ledges to each side, then finish up the slab. Eliminates exist.

10 Unjust Dyno 7B+
Dyno from the sloper to the ledge.
Johnny Peake

11 Ash Pit Traverse ★ **6A**
From either side of the wall, traverse at a low level. A higher traverse is also possible at **4+**.

A little further left are a few more problems, though they are best left until you've done everything else.

12 Rambler 3
The easy slab.

13 Climber And Rambler 4
The crackline leads to the top of *Rambler*. The wall to the left has a very strict eliminate avoiding all crack holds, at around **5+**.

14 Noddy's Crack 5+
The thin left-hand crack. There is also a tough eliminate using only crack holds.

15 Groovy 4
The big flakes.

16 The Thrutch 4
Get onto the ledge.

BROWNSTONES   157

The final area is the Top End, at the left end of the quarry. A last gasp of fun before home-time.

17 The Prow Dyno 7A
Leap from the flat jug to the top.

18 The Prow 5

19 Halt 3+
The crack just left of the prow.

20 Blurt ★ 4+
Super slippy slopey slapping.

21 Fineline 6A
The crack, to the highest top-out.

22 Diane 4
The corner.

23a Dezertion ★ 7A SIT 7A+
Climb the arete on its right, from a sitstart on undercuts. Stay off the right wall, and the crack left of the arete (though you can pull into this to top out). The standing start goes from LH arete, RH undercut. Pull on first, then go for it - jumping off the ground doesn't count.

23b Dezertion Eliminate 7B
Pull on with LH arete and RH small crimp. The sitstart is harder, but probably not a whole grade.
Matt Leigh

24 Dezerit 6A
The obvious crack.

25a Boopers ★ 6B SIT 7A
Climb straight up the face, staying off the arete jug. The sitstart is awkward, especially if you have a thin mat.

25b Boopers Variation 7A+
Start LH as per *Boopers*, RH sidepull near crack. Use a RH sidepull on the rib instead of the *Boopers* crimp.

26 Beano 6A
The crack and left arete, without using the arete jug. You can also head right along the break, this is **Bitto 6A**.

27 Tiptoe 4+
From the right arete of the small slab, traverse left (don't use the top of the slab), pass the corner and continue to the far left arete.

28 Slab Direct 3+
The iddy slab is quite enjoyable. Perfect for beginners.

158 BROWNSTONES

29 The Pock 5
Traverse left, staying below the top. If you stay below the hole, it's **6B**.

30 Obscenity ★ 5+
Just left of the ledges, crimp up the wall.

31a Ridiculous Eliminate ★ SIT 7A+
From the big crack jug, gain the two slopey protrusions, then lay one on for the ledge.
Robin Müller 2005

31a Ridiculous Extension 7B
From the ledge on the left, traverse right below the hole to gain the crack. Then launch into *Ridiculous Eliminate*.
Caleb Ainsworth 2005

32 Ridiculous Dyno SIT 7A+
From the big crack jug, fly to the ledge.
Robin Müller 2006

33 Pocket Hole Wall 3+
Presumably trousers had much bigger pockets when this was first done.

34 Magic Circle 4+
Traverse without using the top. More of a semi-circle, really. Perhaps the other half is invisible. That would be magic.

35 DC10 Ungradeable
If you are feeling stupid, jump from the top of the left wall to a foothold on the right wall.
Paul Pritchard, Anthony Gridley 1980s

36 Test Piece 5+
Mantel it out.

37 Somersault 5+
The wall to the left is slightly overhanging. It's traditionally climbed with a backwards facing legs-over-head manoeuvre, to finish seated on the top.

Ridiculous Eliminate, 7A+ p158

Parr's Crack, 6A+ p154

JR's Soft Shoe Shuffle, 7A p185

23 The Wiltons

The Wiltons pack in over 200 problems. Some are very definitely for locals only, some are much better than they look, and some are really top class. First time visitors will have more fun if they head for the starred problems first.

Access to Wilton 2, 3 and 4 is shared with the gun club - see table on opposing page for details.

APPROACH   3 min
From Bolton, follow the A675 Belmont Rd. Park before The Wilton Arms to access Wilton 1, or take the next left onto Scout Road for 2, 3 and 4. There is parking on the right.

From Blackburn or Preston, take the M65 to Junction 3, then the A675 Belmont Road towards Bolton for 7 miles. Pass through Belmont and continue for just under 2 miles until the first road on the right. This is Scout Road. Turn off here for the smaller Wiltons, or continue to parking just beyond the pub to access Wilton 1.

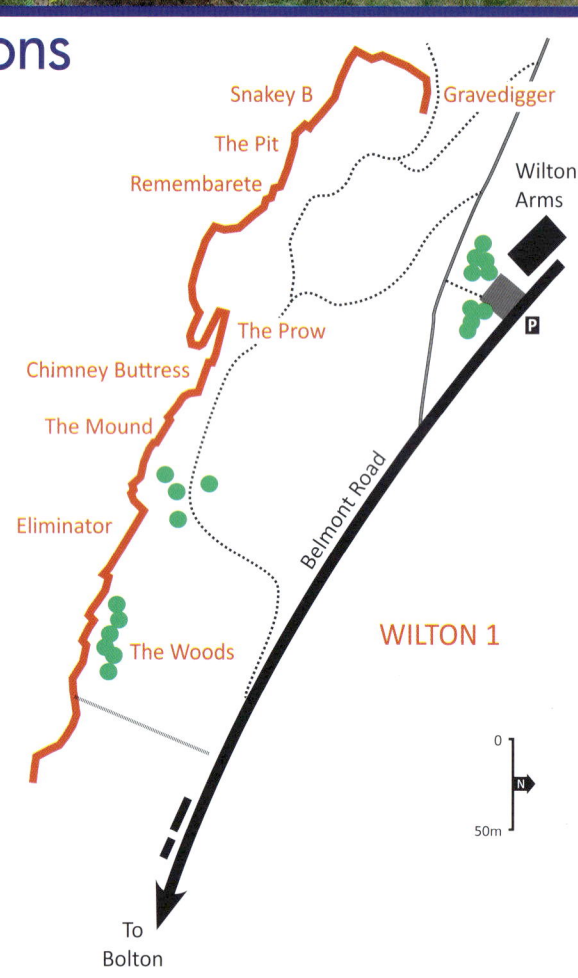

WILTON 1   **161**

To
Belmont Road

WILTON 3

The Square
Final Walls
Small Roof
Orange Wall
Corner Bay
Shiver's Arete
The Slab
Crack And Slab   Grader
The Swine

Scout Road

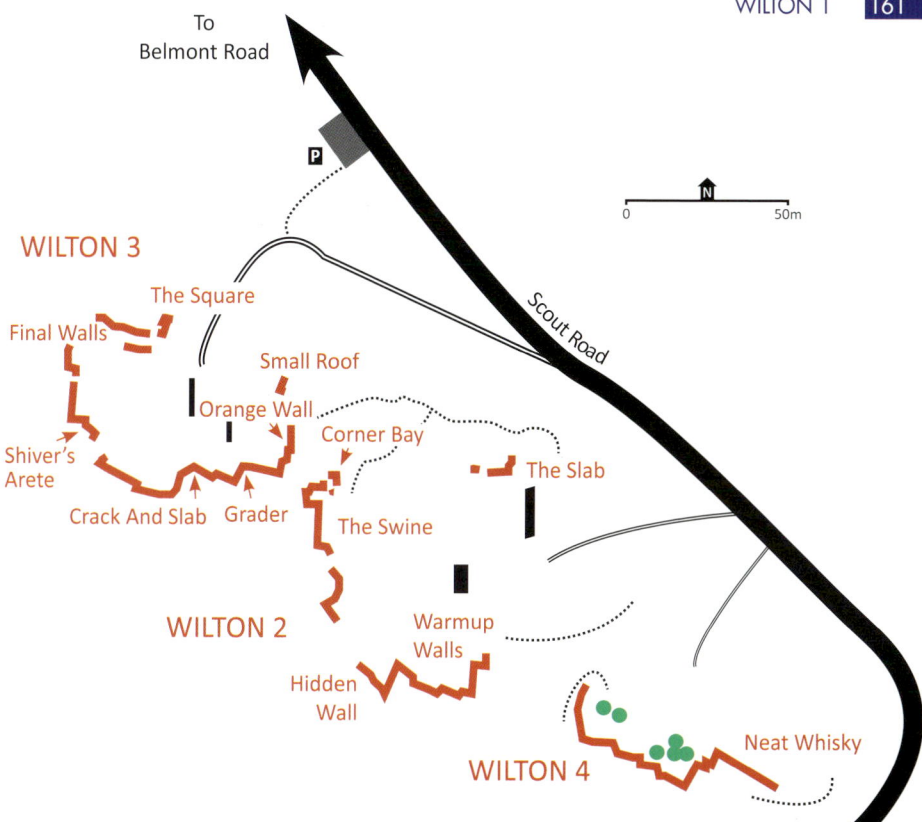

WILTON 2
Warmup Walls
Hidden Wall

WILTON 4
Neat Whisky

Wilton 1
The largest of the quartet is grandest by far. The Prow and Chimney Buttress hold the highest density of problems, but venture elsewhere and you will be rewarded. Midgesquito Crimpelopes, Snakey B and the Gravedigger overhang are all good options on damp days.

Wilton 2
The middle child is amenable to most dispositions. The Swine and The Slab areas are both fast-drying, while the Hidden Wall is sheltered and the Swiss Dreams block is usually in the shade.

Wilton 3
The friendliest Wilton features the wonderful highball block of The Square, as well as a surprising amount of mostly short problems that while often aesthetically unexciting, offer a pretty good circuit. Little here stays damp for long, and on still days this is the best bet for a bit of breeze.

Wilton 4
A small cluster of problems includes good highballs and some stern technical challenges. It gets shade most of the day.

Access Agreement

Wilton 1 is owned by the BMC but 2,3 and 4 are owned by gun clubs. Climbers have priority on the marked days but should give way to shooters on other days, and stay away when the red flag is flying. See the BMC RAD for more details.

	M	T	W	T	F	S	S
W1	✓	✓	✓	✓	✓	✓	✓
W2		✓		✓		✓	
W3	✓	✓		✓		✓	
W4		✓		✓		✓	

WILTON 1

Graveyard

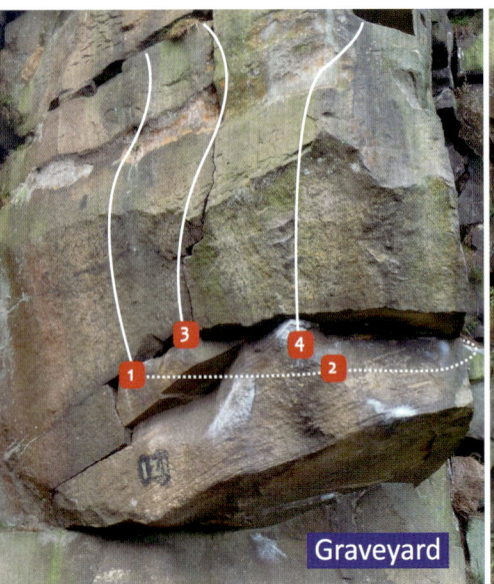

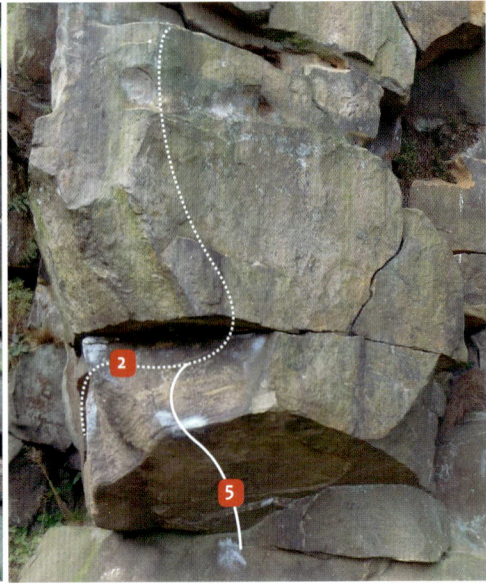

Wilton 1 kicks off with the Graveyard area, in the north-east corner of the quarry. It's usually a safe bet after rain.

There is scope for a good many eliminates, but this has not yet been well developed. Bored wads can try **The Move** footless - still a project.

1 The Very Cheek 6B
The wall left of the crack.

2 Horrorbix ★ 6A
The excellent traverse rightwards to finish up the arete.

3 Overhanging Weetabix 4
The crack.

4 The Move ★ 7A
The wall between crack and arete, via a full power move from a crimp to a sandy sloper.
Robin Müller 2009

5 Horror Arete ★ 6A
A big span from the back leads up the arete.

To the right is a nice wall that offers a few eliminates.

6 Laid Back SIT 6A+
Layback the arete to finish on the jug in the break. Hands on arete only. The block low on the left is allowed for feet.

7 Graveyard Slap 6B
From the central hold and feet on smears, leap for the break.

8 Graveyard Slab 4
Climb up using anything. Top out.

Left of the Horror Arete overhang is a deceptively tricky wall.

9 Squeeze Me SIT 6B
Work upwards to finishing holds beneath the heather.

The Square, 6A p182

Snakey B, 6C+ p165

WILTON 1   165

Beneath the route **Black Mamba** is a useful wall that rarely gets wet. For the uninitiated, "Snakey B" refers to the popular student drink Snakebite and Black, which may be either "lush" or revolting, depending on taste. Much like this wall.

1 Sitting Ducks SIT **5**
Just to the left is a green pillar. Climb this if you are desperate.

2 Baby Fae SIT **6B+**
A fun eliminate. Sitstart the ramp, go for the good hold up and left, then slap to the finishing jug above.

3 Snakey Left Hand SIT **6C**
Sitstart on the ramp and crimp upwards, staying off jugs to the left and the undercut feature to the right. Finish at a good edge.

4a Snakey B ★ 6C SIT **6C+**
Sitstart on the ramp and climb through the undercut feature, using crimps to the left. Finish at the good edge.

4b Snakey B Original 6C+ SIT **7A**
As above, but eliminate the small crimp near the left end of the undercut feature.
Robin Müller 2005

5 Snakey B Right Hand 6B+ SIT **6C**
This time, break right at the undercut feature and go for the big ledge.
Calum Berry pre 2005, SIT Gareth Wallis 2010

6 Thulsa Doom ★ 7A+
Swing left along the ledge, then gain the undercut feature and work into a crux throw for the ledge out left.
Robin Müller 2007

7 Low Traverse 6C+
From standing on the footledge, make a sequency traverse left to gain good holds. **6C** in reverse.
Oliver Müller 2007

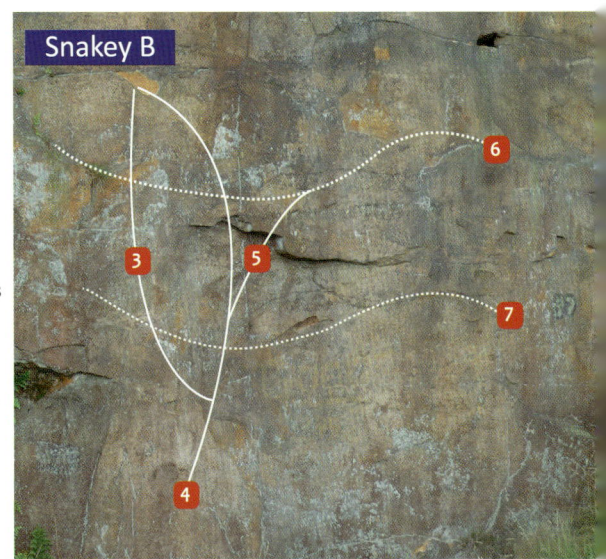

Left of the Snakey B wall, the crag bottom slopes into The Pit. Just before this, a smooth, fast-drying wall offers some entertainment.

1 The Finish 5
Climb the easy finish of the traverse.

2 Midgesquito Crimpelopes ★ 7A+
From holds in the middle of the traverse, climb to the good high edge via small crimps.
Robin Müller 2011

3 Traverse Of The Underlings 7A
From a stance on underclings, swing right across jugs, then tough moves to gain better holds. Finish on the high edge. Stay off the middle footledge.
Robin Müller 2011

The Pit itself offers good highballs. All problems top out, but make sure you are happy to down-climb or jump off. Gets sun in the morning. **The Postman's Daughter** can seep, but the other two problems dry reasonably fast and are excellent.

4 Slanting Hats And Spooky Cats ★★ 6C
Skirt the overlap via a good high undercling, then shimmy leftwards on sidepulls to gain the jug.

5 Grandad's Chin ★★ 7A
Pull through the middle of the overlap, using the right hand sidepull and undercuts.
Robin Müller 2011

6 The Postman's Daughter ★ 6A SIT 7A+
Gain the letterbox and stretch to the top. A fierce sitstart goes from LH crimp and RH sidepull/undercling.
Robin Müller 2011

7 Project
Just left is a smooth slab, which is climbed without the good hold on its right

8 Leaning Wall 5+
A little to the left there is an obvious leaning wall. Climb this on big holds.

WILTON 1   167

Some way left of the pit, the gully opens at a clean-cut arete. This is fast-drying but the Strawberry Kiss walls to the left need several days of dry weather.

1 Strawberry Kiss LOW **6C**
Start on opposing underclings and work up the crack. Finish rightwards at the jug.
Paul Pritchard 1986

2 So You Think You Can Dance LOW **7B**
From good underclings, gain a poor crimp and rockover for the small pinch.
Robin Müller 2011

3 Remembarete Left 5

4 Remembarete ★ **6A** SIT **7A**
The arete has a trick top move, and the sitter needs just one hard snatch. The sitstart footholds may now be buried.
Robin Müller 2011

Opposite is a lone wall poking out of the hillside. This is G Buttress.

5 Side Wall SIT **6B**
Start from underclings.

6 Lone Arete SIT **5+**
The arete on its left.

7 Break Dyno 6A
From break to break.

8 Lone Arete Right SIT **5+**
The arete on its right.

WILTON 1

The Prow

Unlike the rest of Wilton 1, the inside face of the Prow gets sun later in the day. It is clean and dries fast.

1 Big Frenchie 5
Use the juggy gaston to gain the top.

2 Blank Me 5
Span the Blank section with either a rockover or a dyno.

3 Christine's Socks 4+
Climb the easiest line of holds.

4 Ultimate Gnarl SIT **7B+**
The sitstart is made awkward by the slope of the ground. Start from the good RH sidepull and LH pebble cluster. Use one mat only. No footblocks.
Robin Müller 2012

5 Energiser 7A+
Dyno from twin crimps to the top.
Robin Müller 2011

6 Get Your Font Tick Here SIT **6B**
Gain the crimp and sloper, then pull to the jug round the arete.

7 Top Hat ★ 6C+
The wall between crack and arete. Start up problem 6 but reach right to the pocket, then rockover left to gain a small crimp and poor gaston, then the jug. The top is the best bit.
Robin Müller 2011

8 Leading Question 6A
From jugs in the crack, head left to gain the gaston and finish upwards.

9 Bottom Line 6B+
From low slopers, head left below the break to gain the crack.

10 Innominate ★★ 6B+
Punch up pockets to the ledge. Downclimb the crack to the left.
Hank Pasquill pre-1983

11 Cheat SIT **4+**
Start beneath the thin flakeline and pull up it to the break.

12 Yoga for Climbers SIT **7A+**
Climb the slab just right of the crack.
Robin Müller 2011

13 Beneath Deception 5 SIT 6A
The slab using holds just left of the arete, but not the arete.

14 Arete Sitstart SIT 5

15 Recess 3
Bridge up the small recess.

16 Project
Climb the thin back wall of the recess. Tiny crimp dyno!

17 Clamp 4 SIT 6A+
The pillar just right of the recess.

18 Flywalk Slab ★ 7A
Left of the deep foothold, using anything else, crimp up the slab to the oblong pocket. Move right to finish as per *Flywalk*.

19 Phenomenal Monkey 6C
From the deep foothold, climb the slab just left of the arete to the flat hold beneath the big sidepull, then finish easily.
Phil Kelly 1986

20 Flywalk ★ SIT 5+
Sitstart the arete and finish up and left.

21 Sidewalk ★ SIT 6B
Sitstart and pull into the groove. Use the slopey arete (but no holds to the left) to swing up and right to finishing jugs.

22a Veteran Cosmic Rocker ★ 7A+
Start up the undercut arete on its left, gain pinches and turn the arete to finish up the slab.
Mark Leach 1984

22b Project
The arete on its right the whole way.

23 Cosmic Slab Project
Climb the hanging face, just right of the arete

24 Poor Man's Paunch SIT 5+
The low bulge just before the corner.

Opposite the prow is a green wall.

25 Geoff's Wall 6B
Pull up the green wall on positive holds.

26 Nappy Rash SIT 6A
From a good jug, make a nice rockover to the rail. Finish on a good hold just above, or head up and right above a worrying ledge for the E3 tick.

Chimney Buttress Left

1 The Hacker ★ 6A+ SIT 6C
Climb the wall via layaways. The sitter starts from sitting on the rock, LH pinch, RH crimp. Right foot pebble, left foot crack.
Hank Pasquill 1973 (stand)

2 Digital Crusader SIT 6B
The crack to the right, moving left at the top to finish on the Hacker jug.

3 Project
Pop to the sloper, then use the undercut to gain a small crimp. Somehow continue upwards.

4 Shieldbug 7A
Pull on at the slot behind the left arete. Match twin crimps on the shield, then throw to a better hold. Continue upwards.

5 The Shield 6B+
Start LH either of the twin crimps, RH low to the right. Make a reachy lock to better holds.

6 Shields of Glory 6B+
From matched on the right arete, gain the twin crimps and pull up to the jug.

7 Womax 6B SIT 7A
Fingery shenanigans up the tall wall. The sitter is possible via a bunched gaston rockover.

8 The Soot Monkey ★ 6C+
Climb past the left end of the undercut to finish on slanting jugs. A devious wall that gives you lots of options, most of them poor.
Paul Pritchard 1985

9 The Monkey Suit 7A
Pull into the right end of the long undercut, choose holds in the centre, then gain a good edge up and right. Finish at the break.
Robin Müller 2011

10 Builder's Bum 6B
Start matched in the hanging crack, then make strong moves up crimps to the finishing jug on the left.

TRAVERSES

Fans of sideways action will find the Chimney Buttress obliging. The sidewards journey is possible all the way to the far side of the Prow Inside Face. Grades given are French sport grades.

Chimney Buttress Left 6b+
Left to right, finish bridged in the first corner.

Chimney Buttress To Foodle 7a+
Reversing *L'Arete Traverse* adds a bit.

Chimney Buttress To Prow End 7b

Chimney Buttress + Prow Inside 7b+

WILTON 1

11 La Triche SIT **6C+**
Sitstart the arete, swinging onto its left to finish. Stay off the big sidepulls to the left.

12 Le Puriste SIT **7B**
Climb the arete without the big jugs of La Triche.
Robin Müller 2012

13 L'Arete Traverse ★★ **6C**
Superb sideways action. Finish at the jug.

14 Foodle SIT **6C**
Sitstart the arete, using a big LH sidepull. Swing round and finish at the jug.

15 Oodle LOW **6C**
Start RH good right facing crimp, LH low hold. Throw for the arete and finish up this.

16 Fingertoe ★ LOW **7C**
From RH sidepull and LH something rubbish, climb the wall on its left (the arete jug is out) and join Children of Arachne at the good hold.
Robin Müller 2011

17 Children Of Arachne 7A
Devise a fingery sequence to gain a good hold, then a large gaston, then the ledge.
Robin Müller 2011

18 Pocket Wall SIT **6A+**
The wall between the cracks. Sitstart at the jug, work up to a good RH sidepull, then pockets and the top.

19 Sidepull Wall SIT **6B**
Start at the good hold on the left. Climb sidepulls to a flat edge, then crimps to the top.

Chimney Buttress Right

20 Besidepull Wall SIT **7A**
Sitstart the crack to a gaston, then cross to the fat RH sidepull just above and reach holds out left. Stay off the good flat hold on Sidepull Wall.

21 Crack Jack 4 SIT **6C**
Sitstart from the crack to a gaston and a powerful move right to better holds.

22 King of Nothing Muck SIT **6C**
Climb the arete, staying right of the crack. An unlikely LH undercling may be of use.

23 Spider Crack 3
Fun underclinging to the jug.

24 Eyed A Crack 6B+
Crimp up the bobbly wall to gain the big underclings, via a sidepull.

25 Crack 4 5
Slightly highball laybacking. Descend to the right.

26 Crack 1 4
Left of the arete.

The Mound

From Chimney Buttress, head left and climb the heathery mound, which hides this nice collection of easy highballs and powerful lowballs. Though somewhat scruffy, this slightly steep wall is useful because it rarely gets wet.

1 It 6A
From the jug, sketch up the rather high wall.
Mark Leach 1985

2 This 4+
Follow the flake to the top.

3 Snagglepuss 6A
Start matched on the low ledge and climb the wall above, to gain the top via a curving crack.

4a Just a Minute SIT 7A
Start at the large flake and traverse rightwards, with crux moves to gain the mid-way crack sloper. Finish round the far arete.
Robin Müller 2011

4b Went Like Fury SIT 7B+
A low variation to *Just A Minute*, staying beneath the large sloper used on that problem.
Robin Müller 2013

5 Centrefold SIT 7B
Start RH low crimp, LH wierd backwards hold. Make a big lock to gain a decent LH sidepull. Finish matched on the sloper.
Robin Müller 2011

6 Once You Pop SIT 6C+
Start LH tiny edge, RH good hold. Pull to LH pocket and pop to the RH jug. Finish either straight up or by traversing right around the arete.

7 The Mono Project
Sitstart LH slot, RH sidepull. Crimp desperately upwards to a good finishing edge.

8a Greasy Spoon Yard SIT 6B
Start just right of the sidepull matched on a slopey ledge. Traverse the slopes rightwards to finish at a good stance with jugs.

8b Greasy Spoon Yard Hard SIT 7A+
As per *The Mono Project*, start LH slot, RH sidepull. Bump into the slopes and continue rightwards.

The Mono Project p172

Ell's Arete, 6C p176

The Eliminator buttress is the first area reached just after the set back which features the orange pipe.

1 Eliminator Left LOW **6B**
Crouch start matched on the low edge. Head up and left to finish on a flatty near the arete.

2 Eliminator Right LOW **6B**
Crouch start matched on the low edge. Climb straight up to finish on the triangular pocket.
Paul Pritchard 1985

3 Left Bastard LOW **7A**
From underclings, gain the LH crimp and head for an undercling to jug finish.
Robin Müller 2011

4 Right Bastard 7B
Start RH crimp, LH undercling, finish as before. Starting matched on underclings is an obvious challenge. Powerful.
Robin Müller 2011

5 Gravitational Experiment ★ SIT **6C**
Sitstart at the good hold. Pull up the twin cracks, staying off the line of edges out left.

6 Craven 7A+
Climb straight up the face, then press left to finish up *Gravitational Experiment*.
Robin Müller 2011

7 Project
An impressive highball line.

8 Pellet Wall 6B
A couple of tricky moves soon lead to jugs.

9 Knee Butt ★ 7A+
The lower level standing start to *Head Butt* from RH slanty crimp, LH anything. Pull to the flatty and lay one on. Satisfying movement.
Robin Müller 2011

10 Head Butt Wall ★ 6B
Stretch or French start to the diagonal crimp, then up and right.
John Hartley 1986

11 Project
The super crimpy direct sitstart to *Head Butt*.

12 Simon Says SIT **7B**
Sitstart LH crack and RH sidepull. Climb the wall using anything left of the arete.
Robin Müller 2012

13 Snakes 3
The wall and arete. This is also the way down.

Around to the right is a wall that looks half-decent, but the top-out would need excavation.

WILTON 1

The Woods

Keep walking past Eliminator and head into the trees. The red wall marks the start of The Woods bouldering. Its crimpy centrepiece is worth doing.

1 Bean Bag Wet SIT **5**
Up big edges, from sitting. Often wet.

2 Barbara's Man ★ 7B
The vague arete, using crimps and a curving sidepull, with a crux move right to gain the jug on the route *Barbara Ann*. The highball extension is unclimbed.
Robin Müller 2011

3 Project

4 Arete Project
The highball right arete of the crack.

5 Project
Sitstart into the big undercling, then devise a sequence leading to a big move straight up the centre. Lunging out right is easier and not as good.

6 Project
Use the arete, stay right of the crack.

The final wall has some fun easier problems, though top-outs are not always possible due to the mud. If you make it over the top, descend down the slope to the right.

7 Ell's Arete ★★ 6C
The slabby arete on its right. Slap the sidepull and finesse to a romp up slopey crimps - standing on top of the slab is good enough for the tick if the top is buried.
Elliot France 2011

8 The Deep SIT **5+**
Sitstart, climb the cracks and arete.
Les Ainsworth, Dave Cronshaw 1979

9 The Grunt SIT **6A**
Sitstart, mantel, continue.

10 Sideshow SIT **5**
Sitstart, climb up the left of the wall.

Wilton 2

Warmup Wall

On the left end of the quarry, Warmup Wall offers mostly big holds. Just right of the corner, the green slab is also worth a look, but needs a dry spell to be climbable.

1 Oooga Booga That Way SIT **4+**
Start at the far left, traverse right to the big gastons and finish upwards.

2 Wam Bam And Beyond SIT **5**
Climb up on big holds.

3 Bish Bash Bosh SIT **5**
Start at the ledge and gain the top via a slanting edge.

4 The Urkling ★ SIT **6A**
Start at LH crimp RH undercling. Pull up via sidepulls.

5 Concrete Crack LOW **6C**
Pull on to underclings and climb the wall left of the arete. Follow the crack left to a jug. Watch the landing.

6 The Mean Fingers Project
Climb the slab on its left, staying right of the jug. Very thin.

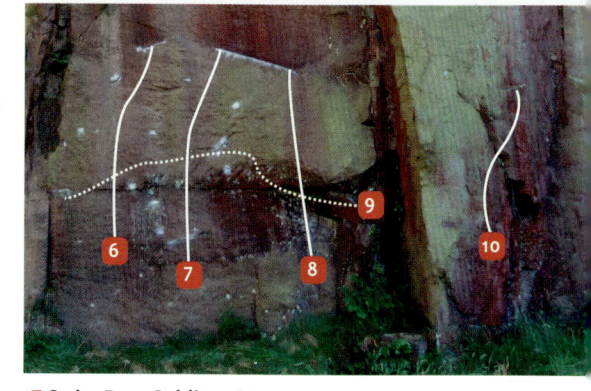

7 Strict Puss Soldiers 6B
Climb the centre of the slab, staying off the bigger footholds to the right.

8 Novice Slab 4+
Keeping left of the slab arete, use underclings to reach the juggy ledge.

9 Project Traverse
Traverse the slab, staying off the high jug line.

10 Derring Do 6B
Pull on to crimps, gain the underclings and finish on a jug above.

WILTON 2

Hidden Wall

In the back left corner of the quarry, beneath the impressive trad line of S Groove is the Hidden Wall.

1 Drag On The Fly 6B+
Follow the break beneath the roof and step off at the far side.

2 Bone Down ★★ 7B+
Start the fierce arete on its left, using a thin RH sidepull. Finish on a good edge obove the overlap. The low foothold right of the arete is off-limits. A sitter looks just possible.
FA Robin Müller 2011

3 Slipstream ★★ 7A+ SIT 7B
Start the arete on its right, from a LH undercling and RH on the low pocket. The sitstart goes from LH arete, RH crimp. Finish on a good edge above the overlap.
FA Robin Müller 2011

4 Pocket Pull ★ 6C
Pull onto the thin pockets and go for a good incut in the break. A tiny gaston is helpful.

5 Project
Pocket LH, undercling RH. Go for the break.

6 Project
Use underclings and sidepulls to gain the break. Stay off the wall to the right.

7 Mouthgaurd SIT 6C
Start on the obvious lip hold. Pull up the left side of the arete. Feet anywhere (a kneebar helps). The jugs on the right wall are off route.

8 Hidden Prowler ★ SIT 6B+
Sitstart at the obvious hold. Pull up the arete on its right. No back walls for feet: if you use the right back wall and the big toe-jams, it's **Hidden Prowler Lite SIT 6A+**.

9 The Curvier 6B
The thin slab just right of the corner. Stay off the layaway to the right and finish on the incut rail.

WILTON 2

The Swine

The back wall is clean, technical and marked by the pocks of misfired shots. Fast-drying. Beware: the boulder problem starts may tempt you into daring solos.

1 After The Shooting SIT **6B**
The pocketed wall.

2 Pigs On The Hoof ★ **7A+**
Step off a boulder to start on jugs at the end of the break. Traverse right with a crux near the far arete. Finish at a hands-free rest on the arete.

3 The Swine ★★ LOW **6B+**
From a crouch start matched on a good edge, pull up the flakes to finish on good edges.
Hank Pasquill 1974-75

4 Iron Orchid SIT **5**
The arete on its left, finishing at a hands-free perch on the chest-height sloper.

5 Dark Side Of The Daisy SIT **6C**
The arete on its right, finishing hands-free on the chest height sloper.

6 From Dirt SIT **6C**
At a slightly higher level, sitstart the tiny wall from a jug, with a tough lock to the top.

7 Carry On SIT **6C**
Start at a sidepull and pull up to the ledge. The footledge is out.

8 Carry Over 6C
Start matched on the arete and the hold just left. Traverse left to reach the jugs, eliminating the big foothold (and the footledge).

9 Rollover Jackpot SIT **7A**
Sitstart the undercut boulder to the right and make a difficult mantel.
Robin Müller 2011

WILTON 2

Corner Bay

The Corner Bay right of The Swine area has a few problems, though they aren't top quality.

1 Limber 5
The leaning double arete feature to a sharp juggy break.

2 Quiver ★ 6B
From the break, work into undercuts then tackle the high face.

3 Floor Work 4+
Sitstart the ledgey arete.

4 Bored at Home 6A
From sitting at a dirty break, climb the thin wall to another dirty break.

5 Grunter 6B+
Sitstart the wall right of the corner, moving up via a thin LH sidepull. Finish on the jug.

6 Moaner 6B+
Sitstart LH on good hold, gain undercuts with the aid of footholds out right and finish on the central jug.

The very small boulder in this bay has an astounding number of problems on it (i.e. more than zero).

7 Rise of the Bums SIT 6B
The undercut boulder starting LH beneath the arete, RH on the lip.

8 The Down Low SIT 7A
From the same start, gain the arete and rock round on its right. Not 7A if you don't do the rockover.
Robin Müller 2011

9 Down Lower SIT 7A
Start LH arete, RH on lip. Work into the start holds of ROTB and finish right of the arete. No rockover required.
Gareth Wallis 2011

WILTON 2

Near the entrance of the quarry is The Slab area. The first few problems here are superb.

1 Purple Feel ★★ **7A** SIT **7B**
The excellent technical arete on its left.
SIT Robin Müller 2011

2 Camille Claudel ★★ **6B**
Just right of the arete, balance up the slab on small crimps. Stay off the arete jug.

3 Smear or Disappear 6B
From the right arete, head left to finish at the far arete niche.

4 The Undercut ★★ **5+**
A great problem. Climb the centre of the slab, using the left end of the undercut if you want to. Gain juggy holds on the headwall and make big reaches to finish. The large ledge out right is off route.
Geoff Hibbert 1995

The next few problems are all on the hanging bloke up and right. Unless specified, all the following problems eliminate the footblock.

5 Swiss Dreams SIT **6C**
Slap up the leaning face from sitting. Hands on the main block only. Use the footblock for feet, but no higher than the obvious ledge.

6 Swiss Air 7B+
Start LH sidepull on the steep face, RH lowest sloper on the arete. Make a hard to hold slap to a good hold on the left arete. Finish easily up the slab.
Robin Müller 2011

7 Hangman 6C+
Hang start: LH face crimp, RH gaston low on the right arete. Power upwards, using feet when possible.

8 Knuckle Shuffle 7A +
Start on large opposing sidepulls, either side of the right arete. Traverse the lip left, eliminating the good crimp higher on the slab. At the far arete, rock right.

Wilton 3

The Square

Right of the entrance track is Wilton 3's star feature, an angular boulder with a climb-me face. The landings are a little awkward on some problems, but this can be sorted with a few pads.

1a Rodin's Requiem ★★ 7B
From standing on the block, use gastons to get established on the face, then reach better holds higher up. Rodin's sculpture 'The Thinker' may provide further beta. This was a great effort for the era and though not well known, probaby the hardest problem in Lancashire at the time.
John Hartley 1984

1b Project
Sitstart without the block. Super hard.

The arete to the left has been climbed on its left by Ryan Pasquill, but although the moves aren't too hard, the landing is frightening and it's definitely not bouldering.

2 The Square Left Hand ★ 6A
Climb *The Square* to the giant sidepull then make a big span left to gain better holds.

3 The Square ★★ 6A
Climb the face via a giant sidepull and big crimps. Classic.
Rowland Edwards

4 Blind Flurry SIT 7A
A direct sitstart to *The Square*. Without using the good crimp out right, climb straight up.
Robin Müller 2009

5 Square-Crow SIT 6C
Sitstart as before, but head right to the good edge. Continue up *The Square*.

6 Common Knowledge ★★ 6C
Razors and small sidepulls lead up the arete.
Paul Robins 2001

7 Common Or Garden Squiggle LOW 6C+
Hang the juggy ledge and power upwards. No footholds on the back wall.

8 Nostriloquy ★ 6B+
Climb the nostril feature with plenty of foot-locking.

The next problems are on the Small Roof, which is directly opposite The Square.

WILTON 3   183

Small Roof

1 The Roof Is On Fire SIT **6B**
Start at the slot, lurch to the lip and pull up the good holds on the face. The starting footledge is allowed.

2a The Starship Wilton ★ SIT **7C**
Sitstart as before, but stay right of the good holds on the face. Gain small crimps and pull to the arete (crux), then onto the slab and a finishing mantel. The starting footledge is allowed.
Robin Müller 2011

2b Stand And Deliver 6B
The finish alone makes a good problem. Start LH face crimp, RH arete crimp, then pull up the slab.

3 Scuffle Bucket SIT **7B**
Sitstart at the lip, throw for the arete crimp and pull onto the slab for the finishing mantel. Powerful.
Robin Müller 2011

Scuffle Bucket, 7B p183

Orange Wall

Here are a few good highballs with slightly dodgy landings. You may want a spotter and more than one pad.

1 Gameplay 6A
Pull on using the arete. Slap for the lip and use slopey holds to rock over.

2 Breakout 5

3. Not Al's Idea At All 5+
The arete is hardest near the top. Don't fall off this one!

4 Not Much Ado SIT **6B**
From sitting on the left, swing rightwards, staying beneath the jug. Rock round the leaning boulder to finish (the low footledge is out).

5 ★ The Pincher SIT **6B**
Start with RH pinch and climb straight up.

6 The Pinchee 6B
Start with LH pinch and climb straight up.

7 Project Crack
Pull into the crack and eliminate all face hand-holds till the finish.

The red wall to the right might offer a problem, but the landing is usually water-logged.

Right of the corner are some short and easy slab problems.

The Grader area is to the right.

8 Roaster SIT **6B**
The tiny arete on its left. The crack is out.

9 Toaster SIT **6B**
The tiny arete on its right. The crack is out but the RH undercling is in.

10 Get Off It SIT **6C+**
The arete on its left, with a crux bunched start. Stand on the jug to finish.

11 Get Down On It ★ SIT **6C**
The arete on its right. A low footlock is useful. Finish on jugs up and right of the ledge.

12 The Grader Direct LOW **5+**
From a low ledge, follow holds to the jug.

A little way to the right there are some problems based around a pointy wall.

13 Marginal 7A
Crimps lead to a jug, via an undercut thumbsprag. The big hold to the left is off limits. Using the footledges makes the problem (only slightly) easier.
Robin Müller 2011

14 Wingspan ★ SIT **6A+**
From sitting with a hand on the right arete, span left and hug up both aretes to reach jugs.

15 Face Front SIT **6C**
From sitting, power up the face without using the aretes.

16 Two Right SIT **6A**
From sitting, climb the two right aretes.

17 Crack and Slab 3
Layback the easy crack.

18 JR's Soft Shoe Shuffle ★★ **7A**
Work up the technical slab using undercuts, small footholds, a thumb sprag and the thinnest crimp known to man.
John Hartley 1984

19 You Heard SIT **6A+**
Sitstart at the flake just to the right and pull left to gain the good hold on the slab. Finish upwards.

20 Some Nonsense SIT **6A+**
Sitstart at the flake and follow it to the top.

Problems 14, 15 and 16 could be made harder by eliminating the large foot-ramp.

WILTON 3

Shiver's Arete

2 Shiver's Arete SIT **4+**
Climb jugs. The shivery bit is much higher.

3 Lock Me Up SIT **6B**
Make a big lock to the slot, then gain the jug. Hands right of the crack but feet anywhere.

4 Lock Me Down SIT **6C**
Sitstart as before, but head right, staying beneath the slot. Finish at a jug.

5 Things That Go Erk SIT **6B**
A fingery sitstart. Stay right of the big pocket.

1a Hold Up SIT **6C +**
The wall between crack and arete. Sitstart just left of the arete with an undercling move. Pull up and left to gain a big sidepull, then reach a sloper and go for the top. The landing has changed since it was first done and is now quite worrying.
Robin Müller 2011

6 Manbumps for Geese ★ **6B+**
From the corner jug, head left, staying beneath the jug finishes of previous problems. Sequency.

1b Project
Eliminate the big layaway. Fingery.

The wall right of Shiver's Arete area has a couple of problems.

7 The Gay Dwarves And Mr Plod Go To The Tupperware Party 5+
From jugs on the left, head up and right via crimps.

8a Lithuanian Lunchbox Luvvies 6A+
No jugs - use only crimps.

8b The Sausage Springs Free 6C
Dyno from the crimps to the top.

9 Great Gritish Flake-Off 4
Sidepull jug and then the top.

A small wall is just right.

10 North Wall 4
Centre of the juggy wall.

11 The Old Wiltonian 4
The wall and arete both have useful holds.

The next problems are on the far side of the bay, centred around an obvious slab.

12 Doozy ★ 4
The lovely slab.

13 Snoozy 4+
The slab on its right.

14 Grovel SIT 6B
Start matched on the left arete, feet on the slab. Slap rightwards, gain the right arete and grovel over the lip.

15 Project
Hang the protruding lip and mantel up the front.

Looking across the bay from here, at a slightly higher level is a low bulge, which should give a nice mantel problem, though it may be somewhat eliminate.

Wilton 4

The bouldering in Wilton 4 is to the left of the quarry. It gets shade most of the day and is a good option on hot summer days.

1 Haig ★ **6C**
A fierce crack highball.
John Monks 1982

2 Johnnie Walker 5
Follow the generous crack ever upwards.

3 The Big Four Project
The centre of the imposing green wall.

4a Long John ★ **6A+**
Climb the crack, using holds on the right.

4a Long John Left 6C
Climb the crack on its left, without any handholds on the right.

5 The Renaissance Men ★ SIT **7B+**
Starting from giant sidepulls, climb the wall just right of the crack, staying off the crack.
Robin Müller 2014

6 Project
More a concept than a project. Pull onto poor underclings and head straight up.

7 Project
From sitting at the arete, finurgle leftwards on underclings to gain *Long John*.

8 Neat Whisky ★ **6B** SIT **7A**
A trick problem, using the layaway. The sitstart begins at the arete and heads left to the layaway.
SIT Robin Müller 2007

9 Burnley Fish & Chips Since 1971 ★ **6B** SIT **6C**
From a sitstart, climb the arete on its left using the high undercling out left. Hint: look for a good low foothold on the right side of the arete.
Oliver Müller, Robin Müller 2007

The next problems are right of the arete.

10 The Ballad Of John Axon 5+
The wall just right of the arete.

11 The Gaston Project
The crack in the middle of the wall.

Cosmic Slab Project p169

Tiny Teets, 6C p192

24 Egerton

A locals' venue, composed mostly of shady bouldering beneath a high brick bridge, though there is also some lower grade bouldering on the upper tier.

APPROACH 5 min
Turn off the A666 at the war memorial, onto Darwen Road. Turn left down Smith Lane, then left where the road turns, then sharp left at the junction. Park on the right in a little bay before the last houses.

From the parking, walk uphill to reach the main footpath. Continue past metal barriers and then duck under a barbed wire fence on the left. A rough path leads down to the bridge. To gain the upper tier bouldering, exit the main footpath on the right and follow the top path round the quarry.

An alternative approach is possible from the north - park on Cox Green Road at the dead end and follow the footpath to the bridge.

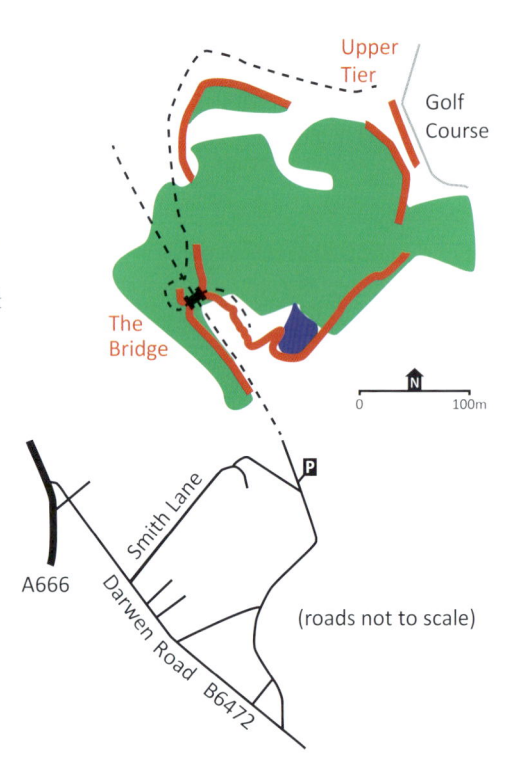

Upper Tier
Golf Course
The Bridge
0   100m
A666
Smith Lane
Darwen Road
B6472
(roads not to scale)

EGERTON 191

The Bridge is sheltered from showers, but often suffers from seepage.

The Bridge

1 Just Out 3 SIT 5

2 Moss of Innocence 3 SIT 5+
The wall between aretes.

3 Mosstradamus SIT 6A
Sitstart on the right and traverse at a low level beneath the jugs.

4 Beneath the Bridge 4 SIT 5+
The arete, staying left of the crack.

5 Twilight Crack 4
The crack, to a jug.

6 Broken Jokes ★ **7B**
From the arete (use anything right of the crack), lurch to the slot in the wall and make a couple of moves right to the jug.
Robin Müller 2009

7 Project

8 Hindsight 7B
Start hands right of ledge crack. Traverse left along the slotted seam and pull up to jugs past the crack.
Robin Müller 2010

9 Reinverting the Wheel 5
Stay left of the crack.

10 Bridge Crack 5

11 Blue Mushroom Warrior 7B+
The dynamic wall and arete, to a high edge on the face, then finishing on the high arete notch. (The good left foothold in the crack is out.)
Robin Müller 2010

12 Project

13 Bridget 6B
Bridge and head to the high arete notch.

14 Spandex 5+ SIT 6A
From just left of the crack, pull to the ledge, then make a big move to the slot.

15 Broken Toe 4
Up the crack, then left to the jug ledge.

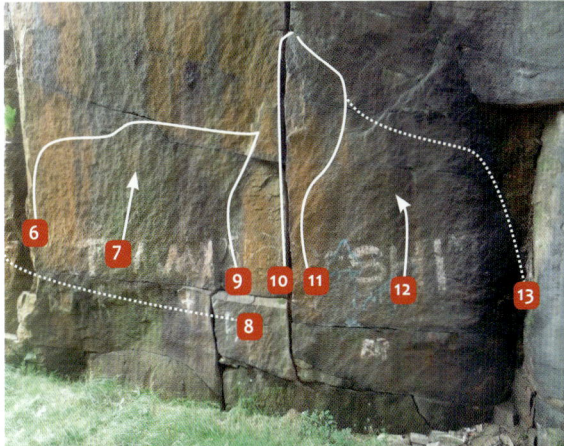

EGERTON

The Bridge

Wood Buttress

Competition Horror Show, 6B+ p193

There is more bouldering on the opposite wall, with a trio of lines attacking the chunky bulge.

16 Tiny Teets 6C
An easy start leads to a hard move right to gain the arete hold, using underclings and small crimps.

17 Project

18 Hit The Buzzer ★ 6B
The central arete, with a big stretch between decent holds.

19 The Nose 5
The right arete, with a giant sidepull.

From The Bridge area, head past the concrete ruins and downhill towards the pool. Wood Buttress is in the clearing on the right.

20 Project
The blank wall on the right looks climbable, but only just.

EGERTON

To gain the Upper Tier, follow the top path to the far side of the quarry. After a short wooden walkway, the path bends left. Turn off the bend via the 2nd of two very small right turns, which leads through vegetation and down a short slope. There is some easy climbing on the first wall encountered, but the good stuff starts on the clean slab further on.

WARNING: The large detached block at the top of the slab does move, so it's probably best to stay off it and finish on good edges beneath.

1 Contorted Filbert SIT **6A**
Make strange shapes to overcome the triangular protrusions. Stay off the crack.

2 Conniption ★ **6C**
The crack on its left, finishing on the slopey ledge beneath the detached block. No handholds right of the crack, but footholds are allowed.

3 Dribbles 4+
The crack and arete, finishing at the ledge.

4 Competition Horrow Show 6B+
Traverse left from the arete to the crack.

A little further right is a clearing, and several fun lower grade lines.

5 Just Out 5
Positive holds lead to a high finish. Watch out - they aren't all jugs.

6 Dingle 5
Start hanging the lowest edge and continue up the arete.

7 Dangle 4+
Mantel and you're done.

8 Dongle SIT **4+**
The right arete.

9a Bringing The Bear SIT **6A+**
Sitstart at the right arete, then swing left along the flatties to finish up the left arete.

9b Singing To Bear SIT **6C**
This time, start RH crack and LH gaston.

10 Reach For The Stars ★ **6A**
A long stretch from the big sidepull gains a good edge. Finish up and left - if the heathery mantel doesn't appeal, you can step off onto the adjacent block.

Project

27 Ousel's Nest

Following council tree felling and water drainage, Ousel's Nest (pronounced "oozel") is now a decent little crag. The bouldering is free of the ferns than run riot in the cracks, and it can be a very pleasant place on a sunny day with a bit of breeze. It is steep enough to offer dry climbing in light rain, and though it does suffer post-rain seepage, some problems stay dry in all but the worst weather. Be warned: cloud and humidity make it dark, damp and midgey. The climbing is mainly on the hard side of vertical.

APPROACH   3 min
From Bolton follow the B6391 Chapeltown Road to a sign for Jumbles Country Park. Turn right into the car park. Take the obvious footpath and then take the first left turn. Cross the grass to access the quarry, which is behind trees at the far side.

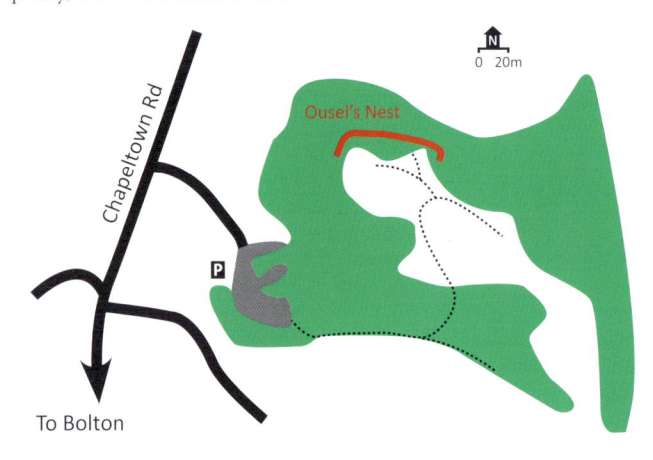

OUSEL'S NEST 195

1 Elliot's Traverse ★ **7a+ (sport grade)**
Start just right of the corner and traverse left at a low level all the way to the block halfway down the crag. Short sections are also good: **Tim's Traverse 6A** starts at **A** (the crack above the bricks) and heads left to finish at jug **B**. **Tim's Even Longer Traverse 6C** goes from **A** to arete **C**.
Tim Greenhalgh 2005, FULL TRAVERSE Elliot France 2014

2 That's The Badger 5+
Big holds lead to a stretch from an undercling to a good jug.

3 Alison's Route ★ **6C+** SIT **7A**
Climb the centre of the wall, staying away from the left arete. A powerful move leads to a good edge, then finish with a fat undercling move to the juggy notch. A French start to the good edge is **6B**.
Tim Greenhalgh 2005, SIT Robin Müller 2013

4 Five Minute Fame 6B SIT **6C**
The left arete to the break. Use anything right of the crack.

5 Faith And Energy ★★ **7A+**
Follow the crack to a high jug. Very sequency.
Andy Griffith 1990

6 Chicken Wings ★ **7B**
The centre of the wall, to an edge above the overlap. The upper wall is an über project for the über strong.
Tim Greenhalgh 2005

7 Project
Climb the arete to a crux finish matching the slopey ledge. Keep right of the crack.

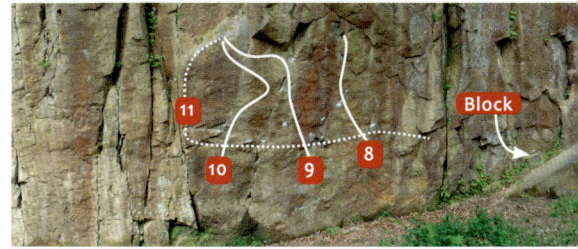

8 Tappings Of Power 6C
Use the slanting undercut to gain a small higher sidepull, then finish on the RH pinch. Tap the back of your hand in a confident manner, then jump off.

9 Zendik ★ **7A**
Gain a crimp below the peg, then reach left to a good finishing hold partway along the slopey ledge.
Robin Müller 2014

10 Reach For The Stairs 7A+
Get the slot as a RH pinch and throw to the top.
Robin Müller 2014

11 Yahoo! 6A
Layback the arete to good holds. A low traverse across this wall and up the arete is **Introduce The Moose 7A**.
TRAVERSE LINK Robin Müller, Oliver Müller 2014

Project p198

26 The Jumbles

A very conditions-dependent venue that can present either pleasant wooded bouldering or a midge-ridden jungle swamp, depending on recent rainfall and plant growth levels. Some walls dry fast, while others stay damp for ages. Dry spells in winter give the best conditions, when leafless trees allow more light into the quarry. All climbs are detailed online in the Jumbles bouldering wiki.

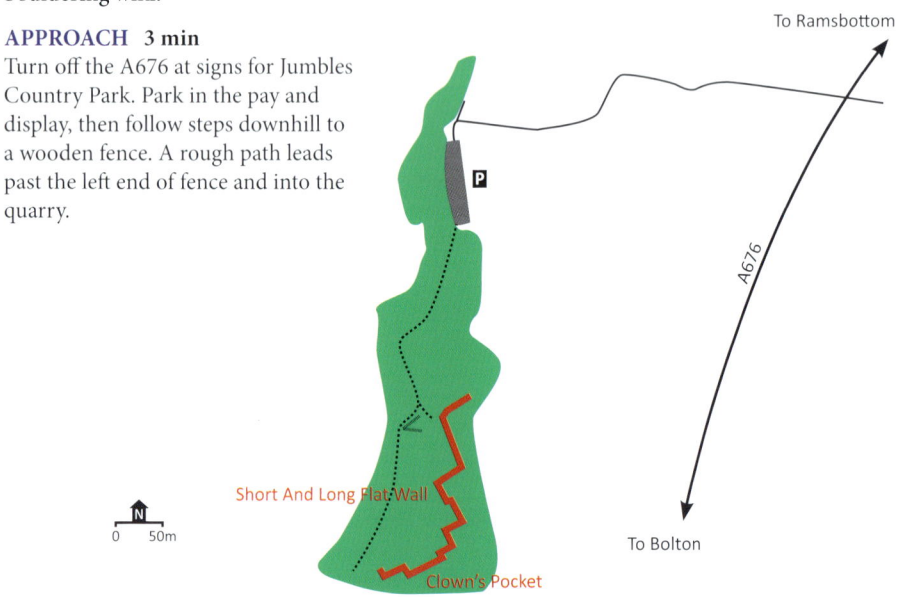

APPROACH 3 min
Turn off the A676 at signs for Jumbles Country Park. Park in the pay and display, then follow steps downhill to a wooden fence. A rough path leads past the left end of fence and into the quarry.

To Ramsbottom

A676

To Bolton

Short And Long Flat Wall

Clown's Pocket

JUMBLES 197

Short Flat Wall

The left end of the quarry has some routes on dodgy-looking rock, but most will walk past it to this wall of decent easier problems. The first three finish at the ledge.

1 Leaning Back is Cheating 5
The wall right behind the tree.

2 Tadpole 5
The line just to the right.

3 Bryn 6A+ sit **6B**
From sitting at the obvious slot, climb via the pocket in the break and an undercut.

4 Coalition 5+
Sidepulls and a crimp lead to a top-out by the stake.

5 Shreddies 5
Use the *Coalition* crimp with LH. No arete.

6 Left Arete 5+
The arete on its left.

Pursuit Of Slappiness, 7A p199

JUMBLES

Long Flat Wall

The Long Flat Wall starts round the corner and features several highballs.

1 Shadow Bands 5+
Thin crack climbing.

2 Bolide 5

3 Twin Cracks 4

4 Madrigal 4+
Another thin crack.

5 Undiscovered Dyno 6B
Dyno from the V-shaped hold to the flatty.

6 Jacob's Ladder 5+

7 Cracked Groove 6A
This crack is a little steeper than the rest.

8 Project
Follow the disappearing crack into the high and blank upper wall.

9 Laying Into 5
Break right from the crack to finish up the next problem.

10 Impending Groom 5+
Follow the crack to the top.

11 Tiny Feet Traverse 6A+
Cross the wall at a low level.

More lines have been climbed between here and the Clown's Pocket area, but have not been described as they are mostly dirty, a bit high or cursed with poor landings. If you see something that inspires you, check the wiki for info. There is nothing harder than **6A**.

JUMBLES

The most popular bouldering area is on the final stretch of rock.

1 Pursuit Of Slappiness ★ 7A
Climb the arete on its right. No holds left of the crack.
Robin Müller 2012

2 Project

3 Steep Start Wall 5+ SIT 6C
Stay between the cracks.

4 Crescent Of Embrace ★ LOW 7A+
From a crouching start on low holds, crimp up the face to good ledges. A morpho French start uses RH undercut to pop for the high edge - this is **Flight 93 7A**.
Gareth Wallis 2010

5 Lollymack 6C
Layaways lead to a high rockover.

6 Cheeky Constable 5+
Right of the tree, to a finishing ramp.

7 Hitchcock 5+
Climb via the big sidepull, staying right of corner jugs.

8 The Advent Of Hayden 6B
From the low rail, gain a sidepull, then head up and right.

9 Clown's Pocket Direct ★ 7A+
From the rail, rockover and undercut through the roof. No arete.
Nik Jennings 2010

10 Clown's Pocket ★ 6C
Use the arete to gain the pocket, then up.
Nigel Bonnet 2010

11 Pearl Oister 6B
The arete to the break, then left and up.

12 Careless Wispa 6C+
Climb the wall, using the arete.
Ste Li 2010

13 Sit Thee Down ★ SIT 7A
Start matched on the big low sidepull. Various methods exist.
Robin Müller 2012

14 Unfinished Wall 5
Follow the crack.

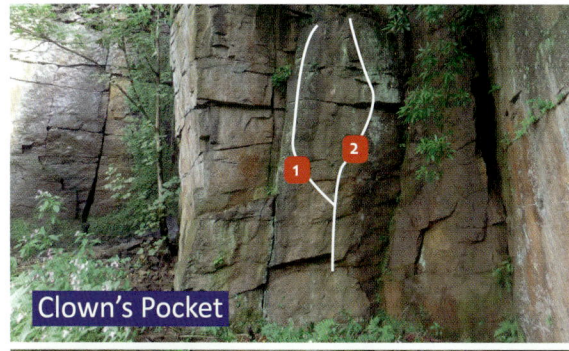

Vesuvius, 6B

27 Parbold

Tucked away in the non-rocky side of Lancashire, this quarry gives locals something to moan about. The rock is hard sandstone, though not all that different from most quarried grit. Trees block out much of the light, so bouldering here can be an atmospheric affair. The ground is muddy after rain but the main wall is fast-drying, with a handful of decent established lines.

APPROACH **10 min**
From junction 27 of the M6, follow the A5209 towards Parbold. After 2 miles, park opposite a steakhouse at a local viewpoint. Follow the footpath downhill from the east end of the parking area. After 400m this leads to the quarry.

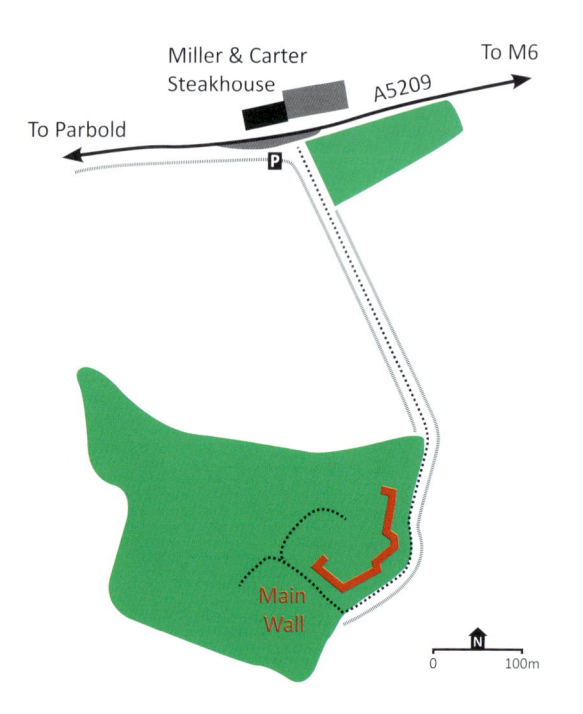

Miller & Carter Steakhouse
To M6
A5209
To Parbold
Main Wall
N
0   100m

PARBOLD 201

The Main Wall is on the right side of the quarry. The first problem is on an adjacent wall, right of the corner.

1 Parboiled ★ 7A
Starting to the right of a square-cut hole, crimp upwards to a finishing jug 2 metres above the break.
Alec Taylor 2013

2 Project

3 Project

4 Mentalist SIT 5+
Follow the crack up then left.

5 Mentalist Direct ★ SIT 7B+
Sitstart LH crimp, RH slot. Grimace upwards via the bad sidepull. It may be possible to dyno from the start to the top at an easier grade.
James Jennings 2011

6 Fundamentalist ★ SIT 6B
Sitstart from the two slots.

7 Fundamentalist Left Hand 6A
Start RH slot, LH crimp.

8 Project

9 St. Helens SIT 5+
Sitstart the slab, using the arete. Without the arete it's a contorted 6A.

10 The Arete SIT 6A+
Climb the arete on its left, from the low jug. Use arete holds only.

11 Etna SIT 6A
Erupt from the back. No sidewall.

12 Vesuvius 6B
Traverse to finish up the slab.

13 Pompeii 6A+
The steep rib.

EAST LANCS MOORS

But waved the wind on Blackstone Height
A standard of the broad sunlight
And sung that morn with trumpet might
A sounding song of liberty!

The Blackstone Edge Gathering - Ernest Jones, 1846

Troy A Little Tenderness, 7A p209

Troy 28

A popular spot with fine fast-drying burnt red walls, a friendly pinnacle for lower grade action and a few excellent harder challenges slotted in between neglected trad areas.

APPROACH 10 min
Turn off Grane Road at Heap Clough - there is a sign that reads "Quarry Entrance". Park in the obvious spot and cross the stile to walk down the road. Turn right at the next stile and take the right hand footpath, which leads to another stile. Turn left to enter the quarry. Some of the problems can be accessed slightly faster by approaching the quarry from the left hand footpath (see map).

Lone Wall
Recessed Bay
Little Buttress
North Walls
Cheeky
Nose
Pinnacle

0   50m

To Grane Road B6232

TROY

The obvious pinnacle is fast-drying and full of lower grade lines, some fairly high but others quite friendly.

1 Steptoe And Son 4
Follow the good ledges to the top.

2 Highball Paul 4+

3 Urban Skiing 5

4 Wellington Wall ★ 5
The tall front face.

5 Ee Am Reet Good 5+
The arete on its right.

6 Ee Am Reet Better 5
The left side of the arete. No bridging.

7 Layback That Crack, Jack! 5
Pumpy at the grade.

8 Shelf N' Crack 4
Onto the shelf, then guess what comes next...

8 Tray's Wall 5+
The wall between cracks.

10 Skinny Minny 4
The little groove.

11 Pinnacle Girdle 6A
Start at the arete and girdle the pinnacle, finishing at *Skinny Minny*. Sometimes the first face is wet, but starting on the next face is still a worthwhile **5+**.

12 Crawl From Your Hole ★ 6A+
Attack the central weakness. High at the top.

13 Distraction 6B
The arete on its right.

The Recessed Bay is reached from the Pinnacle by traversing across the nearby boulder pile at the edge of the water.

12 Project
The arete is high and looks flippin' brilliant. Sadly the landing isn't. A stack of four or five folded pads might fill the drop.

13 Project
The other arete. See above.

14 Project
Sitstart the clean wall.

Further round and just above water level is a small undercut wall. This is best reached by dropping down from the top.

15 Stilt House SIT **6A+**
The short wall. Eliminate the left footblock at **6B**, or the right footblock for **6B+**.

16 Stilton SIT **4+**
Climb the arete front on.

Finickitea Time, 6B+ p209

The Nose is at the top of a small bay not far from the North Walls.

1 Always A Giggle 6B
Use the left arete and finish on a hidden hold.

2 Project
The wall between arete and crack.

3 Stentorian 4+ SIT 6A
The upper crack on its left. Drop off at the crumbly break.

The Nose

4 Project
The crack on its right has an uneven landing.

5 The BNC SIT 7B+
Start at the back ledge and climb through the roof to finish up the left arete. Holds on the right arete are out.
Robin Müller 2012

6 Facial Flaring ★ SIT 6C
Start at the back ledge and clamp along both aretes to the top. Eliminating the big right heel placement is **7A**.

7 Chin Dweller SIT 6A
From the same start, it's possible to sneak right to the big jug and pull up the side wall.

Cheeky Sitstarts

The Cheeky Sitstarts are on the slope just before the North Walls. Walk on unless you've done everything else.

8 Zebedee SIT 7A+
Sitstart at crimps. Dyno. Don't use the wedged plate (it doesn't look safe).
Robin Müller 2012

9 Corset SIT 7A
A tight line. Start using LH crimps and RH in the small cracks. Pull to the slopey lip, then get jugs further back. Jumping to the jugs on the left is **6B**.
Robin Müller 2012

10 All Your Base Are Belong To Us SIT 5+
The big crack.

11 Haul Away For Rosie 4+
The arete taken front on.

12 Dance For Your Dinner 4 SIT 7A
Sitstart the aretes.
Robin Müller 2012

Just right, the North Wall offers a few problems.

13 Eloping Via Woking SIT 6A
Start at a sidepull and pull up surprisingly slopey holds.

14 Finickitea Time SIT 6B
Sitstart the undercut face. Sadly, it's easy after the first move.

15 The Perambulatick SIT 6B+
Start as before, but stay beneath the jug and traverse left to finish up *Finickitea Time*.

The wall to the right has a good one.

16 Troy A Little Tenderness ★ 7A
Pull on at the left arete and good central sidepulls. Make technical moves up and right to gain the crack and an easy finish. The giant ledge in the groove to the right is (obviously) off route, but all other footholds are in.
Robin Müller, Oliver Müller 2012

Little Buttress is best reached by the boulder bridge.

17 Magic Beans ★★ SIT 7C
The highball hanging prow is one of the best. Sitstart from the back break, without walls to either side. The top section is easier but scary.
Robin Müller 2013

18 Project
The arete on its left. Super hard.

19 Meat In The Middle ★ 7B
The pillar, without the left arete or holds in the crack on the right. Get your technique award here.
Robin Müller, Dawid Skoczylas 2012

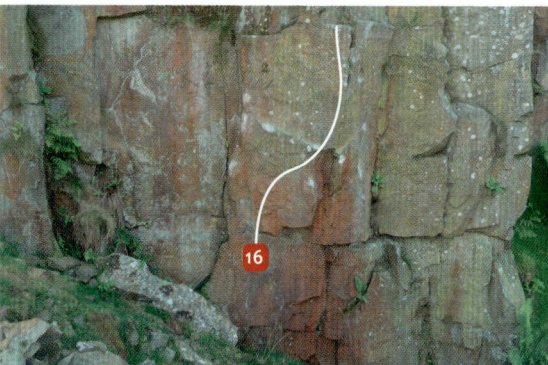

20 Smoke on the Water 6A
Use the left arete.

21 Project
This small hanging arete can only be reached from the other side. Back around!

Heel The World, 6B p214

Holcombe Moor 29

Dotted around the steep sides of Holcombe Moor are various short accidents of gritstone. Ultra-lowball sitstarts are the order of the day. Although there is not much here to shout about, locals might at least grunt with some measure of satisfaction. There are a few entertaining problems and the boulders have the advantage of drying faster than all the nearby quarries.

APPROACH **10 min**
From Ramsbottom, turn off the A676 onto Holcombe Old Road. Park in the parking area. Cross the road to the footpath, then turn right at the end and follow this road to a side road. Turn left here, then turn right onto the uphill footpath, from which various paths lead to each small area.

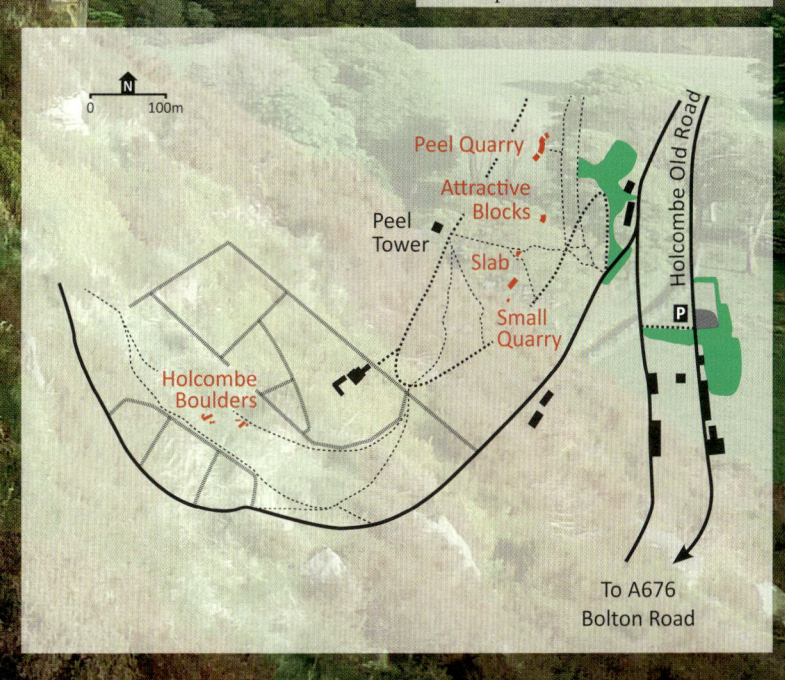

N
0   100m

Peel Quarry
Attractive Blocks
Peel Tower
Slab
Small Quarry
Holcombe Boulders
Holcombe Old Road
P

To A676
Bolton Road

HOLCOMBE MOOR

Peel Quarry

3 Weight For Me SIT **6A**
Pull up, then turn the arete to finish up its left.

4 Arms For The Poor SIT **6A+**
The undercut arete on its right. Finish rightwards.

5 Project
Pull away some brambles and sitstart the wall.

6 Sides of Ham 4
Pleasant wall.

7 More Words For Less Moves SIT **4+**
The crack on its left.

8 Traipse SIT **4**
The crack on its right.

9 Ultra Low Tech SIT **7A+**
Sitstart from the sidepull and traverse left beneath the break to gain the two central edges, then the top. Keep feet right of the crack. Lowball!
Robin Müller 2013

Peel Quarry is just off the path and makes a good start to the circuit.

1 Project
Climb the thin end face, past a sloper in the break. More than one pad is needed.

2 Project
The arete on its right.

10 Off Road, On Track SIT **6C**
Start from the sidepull.

20m left of the quarry is a cracked wall.

11 Slit Slat Slot SIT **4+**

HOLCOMBE MOOR 213

Another 80m beyond the cracked wall, hiding slightly downslope, are a couple of small, steep Attractive Blocks. Probably Holcombe's best bit.

1 Scratchplight SIT **6A**
From the back break, work left to the lip then back right to mantel.

2 Turntabla SIT **6B**
From the back break, pull through undercuts into the mantel. Side-blocks are out.

3 Mashup Muddley SIT **6B**
Start up *Scratchplight*, then traverse both lips to the far right arete. Top out here.

4 Goldkick ★ SIT **6C**
The arete, with a dynamic move off the ground. Follow the lip right to an easy top-out.

5a Wing Wang ★ SIT **7A**
Starting with a hand on each arete, wing it to the top.
Robin Müller 2013

5b Wing Wang Low SIT **7A+**
Start LH undercling, RH arete. Adds burl.
Robin Müller 2013

The Slab is 30m further round the hill from the Attractive Blocks.

6 One For Hobbits SIT **6C**
Sitstart the small undercut face from RH arete, LH lower crimp. Keep feet off the wall to the right - with this it's **3**.

7 Two For Hobbits SIT **6C+**
Use any crimps and slap the very top.

8 Dance For The Scones 4
Start on the jug right of the crack and traverse the top all the way to the left.

9 Crack In The Day SIT **5**
The crack.

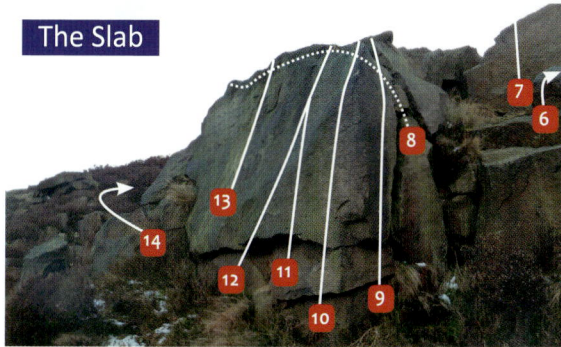

10 Over The Hill ★ SIT **6A**
The arete on its left, without the crack.

11 Dungarees For Danglers SIT **6B**
Climb just left of the arete, starting from a good LH hold under the overlap and RH mini-arete pinch.

12 Come All You Disgraceful SIT **6B+**
Using a sneaky LH undercling and RH good edge, sitstart the slab without the footledge low on the right.

13 Amber Rambler 3
Anywhere up the slab.

14 Fletcher Memorial SIT **4+**
Also fun and slightly harder without the left arete.

214 HOLCOMBE MOOR

Holcombe Boulders

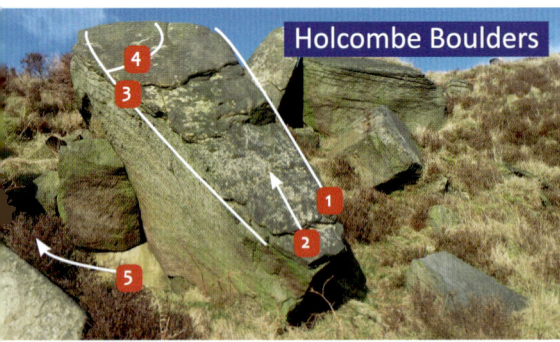

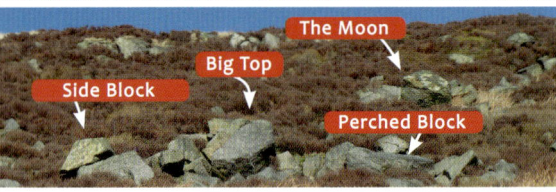

To access the Holcombe Boulders from The Slab, head up to Peel Tower, then take the path that leads downhill past the hilltop houses. Cross the stile, then take the smaller path that follows the wall. After 200m, the top of the first boulder is visible on your left, near to the path. Warning: these boulders are small!

1 Greening From Ear To Ear SIT **4+**
Lip traverse the easy side.

2 Feel The World 3 SIT **6A**
The slab, tackled front on from sitting.

3 Heel The World ★ SIT **6B**
Follow the lip to a good jug and rockover. Eliminate the undercling on the slab - with this it's **6A**.

4 Sketch Artist ★ 6C+
Start both hands on the lip at the top section of slab. Swing up a foot and rockover. Stay off the undercling, the back arete and juggy lip holds.

5 Hugs For The Soul SIT **7A+**
The clampy rock, without the footblock. With the footblock it's a nice **6A**.
Robin Müller 2013

The other boulders are 30m further on, at a slightly lower level.

6 Dark Side Of The Loon SIT **6A**
Start LH arete, RH lip.

7 Mooned Landing SIT **6B**
Start matched on the large crater. Footblocks are not allowed.

8 Sunken Gold ★ 2 SIT **7A+**
Sitstart matched on the lip and somehow pull onto the slab. Try a toe-hook. Super lowball but suprisingly involved.
Robin Müller 2013

9 Slappers On The Slope SIT **6A**
Sitstart off the rock, starting with one hand on each seam in the slab.

10 More Slaps Than A Girl's Night Out SIT **4+**
Start at the slight arete.

HOLCOMBE MOOR 215

11 Something More Civilised SIT **4+**
The short upper arete.

12 Perched Lips SIT **5+**
Start RH on the big sidepull and feet on the footblock. Pull over the lip.

13 The Pout Rowt SIT **6A**
From the same start, traverse left to the blob then top out. The footblock is in.

14 A Proper Grovel SIT **6C+**
A direct sitstart without the footblock, staying off the good sidepull to the right and the good blob to the left.

15 Grab And Go SIT **6A+**
Sitstart without the footblock. Make a move to gain the blob, then over you go.

16 Nose Job SIT **5**
The short arete, rocking onto its right.

17 Pah SIT **4**
Start from the break, pull round to finish.

18 Pink Floyd - The Arete SIT **6A**
Start from the break and pull up the aretes. Stay off the break sidepulls.

The last boulder is another 20m further on, at a slightly lower level.

19 Crunch Time SIT **5**
Use the undercling on the bottom lip and a hold on the face. Or you could try to jam up the crack...

20a Bingly Bingly Bong SIT **4+**
Swing up the arete and rockover.

20b Minimergence SIT **7B**
This time, no footblock. Start with hands low on the left.

Robin Müller 2013

Trouser Ripping Sitstart, 6B+ p217

30 Harcles Hill

Most of the bouldering at Harcles Hill is a little short, but there are some decent moves on sound rock. The small quarry is fairly fast-drying.

APPROACH 10 min
From Ramsbottom, turn off the A676 onto Lumb Carr Road. Park at the north end of Holcombe village, beneath trees near the primary school. A footpath beside the school leads uphill to a rough farm track. Turn left, then turn right to cross a stile and head uphill again. Once out of the fields. turn right onto another track, then left towards the quarry.

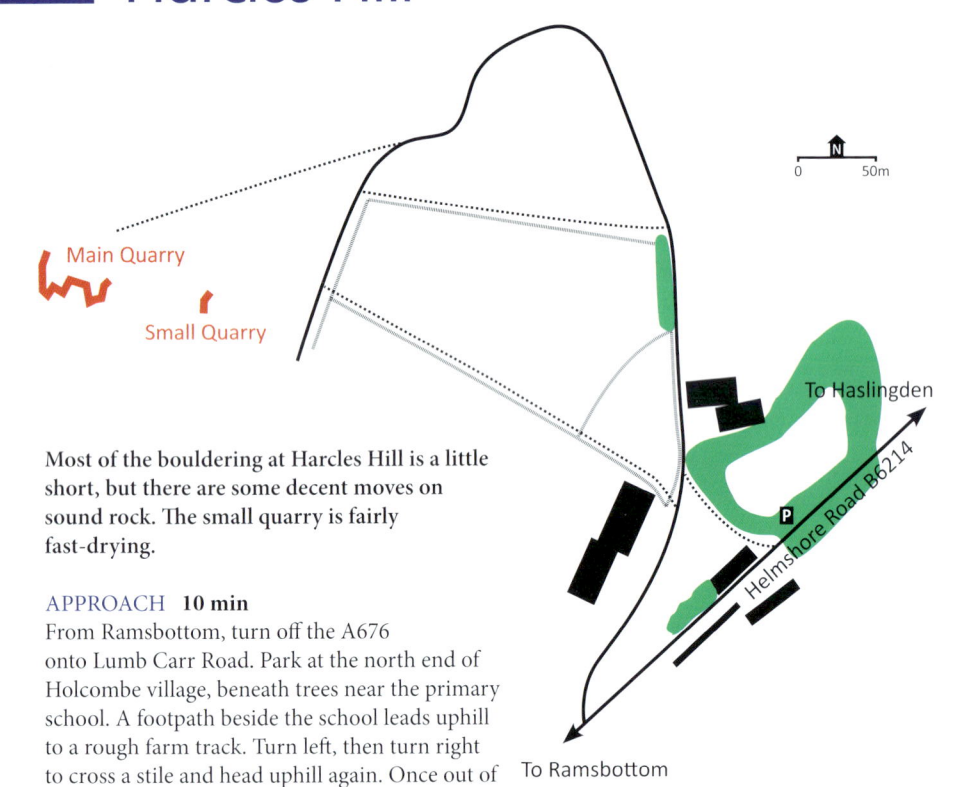

HARCLES HILL

Small Quarry

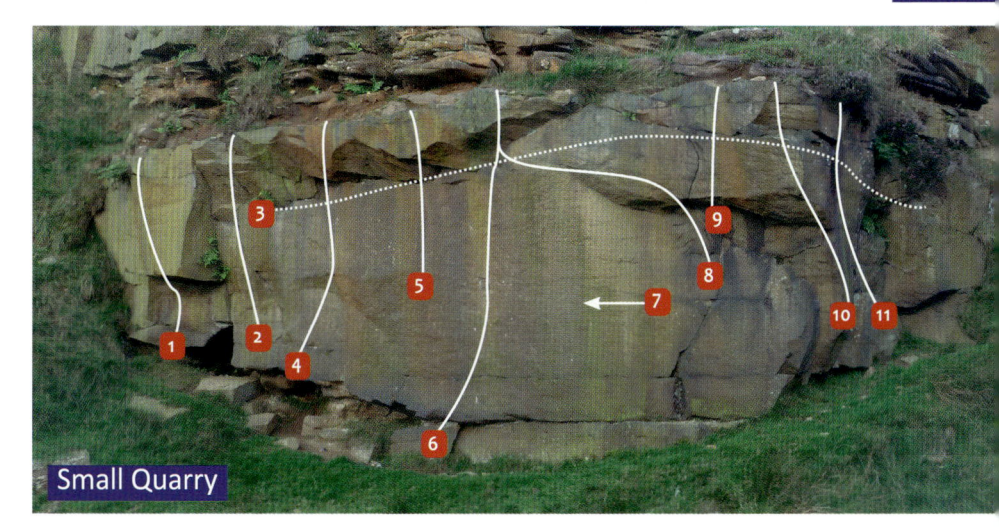

The Small Quarry holds a compact selection of short problems.

1 Big Scary Monsters SIT **7A**
Sitstart from hands on jugs beneath the small arete.

2 Cold Crags and Colder Grit SIT **4**
The arete from sitting at a good low jug.

3 Traverser La Rue 5+
Traverse the break from left to right, stepping down at the far end. Stay beneath the top.

4 Trouser Ripping Sitstart SIT **6B+**
From sitting, make a wierd rockover to gain the sidepull and the top. The footblock attached to the crag is allowed.

5 Bit of Both 6B
Pull on with LH tiny sidepull, RH crimp.

6a Superfly ★ 7A+
From the chipped crimp, make a fingery dyno to the jug.
Robin Müller 2005

6b Superflea SIT **7B**
The sitting start has a different name and grade, but the crux is the same.
Robin Müller 2009

7 Project
Step left from the footledge to make a super thin traverse, staying below the break all the way to the end.

8 The Lightning Bolt ★ 6A+
Pull left below the break to reach better holds, then the top.

9 Cracking Cheese, Gromit 5
Straight up.

10 Tennis Players Beware SIT **6C**
Sitstart at the low jug on the right and pull into the arete holds, without using the crack.

11 Fingerlockin' Good SIT **4+**
Sitstart from the jug and climb the crack.

HARCLES HILL

Main Wall

1 Lord Foul's Bane 5+
Rockover to the break.

2 Project
The left wall of the prow, to the break.

3 Caress of Steel SIT **5+**
The wall right of the arete.

4 The Judge 4+
Mantel onto the shelf and reach the ledge.

5 Blue Lamp 3
Easily up the short arete.

6 Project
Sitstart with RH in the slot and LH on the big hold to the left. Rock into thumb sprags and go for the notch. Reach-dependent, but great moves.

7 Skirts and Ladders SIT **5**
From the slot and the crack just right, sitstart and head for the notch.

8 Jailbreak 4
Climb to the break.

9 Wotsit SIT **5**
Sitstart, then pull up and left via a good crimp.

10 Hallucinogenics 5
The thin wall right of the grassy ledge. No cracks allowed, nor the big jug on the right.

11 Strict Late Night Mob SIT **6A**
Start the bulging arete from low holds. Don't use the crack to the right or anything to the left. Finish standing on the bulge.

12 Bastille Traverse ★ **6A**
Traverse from jug to jug in either direction.

13 Project
The landing requires spotters.

14 The Jeff Bomb ★ **6B** SIT **6C**
The right arete of the short wall, which starts as a crack. Don't use the other side of the crack, or any footholds in the crack. The short LH crack is allowed.

Bastille Day Buttress

The Lightning Bolt, 6A+

Sunday Morning, 4+

31 Pinfold

Pinfold offers a reasonable but limited bouldering area, on quick drying rock.

APPROACH   10 min
Head north out of Bury on the A56 Walmersley Road. After 2 miles, turn right in front of the post office onto Walmersley Old Road (signposted as Old Road). Follow this for just over 1 mile, often on cobbles. First pass the Mason Arms pub, then the Lord Raglan when the road becomes known as Bury Old Road. Park when the road finally turns into a rough track. Walk down the track for 200m to a double gate on the right. Climb over and follow the stone wall to the end of the field. Go through a gate and turn right, following the fence to a stile that leads into the quarry. Do not shortcut through the farm.

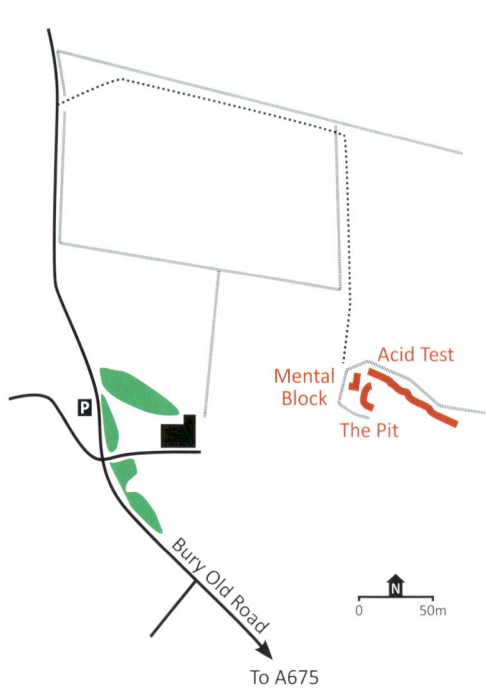

Acid Test
Mental Block
The Pit

Bury Old Road

To A675

0   50m

Mental Block

1 Blocked Mental 4+
The arete.

2 Monty Blonx ★ 5+
A tricky pull up the centre leads to jugs.

3 Physical Phil 5
The right arete on its left, with a dodgy landing.

4 Sunday Morning 4+
The arete on its right.

5 Saturday Night 6A
Climb between the slot on the arete and the square jug on the right.

6 Automatic Daffodils 5+
Climb up and left from the square jug.

7 Livin La Vida Loca 6C
LH square jug, RH slot, make a big move to the ledge. Sadly, the recent shotholes have reduced the difficulty.

8 Pendulum ★ SIT 7A
Start as per **9** and follow the seam holds leftwards to a crimpy pull for the arete slot.
Gareth Parry, Matt Nuttall 1995 (prior to foothold changes)

9 Her Back Yard SIT 6B
Sitstart RH pinch, LH low crimp.

10 Pyscho Time SIT 7A
Start LH on the left end of the undercut, RH on the biggish hold to the right.
Robin Müller 2012

11 Pit Stop SIT 4+
The flake in the pit.

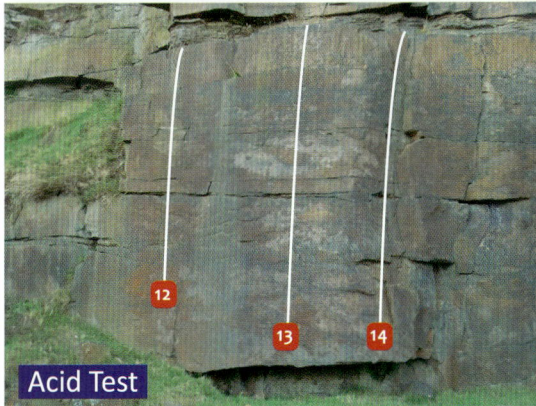

The Pit

Acid Test

12 Acid Test 4+
The arete, to finish on good holds over the lip.

13 Madman's Paradise ★ 6A SIT 6C
An awkward sitter into a thin upper section. Sneaking left at the top drops the standup grade to **5+**.

14 That Little Bit Of Rock Right Of David's Route SIT 4+
Sitstart the groove from big holds.

There is also a traverse from the groove to cross the wall to the right. This is **Traverse Of The Bods 6C**. It can be continued to the end of the crag.

32 Ashworth Moor

Esoteric bouldering for locals, with some fine get-past-the-lip challenges on the East Side and a good easier circuit on the West Side.

APPROACH 10 min
Turn off the A680 Rochdale to Edenfield road, onto Croston Close Road (600m west of Ashworth Moor Reservoir). Park either at the small bay or wherever you can get off the road. Don't block any gates. Follow the footpath downhill and turn right through a gate to gain the West Side, or to access the East Side, cross the bridge and keep to the footpath above the fence, until it is possible to drop down to the top end of the crag.

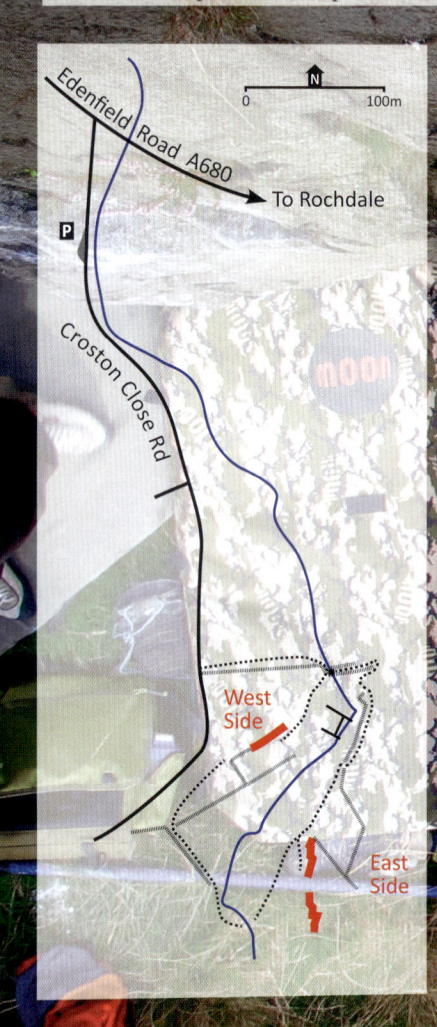

Black Hole, 6A+ p225

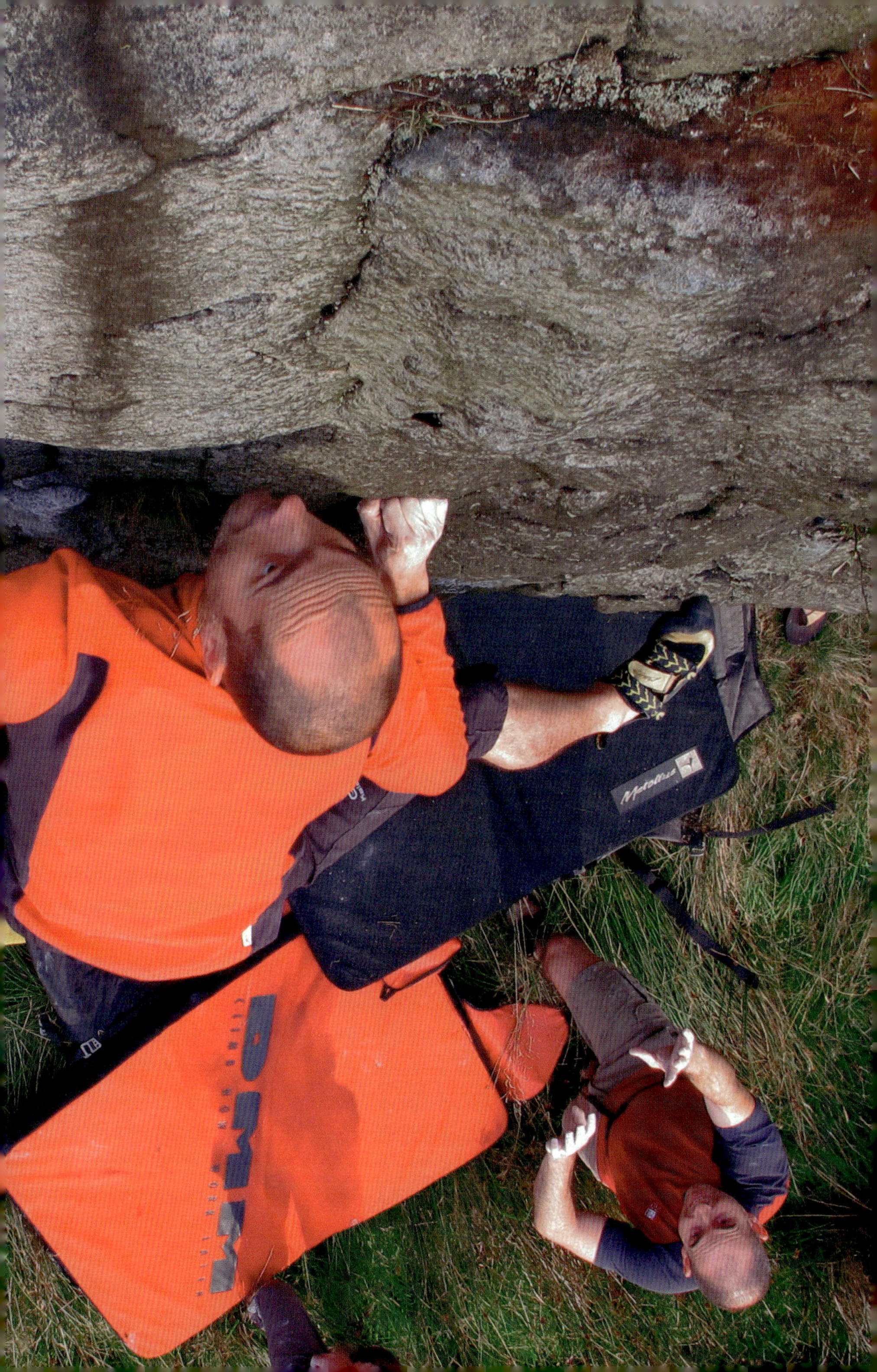
DMM
CLIMB NOW WORK LATER

ASHWORTH MOOR

East Side

Rock This Country, 6B+ p225

1 Mountain Ear 4
The arête is fun. The summit calls...

2 From Concentrate SIT **6A**
Sitstart just left of the protruding jug and rock leftwards to a small sidepull/crimp. Stand up to finish. One squeezed in move, but satisfying.

3 Yawning Arms SIT **5+**
Start on the protruding jug and make a big reach up to the crimp on the face. Finish easily.

4 What's That, Skippy? SIT **7A**
Feet low, dyno from the sloper to the good edge.

5 Whodunnit SIT **6C+**
A strict line that was previously very overgraded. Match the sloper, reach the small crimp, then pull to the good one. Keep feet low for the hard moves. (It was the butler, in the pantry, with the crimp.)

6 Into the Cleft SIT **6A**
Layback the crack to reach the top. Strenuous.

7 Fib of the Lips 6C
From the hold beneath the break, climb the thin wall between cracks.

8 Dirty Crack ★ 5
Not actually that dirty. You can finger jam if you are feeling keen.

9a Us Fellows 6C
From the jug on the arete, drop down to traverse beneath the break to gain problem **3**. An eliminate uses only the three slopey holds at **7A**.

9b Ragged Rascal SIT **6A+**
From the start of problem **3**, traverse right to the arete jug. Finishing up problem **13** is **6C**.

ASHWORTH MOOR | 225

10 Rock This Country ★ **6B+**
Rock into and slap up the arete. Stay off the crack to the left. Great stuff. Reverse problem **9** into this at **6C**.

11 Oli's Problem 6C
Trickiness to the right of the arete.

12 Black Hole ★★ **6A+**
Climb via the juggy pocket. Beware cosmic phenomena.

13 Kneerly Kneerly 6B+
A bit of jump-footing will see you right.

14 Temple of the Tooth 6C
Traverse to finish up **10**. Using no feet below the roof is **7A+**.

15 Flutter 5+
Reach through the roof to holds on the arete. Poor landing.

16 True Colours 5
The high wall on the right is climbed easily via the ramp. Careful of the blocks low down.

17 Grass Crack 4
Scrabble past the grass.

18 Right Arete 4

Black Hole, 6A+ p225

ASHWORTH MOOR

West Side

The short walls on the West Side of the valley offer some great low-grade esoterica, but be careful of the landings - some drop away alarmingly.

1 Ledgislation SIT **4+**
Sitstart the left side of the wall. Without footblocks this is **5+**.

1 Wotsamoov SIT **4**
The short wall.

3 Riff-Ruff 5+
The left arete and face. No holds on the right arete.

4 Twiddlicus SIT **5**
The right arete.

5 Greenee 3
The juggy green wall.

6 Schmeesy 4
An easy wall, but be careful of the loose block at the top.

7 Cracksaknack SIT **5**
Start at the break and pull up the crack.

8 Underslander SIT **5**
Sitstart and climb via the flake undercling.

9 Undercadabra 5+
The blank looking face has magic undercuts.

10 Grüvy ★ 5+
Up the groove.

11 Sydeswype 6A
Crimp up the face, no holds in the groove.

12 Phaseleft 5
Layback the crack and step around the arete to finish over a good hold.

Kneerly Kneerly, 6B+ p225

ASHWORTH MOOR

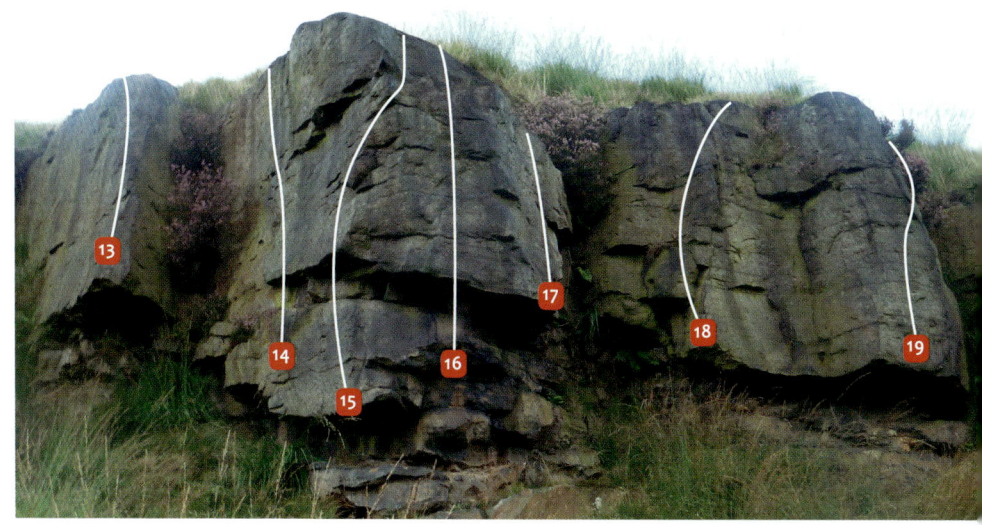

13 Strawbogen ★ 5
The thin arete, with big holds on the face.

14 Plexify 5
The sidewall gets high and the top is a bit worrying.

15 Nanimiles 6B
The grade is for undercutting past the loose crimp.

16 Squeezabules SIT **6B**
Slap up the front.

17 Skirtingus 4+
The sidewall is much easier.

18 Stepsakross 5
Awkwardly does it.

19 Fiddlipop SIT **6A**
Pull to the right to finish.

20 Woops-A-Crazy ★ 6A
Good edges lead up the airy wall.

21 Team Time 6A+
The high front face. Bring many pads.

22 Project
The arete on its right. Bad landing.

23 Campus Jugs 5+
Reach big holds and swing upwards.

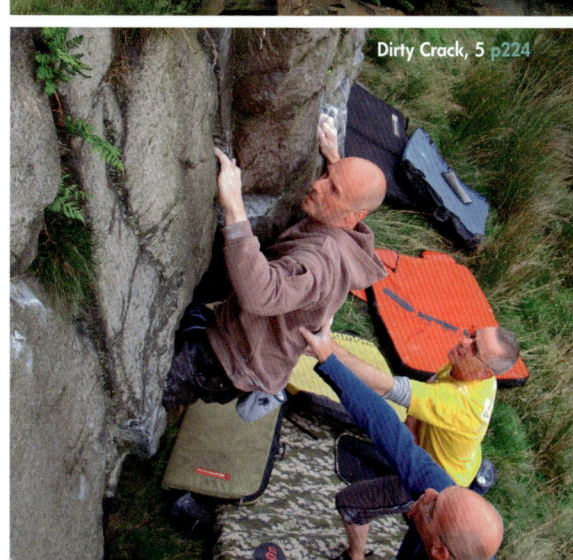

Dirty Crack, 5 p224

Digging For Deeply, 6A+

33 Deeply Vale

In the 70s, Deeply Vale played host to the Free People's Pop Festival, attended by a crowd of 20,000. Those numbers might never again descend on this unlikely venue, but a steady trickle of climbers keeps the music alive. Rock on, Deeply Vale! Following a clean-up and excavation operation by the Mountaineering Club of Bury, it now makes for a worthwhile evening hit. There is a good highball bay, plus a few other bits of fun - check the internet for details of even more problems. The outlook is scenic and the crag gets sun in the morning, then shade later on.

APPROACH   10 min
Head north out of Bury on the A56 Walmersley Road. After 2 miles, turn right in front of the post office onto Walmersley Old Road (signposted as Old Road). Follow this to the Mason Arms pub, then turn right off the steep bend onto Bentley Lane. Pass under the motorway bridge and half a mile later take a right turn down a bumpy road. Turn left at the end, then after a little way park by a gate on the right (don't block the gate or the road - extra parking is available back by the T-junction). Follow the footpath, which turns right after a stile. The quarry is soon visible on the right.

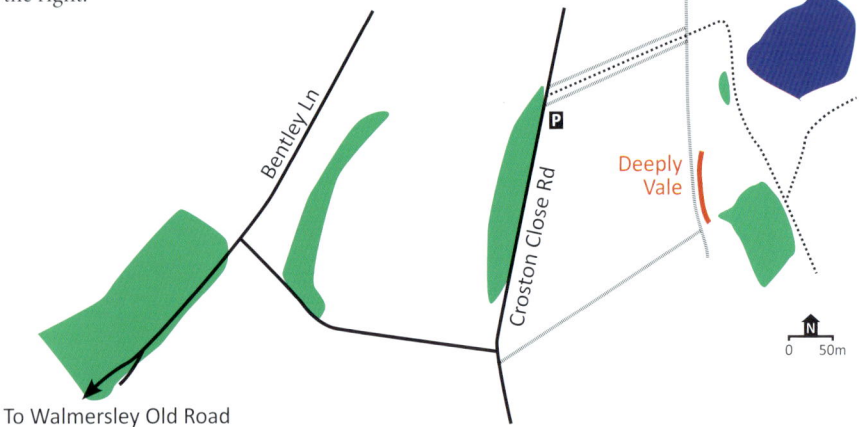

DEEPLY VALE 229

Highball Bay

The left-most wall has good vertical highballs with flat landings.

1 Blunt 4
The arete, from a pair of spread sidepulls.

2 Leggy Turd Wax 3
Climb just left of centre.

3 Tiger Antonio 3
Right of centre, but without the crack.

4 The Gutter 2
The corner.

5 Central Line 4
Up the middle - harder if you are strict.

6 Festival Arete 4+
The arete on its left.

7 Kestrel Arete 5
The arete on its right - finish on the left.

8 Archeological Treasures 5
Climb just right of the arete - downclimb or jump off near the top to avoid a loose finish.

9 The Pod 5
Follow the big sidepull left of the corner. Stop at the hole - above looks loose.

10 Excavator Wall ★ 6A
The wall between the crack and arete - left and right variations possible.

11 Farthing Arete ★ 5+
The arete isn't too hard, but is a little scary.

Inflexion

12 Digging For Deeply ★ 6A+
Traverse left to the far end. Staying below the break from the central arete is **6B+**.

Further right is the Inflexion wall.

13 Derivation 5+
Gain the arete, then finish at the slot.

14 Inflexion Direct Start ★ 6A+ SIT 6B
Climb on largish holds to finish at the slot.

15 Resurrection ★ 7A
Stretch to a sharp RH crimp and strange LH hold. Choose a foot nubbin and go for the ledge. Rockover on this to finish.

16 Resurgence ★ 7A+ LOW 7B
A lower left start to *Resurrection*, staying right of the cracks. The even lower start is from the break.
Robin Müller 2014

17 Inflexion Traverse SIT 6B
Follow the break line, then rock around the arete.

Further right is a good small arete. From a sitstart on its right, this is **Lonely Arete 6A**. Sitstart the wall just right of the arete for **Lonely Brother 6C**.

Black Beauty, 7A

34 Birtle Boulder

Surreally positioned just outside Bury, the lakeside setting of the Birtle Boulder seems a million miles from terraced houses and busy streets. This is a very minor venue, but it's a pleasant spot with pleasant sport and a good crimping centrepiece. The boulder is on private land so keep noise to a minimum and make sure you don't leave any litter.

APPROACH 2 min
Turn off the B6222 Rochdale Old Road onto Castle Hill Road. At the T-junction turn right and park just beyond the first buildings, near a gate (but without blocking it). Walk down the road to a small swinging gate on the right, by a public footpath sign. Go through this and head leftwards through the field to another gate. Go through this and the boulder is soon visible on the left.

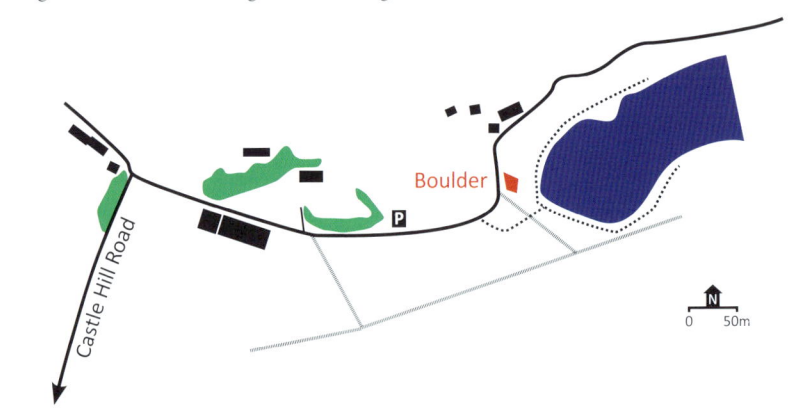

Castle Hill Road

Boulder

N
0 50m

To Rochdale Old Road

BIRTLE BOULDER 231

1 Organise By Vegetable 4+ SIT 5+
Squat on the low footledge for the sitter.

2 James And The Giant Reach LOW 6C
From underclings, pop for the ledge. The grade is likely very height dependant.

3 Black Beauty ★★ 6C+ LOW 7A
The central line on the block, with a low start from underclings to a hard move past fierce crimps.

4 Swan Lake 6C+ SIT 7A
The arete yields to a nice bit of slapping but the landing isn't the best. Don't use the ground rock for feet.

5 Farromatic 4+
The green slab.

6 Cheesy Rider 4
The arete on its right.

7 Herbie Goes Bananas 4
The juggy bulge.

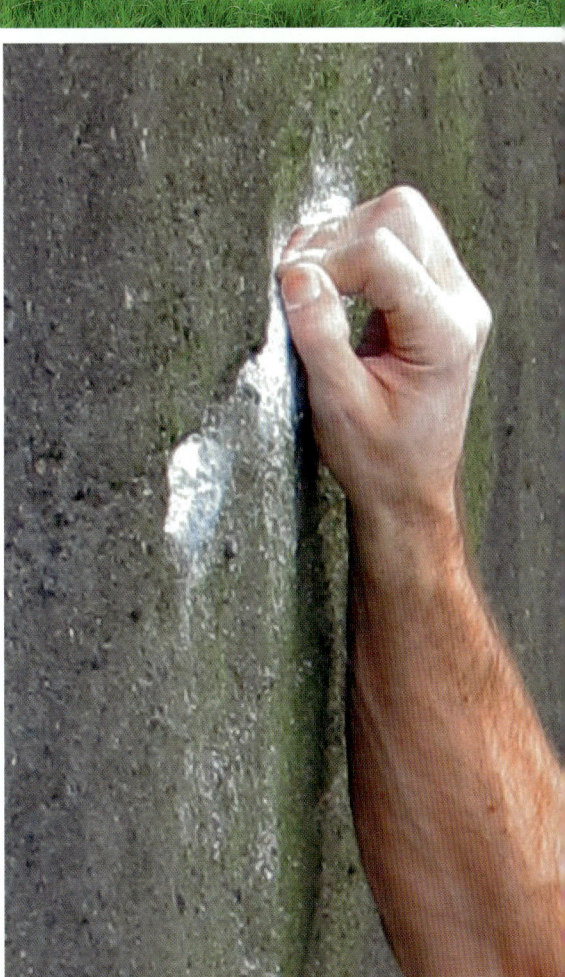

35 Lee

Here is a quarry with an epic feel, where a few nice boulder problems are dwarfed by tumbling chossy cliffs and framed by rock-dotted ponds. Custom-built tracks have been installed for mountain bikers, so expect to share the place with plenty of two-wheelers on sunny evenings and weekends. Much of the bouldering is fast-drying. Expect small holds and more steep problems than the usual quarried fare.

APPROACH 15 min
Turn off the A681 Newchurch Road at Futures Park. Park at the dead end fork and walk up the road, which soon becomes a footpath.

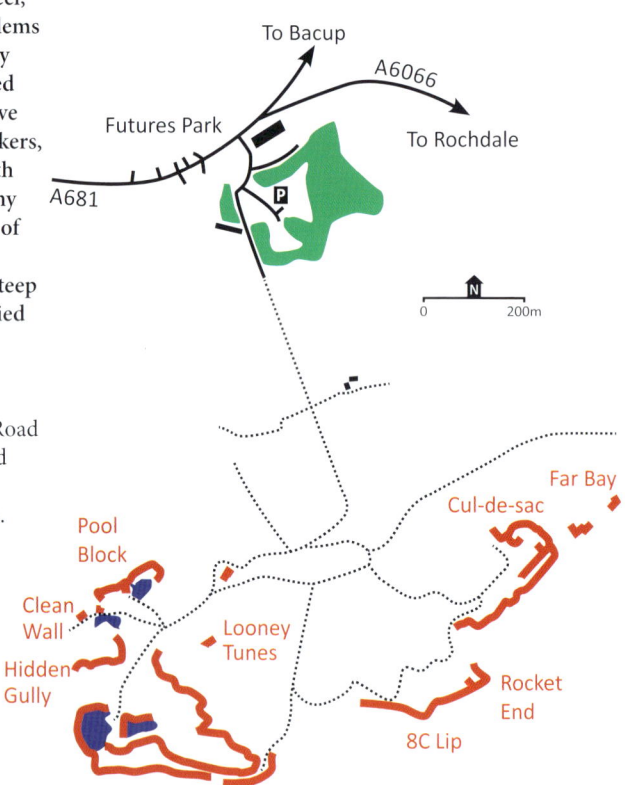

LEE

For the Pool Blocks, follow the main approach path and continue through the quarry until both pool and boulder are visible on the right.

1 Project
Sitstart using the lowest footblock and pull on some hideous crimps. No undercutting the low lip.

2 Ovine Communion SIT **5+**
Sitstart and undercut up to the scoop, then left to the ledge.

There are several variations to this problem, all of which get another step closer to the project sitstart.

3a Ovinity Phase 1 SIT **6B**
Sitstart and climb the wall without any undercuts. Stay away from the ledge up and right, and holds on the arete.

3b Ovinity Phase 2 6C
A standing start from LH low crimp and RH slopey edge. Same rules as before, but this time the lower footblock is not allowed.

3c Ovinity Phase 3 7A
...And this time no footblocks at all. Hang the slopey edge footless, then campus to the scoop, engage your feet and continue leftwards. Campussing to the ledge straight above is **6C**.
Robin Müller 2013

3d Project Phase 4
Sitstart without the lowest footblock. Dirty hard crimping.

4 Good Lass ★ SIT **6C**
Sitstart and pull to the lip, then up the arete. Rock onto the slab to finish.

5 Bad Lad ★ SIT **6B**
Sitstart to lip holds, then head for the front face and pull straight up.

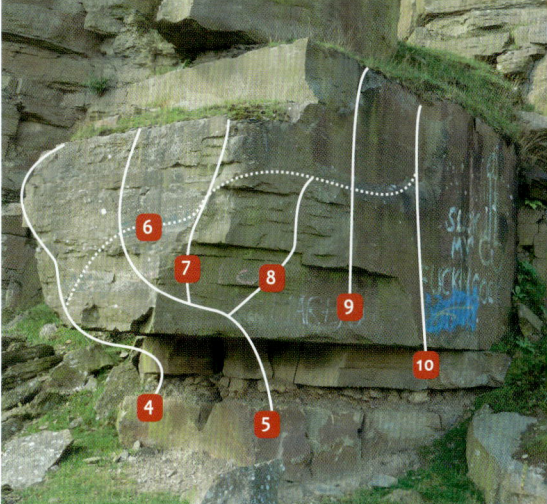

Pool Block

6 Matchmaker SIT **6C+**
Start up *Good Lass*, then traverse right, staying beneath the high jug. Turn the arete and finish along the ramp.

7 Ladels And Jellybeans SIT **6C+**
Climb the right arete, staying off big holds to the left.

8 Project
From the lip crimps, power into the gaston.

9 Rocksucker ★★ **7A**
LH sidepull, RH low crimp, pull on, go for it. Very satisfying. The sitstart is a hard crimpy project.
Robin Müller, John Wilson 2013

10 Project
From undercuts to the ledge.

LEE

Clean Wall

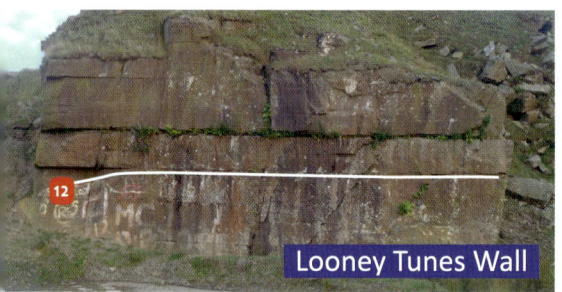

The Clean Wall is a little further along the same side of the quarry as the Pool Block. It has lots of short, easy problems. Top-outs are currently not so clean, so either drop off or go grass swimming.

1 Beginning Galvanized 2
Walk up the slab.

2 Manual Of The Afterglow 4 SIT 5+
Sitstart from RH sidepull in the crack and a good LH hold.

3 Bull Bakes Best 4+
A good sidepull aids progress.

4 Puzzle Paper 4+
Follow edges to the top

5 Stereo Reindeer 4
Use the low slanting crack for RH.

6 Potential Cockroach 6B
From right of the low slanting crack, follow the break left to the rock round the arete, without using higher holds.

7 Relic Of Jester 3
Use the low slanting crack for LH.

8 Suspense Of The Complicated 2
Just step up.

9 Plight Of The Pliers SIT 5
Sitstart at the ramp

10 Sweet Panda SIT 4+
Sitstart at the low sidepull.

11 Lethargic Era 6A
From far right, traverse the wall beneath the top, to rock around the far arete.

Opposite Pool Block is the Looney Tunes Wall.

12 Project
Traverse the lower break.

Approached along a footpath from the west, there are several small scrappy sections in this bay that might be climbable with a bit of cleaning, but the most impressive line is near the start of the big drop. It seeps during wet periods.

1 Project
Is this possible? A big span to a sidewards undercut below the lip, then another metre of blankness to holds in the break.

1 Project
The arete on its right looks a lot easier, but still hard by most people's standards.

At the east end of the same bay is a short section at right angles to the main wall. This is Rocket End.

3 Project
A wild-looking dyno, with a poor landing. It's steep, juggy and oh-so tempting, but you'd want a good few pads to level out the landing.

4 Project
The leaning wall.

Continue to the far end of the quarry and you will reach the Cul-de-sac bay, near a historical ruin. Walk down the slope to enter this bay and turn left to encounter a wall with probably the longest sloper you've ever seen. The top-out needs cleaning.

5 Project
Several lines are possible.

There are also some project lines on a clean wall in the Far Bay. To reach the Far Bay from the Cul-de-sac, head for the east-leading path below the quarry. Follow this for a little way, then turn right when another bay becomes visible between grassy banks.

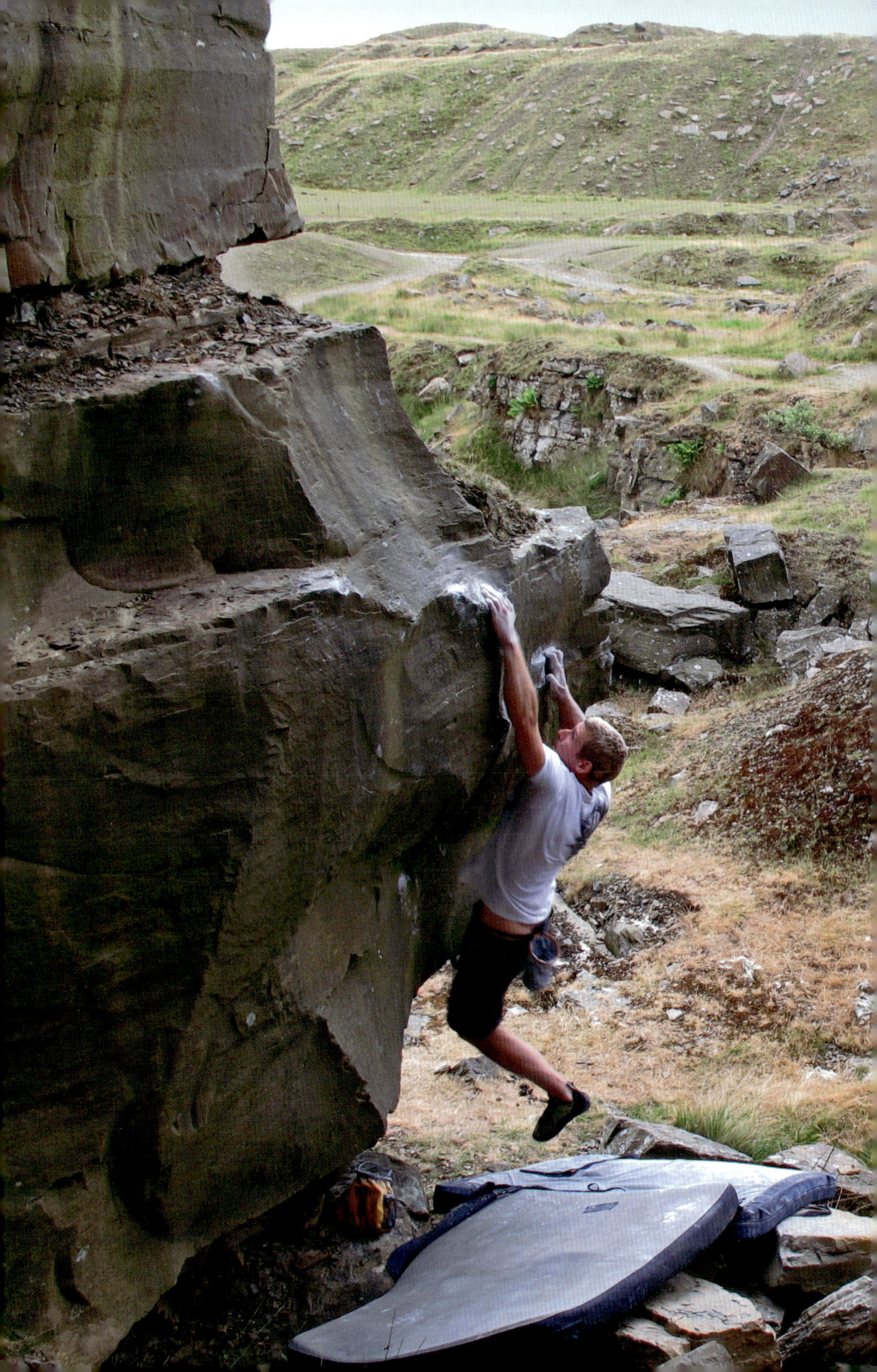

Ovinity Phase 3, 7A

Orchasm, 6B

36 Orchan Stones

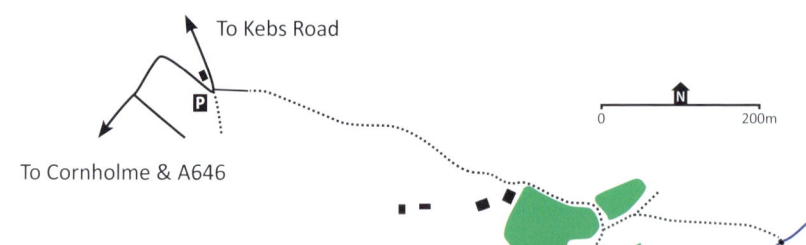

Not far from the Bridestones is this often overlooked venue. It's a higgeldy-piggeldy mound of boulders, with no real stunners but lots of quirky climbing. With a smattering of steepness and better rock quality than Brideys, the Orchan Stones provide a worthwhile fast-drying alternative for an evening session. Besides the problems described here, super easy lines are possible all over the place.

APPROACH 20 min
The fastest approach is from the road between Kebs Road and the village of Cornholme on the A646. From either end, this road is signposted to Shore. Follow it to a hairpin bend, where there is a small parking space between road signs for Bluebell Lane and Pudding Lane. Walk down Bluebell Lane (not the path beside the parking) for 400m. When the lane leads into trees, turn left before the farm buildings. Cross the stile then turn right along a large footpath which leads to a small bridge. Turn right after the bridge and follow the footpath round the hill until the rocks come into sight on your left. It is easiest to keep to the path until you reach the south side of the crag.

ORCHAN STONES 239

The bouldering begins on the south-east side of the hill, at a slopey-lipped boulder.

1 Sloping Duty SIT **6B**
Reach a slopey dish and mantel the lip.

2 Moping Beauty SIT **7A+**
From lip slopers, head left to the arete and top out using this.
Robin Müller 2013

3 The Brunt Of All Woes SIT **6A**
From the break at the back, gain the lip and pull over.

4 The Elf Shelf SIT **7A**
From jams under the left side, reach the lip and pull to the top. Stay off other footblocks.
Robin Müller, Matt Nuttall 2013

5 Posh Chocolate SIT **5**
Go straight over the top roof. Stepping left is easier. Footblocks allowed at this grade.

6 Hot Chocolate SIT **6A+**
From far right and using the right-most footblock, traverse left to finish up *Posh Chocolate*. No other footblocks are allowed.

7 Chocolate Bar SIT **5+**
Climb the right-hand block from the same start. No other footblocks are allowed.

8 Orchknee Island Wall 5+ SIT **6A**
Climb the slopey shelves. No footblocks.

9 Orchasm ★ SIT **6B**
At the back of the boulder is a cranny. Sitstart the centre of the leaning wall.

10 Hobbes LOW **7A**
From the back wall, finish up the side wall.
Jordan Buys 2004

11 Something Under The Bed Is Drooling ★ LOW **7C**
From the back wall, climb the prow to its end. Bring spotters - there's a drop!
Jordan Buys 2004

Body Bionics, 7B p242

37 Lobb Mill

Lobb Mill is an awful chosspile of a quarry. Luckily, the nearby boulders are much better. Situated on a hillside, the boulders are fast-drying and get evening sun. There are numerous turn-the-lip 6's and a few much harder challenges.

APPROACH   10 min
From the centre of Todmorden, take the A646 Halifax Road. Follow this for 1 mile, then turn right down Woodhouse Road - opposite a sign for Bikers Cafe-Bar. Cross the bridge, then just after the bend park sensibly by a long stone wall. Walk up the road and turn left between houses, up an unpaved road that leads steeply to a footpath sign and a stile. Cross the stile and head straight up the hill. Turn left on the track at the top and follow this to the end of the field. The boulders are below the path.

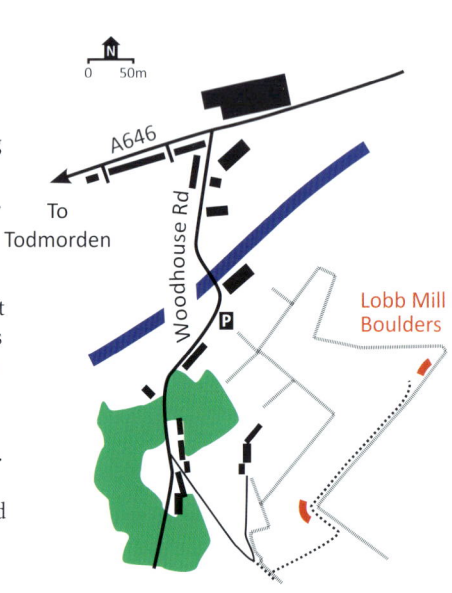

LOBB MILL | 241

1 The King Has Entered the Building 6C
Traverse from the low shelf on the left to finish up the right arete, on its right.

2 Lost Propriety ★ 5+ LOW 6A
From good holds at the back, make odd moves to get established on the slab.

3 Brutus 6B+ LOW 6C
From the crack, reach slopey crimps and make a hard move to better holds above.

4 Too Mental To Mantel 6B LOW 6B+
From the break, gain poor holds around the lip and use these to pop for decent crimps. A tricky foot-up move follows. Stay off the bigger holds to the right.

5 Better Than Tele 6A LOW 6B
From the break, climb the arete on its left.

6 Side Reel 5+ SIT 6A
From the break, climb the arete on its right. Can also be done without the arete at **6B**.

Too Mental To Mantel, 6B+ p241

7 Funkatronic ★ 6A SIT 6C
Make a hard move from a low sidepull (not the loose one) to gain the arete and rock onto the slab. You can put your feet on the chunky strip of rock attached to the main wall, but not the big block left of this. Obviously, the footledge is not allowed.

8 Body Bionics ★ ★ SIT 7B
Start as per *Footloose And Fancy Free*, then head left to slap along the the arete and finish up *Funkatronic*. No footledge.
Robin Müller 2013

9 Project
Straight up from the slopers. Jump into a mantel?

10a Footloose And Fancy Free ★ 6B SIT 7A
Without the footledge, start LH break slot, RH lip. Gain the sloper and rockover via the RH crimp. **6B** with the footledge.
Robin Müller 2013

10b Extra Bacon ★ SIT 7A+
Without the footledge, start at the break jug beneath the lip on *Press For Success*. Head left to finish up *Footloose And Fancy Free*.
Robin Müller 2013

11 Press For Success ★ 6B+ SIT 7A+
Use the big RH sidepull to get over the lip. The sitstart involves heel trickery.
Robin Müller 2013

12 Tantalicious 6B+ SIT 6C
From a good jug at the top of the footledge, reach unhelpful holds and use them to progress.

13 Swelter Style SIT 6B+
From a sloper start, get the good RH edge, then find a way to the break. The footledge is allowed.

14 Make Yourself Small SIT 6B
Starting LH on the good edge and RH on a backhand sloper, power up to the break. The footledge is not allowed. Proper lowball!

Press For Success, 7A+ p242

Keeping Trim, 6A p247

38 Holder Stones

A mini-crag of strange folds and sublime slopes. Lots of it doesn't quite work but the bits that do are great. There are brilliant slopey highballs from easy to hard and a few interesting normal height problems.

APPROACH 40 to 60 min
1.The fastest but steepest approach is from Mankinholes near Todmorden. Turn off the A646 between Todmorden and Hebden Bridge, onto Woodhouse Road (signposted to the Youth Hostel). Follow this to its end and turn left. Park by two concrete sheep on Mankinholes Bank - don't block any gates. Follow the lane towards the hills and through the gate at the end. Turn left up the hill. At the top, turn right onto the Pennine Way. Head over the moor to a crossroads. Turn left here in front of the ditch. Follow the ditch until you see a stile on the other side. Jump the ditch (big jump!), hop the stile and head uphill to the Holder Stones.

Easier but slower options:
2. From Withens Clough Reservoir, start at the free car park on Rudd Lane. Take the path on the north side of the reservoir, which leads to the Pennine Way. Follow route 1 from here.
3. From the north end of Warland Reservoir (see directions for Stony Edge), continue on the Pennine Way instead of turning right for Stony Edge. Follow this to a crossroads and turn right to continue beside the ditch to the stile described in route 1.

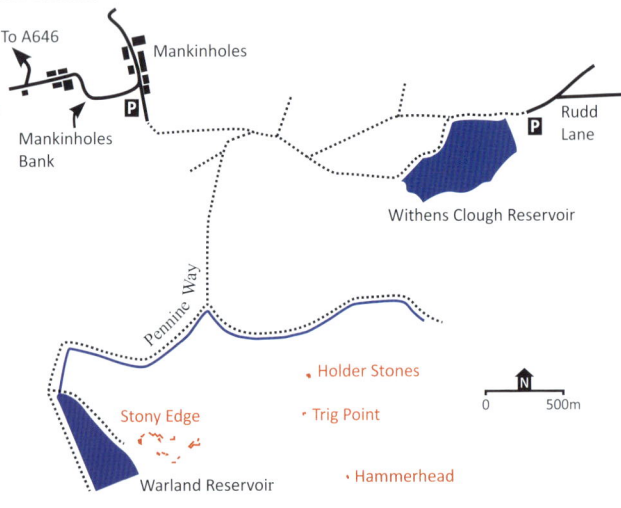

Big Wind, 6A p246

HOLDER STONES

The south end of the crag is a good place to warm up on small rocks.

1 Murky Rising 3

2 Stacked For Pleasure 4+

3 Thinking In Stone 3+

From here, circle rightwards to a gully.

4 Big Wind ★ SIT 6A
From a good hold, work up the ripples with a big stretch to slopes near the top.

5 Little Wind SIT 5
Just right is an easier version.

6 Lie 'n' Cling ★ 6C SIT 7A+
From sitting, pull into a wedged lying position on the low shelf, to set up for a reach to higher holds. Then head for the arete and rock left into the scoop to finish. A spotter is useful for the top-out.
Robin Müller 2013

Further right there are some slopey highballs above the rock platform.

7 Run Away 6C
Up the left side to a slopey top-out, which leads you close to a worrying landing.

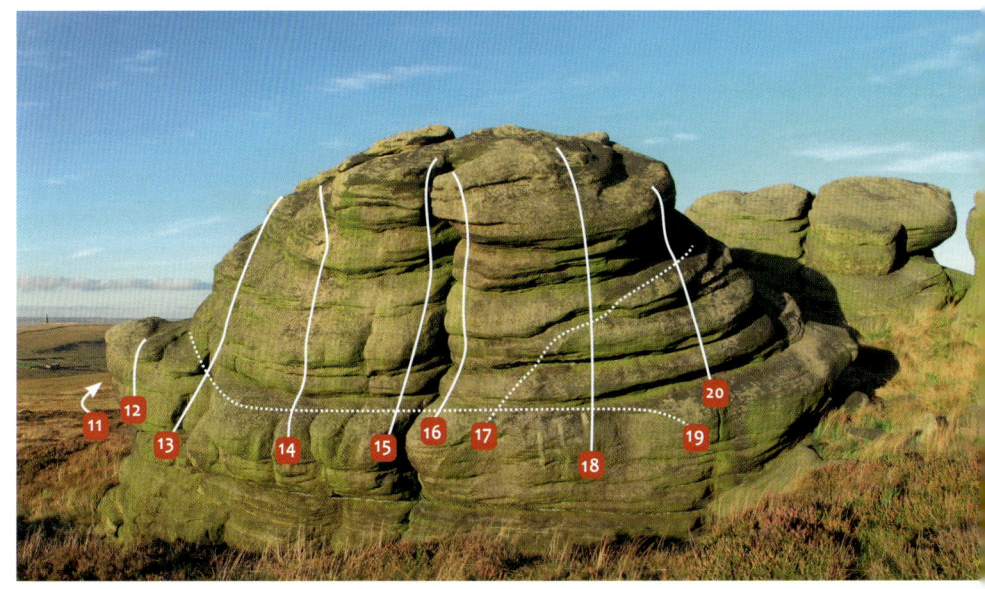

HOLDER STONES

8 Project
Up the right side to another slopey top.

On the dark side of the adjacent buttress is a short leaning wall.

9 Shady Dealings 4+
Pull up from crimps on the small dark wall.

10 Master Mutter SIT **6A**
Start LH on a good sloper right of the crack and traverse right along the crimpy break just below the top. Top out at the end.

There are some super easy slabs on a short wall to the right, but the reason you came here is the amazing stack of slopey shelves on the sunny side of the crag. The landings are mostly good, but you'll need your highball head on.

11 Big Man's Nose 5+
The overhanging nose tackled direct, with a slightly worrying top move.

12 Blades Of Green 5
Climb the right side of the nose to a crux top-out using the grassy crack.

13 Pillow Talk ★ 4+
Start up the groove and smear delicately up the rounded folds above.

14 Sultans Of Squirm ★ 6C
The wall left of the cleft has a difficult mantel start.

15 The Bum At The End Of The World ★ 4
The big cleft directly.

16 The Cherry On Top ★ 6B
The right arete of the cleft.

17 Action And Refraction ★★ 5
Traverse the rising line of ripples.

18 Project
The standout sloper-riddled wall. That top-out looks spicy!

19 Slip, Slap, Slope ★ 6A+
Step off the rock to hand-traverse the low shelves. Up to the cleft is easy - the trickiness comes in the second half.

20 Keeping Trim 6A
Step off the rock and undercut to get established. The top half is easier.

39 The Hammerhead

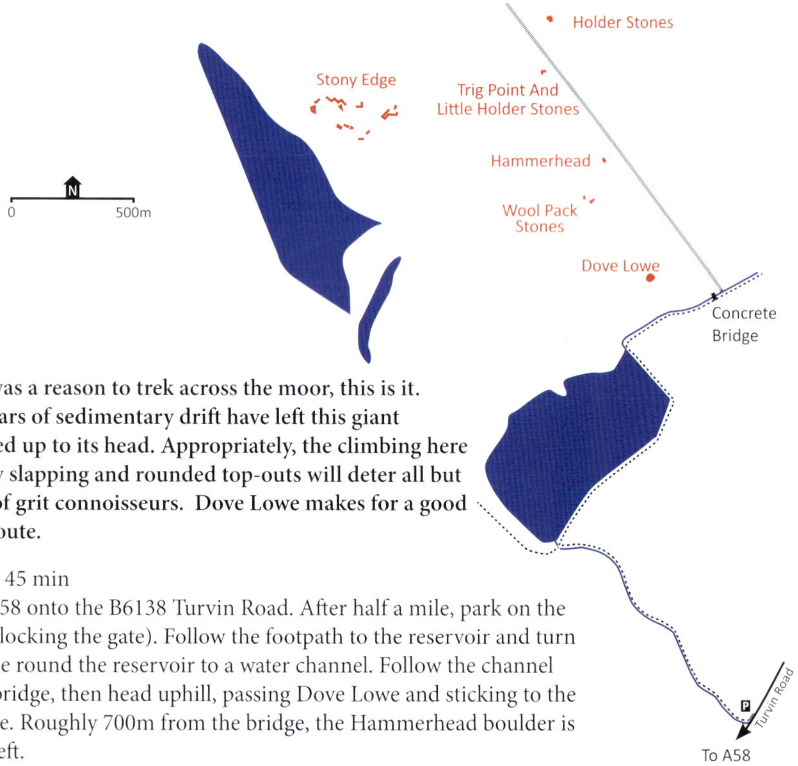

Holder Stones

Stony Edge

Trig Point And Little Holder Stones

Hammerhead

Wool Pack Stones

Dove Lowe

Concrete Bridge

0   500m

If ever there was a reason to trek across the moor, this is it. Millions of years of sedimentary drift have left this giant hammer buried up to its head. Appropriately, the climbing here is hard: slopey slapping and rounded top-outs will deter all but the gnarliest of grit connoisseurs. Dove Lowe makes for a good warm up en route.

APPROACH   45 min
Turn off the A58 onto the B6138 Turvin Road. After half a mile, park on the left (without blocking the gate). Follow the footpath to the reservoir and turn right. Continue round the reservoir to a water channel. Follow the channel to a concrete bridge, then head uphill, passing Dove Lowe and sticking to the left of the fence. Roughly 700m from the bridge, the Hammerhead boulder is visible to the left.

Turvin Road

To A58

HAMMERHEAD 249

1 Flystorm 7A
Start LH small incut dish, RH anything.
Robin Müller 2014

2 Project
The arse end of the boulder.

3 The Gritmare 6C+
Slap along the lip until you can top out.
Robin Müller 2014

4 Whistle Test 6A
Use a good ripple to gain the top.

5 Gristle Test ★ 7A+
LH crimp, RH sloper in the slight scoop. Make a tough pull-on and slap the top.
Robin Müller, Dawid Skoczylas 2013

6 The Knockdown ★ 7B
LH in the low eye and RH somewhere on the arete. Slap up and left, then shuffle left until you can top out.
Robin Müller, Dawid Skoczylas 2013

7 Berth Of A Tool ★ SIT 7A+ LOW 7A
Sitstart (or crouch if you can't reach) using a RH finger slot and LH on the shelf. Gain the eye, then make a hard move to the lip. Traverse off right to finish. The low start is from lying on the shelf, with LH in the eye and RH undercutting the shelf.
Robin Müller, Dawid Skoczylas 2013

8 Lost And Proud 6C
Without the shelf for feet, mantel the lip using the good hold.

The Wool Pack Stones are 100m downhill (at 90 degrees from the fence). A block near the bottom end of these has some lowball problems.

9 Butterfingers SIT 7A+
Traverse right and top out. Starting *Rear View* and finishing up the groove left of *Cheeky Arse* is **Droll Sergeant SIT 7B**.
Robin Müller, John Wilson 2014

10 Mardy Bum SIT 6B+
Climb straight through the slopey lip. The left arete on its right is **Cheeky Arse SIT 6B** and the right arete on its left is **Rear View SIT 6A**.

11 Rough Dough SIT 4+
Sitstart the rounded flake on the arete.

The Epic Lip Project p260

40 Stony Edge

Stony Edge is a real gem of a crag, hidden away behind a moorland reservoir. There are problems at all grades, from the joyfully easy to the hideously hard, and all angles from desperate roofs to sublime slabs. This crag has been one of the area's best kept secrets for many years, but it really deserves more attention. Expect a bit of scrittle, which should clear up with traffic.

APPROACH 30 min
From the A6033 Rochdale Road, turn onto Warland Gate End. Follow this road as it passes over a canal, between houses, then turns steeply uphill. Park on the left opposite a gate and sheds. Now walk up the road 50m to the iron gate of Calf Lee House. A small side gate allows access to walkers. Continue up the road to the last house on the hillside (passing through another gate and then over a stile). Walk round the back of the house to a stile. Cross the stile and follow the footpath uphill. Pathside Roof is reached shortly. For Stony Edge itself, continue along the footpath and turn left where it splits. Follow the track round the water to Stony Edge.

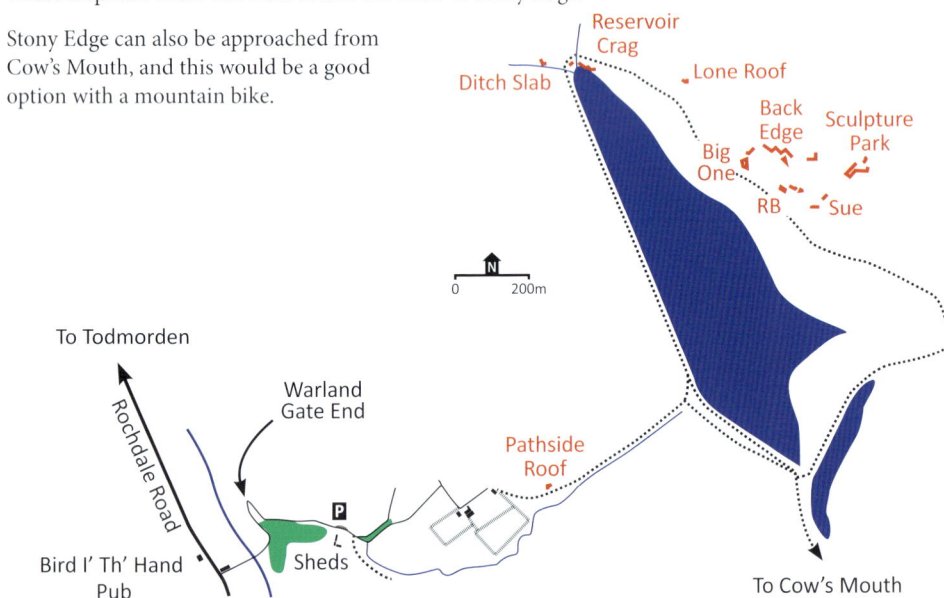

Stony Edge can also be approached from Cow's Mouth, and this would be a good option with a mountain bike.

STONY EDGE 251

Pathside Roof

Pathside Roof is next to the main path. It is best accessed by keeping left of the fence which appears after the left bend in the track. Only a ten-minute walk from the car, it makes an ideal quick hit.

1 First Gear SIT **4+**

2 Manhandle SIT **4**
From the low jug, go straight up.

3 Think Of England SIT **6C**
From the low jug, pull up and right to match poor holds, then go for the top.

4 Back Dance SIT **6C**
From the back break, head for low crimps on the arete, then up and left to the top via a good high hold.

5 Project
The central challenge requires fierce pebbly crimping.

6 Fanfare ★★ SIT **7B**
From the ledge jug, reach the arete and climb it on its left.
Robin Müller 2013

7 Feet Of Strength ★ SIT **6B**
From the ledge jug, gain the arete and climb it on its right. The clue is in the name.

8 Harumph SIT **4+**
From the break, reach the top. Stay off the footledge on the right.

252 STONY EDGE

As you round the corner of the reservoir, across the ditch you'll see some rocks to your left. There is one decent slab to do.

1 Project

2 River Witch SIT **6B**
From low jugs, use holds just left of the arete, but stay off the arete.

Ditch Slab

Reservoir Crag

Down in the reservoir itself, the short crag has a wonderful seaside feel after dry periods when the water is low.

3 Warland Slabside ★ **4**
Use the arete near the top.

4 Reservoir Slab ★ **4+**
A peach of a slab.

5 Beach Bum 4 SIT **5**
Use the right arete.

6 Intro Slab ★ **4+** SIT **5+**
Pull up the centre, starting from the large low sidepulls.

7 Strange Habits SIT **6B**
Start from the slopey arete and grind over the top. The massive footledge to the right is off limits.

8 Sandy Hobbits SIT **6A**
Start from the big hold on the left and pull right to whale over the top.

Down at the left end of this crag is a clean wall just right of a tunnel. This has some easy up problems and a possible super hard vertical sitstart.

Continuing on the main path, about 100m before Stony Edge proper, there is one good isolated boulder. This is the Lone Roof.

9 Smash Patrol ★ SIT **6C**
Sitstart from the jug, without using the ledge. Burly moves lead to a slopey top.

10 Fisticuffs SIT **6C**
From seated on the ledge, start with RH jug and LH slopey arete pinch. The ledge is not allowed for feet. Finish on the left.

11 Find Your Own Shield SIT **5**
Start matched on the large hold.

Lone Roof

Warland Slabside, 4 p252

254 STONY EDGE

Big One

The Big One is the left-most block at Stony Edge, and one of the best.

1 Ramble Rouser SIT **4+**

2 Stair Trek SIT **5**

3 Grip Of The Wild SIT **5+**

4 Standing On A Stomach 4+

5 Grab The Hat 5
Pull from the slopey ledge to the top.

6 Do Like Zoidberg 6A LOW **6C+**
From a low sidepull and anything near it, climb the wall right of the crack, passing horizontal pinches to a great lip jug.

7 The Right Side Of The Flaw 5
The crack, started on its right.

8 The Wrong Side Of The Flaw ★ 4+
The crack, started on its left.

9 Longship ★ 7A
Sitstart (be strict) using a LH sidepull and RH mono. Make a hard move to pull off the ground and a harder one to better holds. Footholds can be green.
Matt Nuttall, Robin Müller 2013

10 The Kingdom Of Slope ★ SIT **6B+**
From lip jugs, enter a slopey world.

11 Argle Bargle ★★ SIT **7A+**
Start crouched beneath the roof, gain the right-hand lip and then reach past the arete to access the rising line of holds that lead to a juggy exit.
Robin Müller 2013

12 Project

13 Project

14 Baby Bouncer ★ 5 LOW **6C+**
Start with hands on the lower seam and feet on the ledge at the back. A fun cutloose leads to bigger holds.

15 Molly The Moocher SIT **7A**
From the jug, head right to gain the groove. The footledge is not allowed.
Robin Müller 2013

16 The Grit Exam ★★ SIT **7A+**
From the jug, negotiate the very awkward bulge. The footledge is not allowed. A real test!
Robin Müller 2013

The next problems are on the smaller boulder near the Big One.

17 Laugh A Minute SIT **4+**

18 Hush A While SIT **5+**

19 Stop A Second SIT **5**

Flute Note, 6B p256

STONY EDGE

Back Edge

The Back Edge has friendly easier problems.

1 A Is For Aardvark ★ 6A
The slopey left side of the wall.

2 Flute Note ★ 6B
Use the shelf and slight rib to reach a higher shelf.

3 Echo Mute 6B
Use a RH undercut to gain the higher shelf a little further right.

4 To Heck 4
Easy arete.

5 Scribble 3
The back wall.

6 Big Stroke 4
The slab on its left.

7 Big Purr 4
The slab on its right.

8 Culminate 2
End wall.

9 The Middle Book 6A
The hemmed-in arete, on its left.

10 Updraft 4
The slab, staying left of the arete.

11 Slow Dance 3
The slab on its left.

12 No Dance 2
The slab on its right.

13 Jiggery Slopery ★ 6A SIT 6A+
The left side of the roofy wall has a slopey exit.

14 Summit Fever ★ 5+
Climb steeply to the apex.

15 Steep Size 6A
Top out on the left side of the arete.

16 Gritworm ★ 6B LOW 6B+
The fun wall left of the arete, via the fat nematode. The low start goes from obvious protrusions.

17 Shy Side 6A SIT 6A+
The arete on its left.

18 Ballet Shoes 4+
The slabby face.

19 Cakewalk 2
A good way down.

20 Get A Grip 3
Nice moves up the layered arete.

There is a short overhanging wall on the boulders just in front of the Back Edge.

21 Everything But The Sink SIT 6A
Start on good holds just right of the arete. Better if you mantel direct, rather than using the arete.

STONY EDGE 257

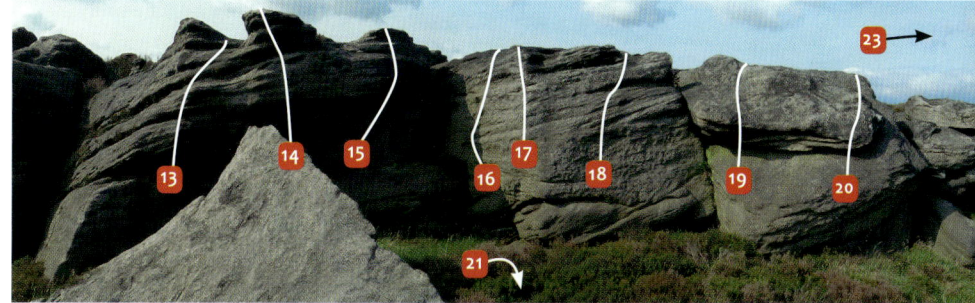

22 Rocket On The Brink SIT **6B**
Slap the top from green edges, then launch into mantel mode. Harder the further left you try to top out.

About 20m right of the Back Edge is a low undercut block.

23 Bruce Almighty SIT **7A**
Sitstart matched on good lip holds. Rock into arete holds and stand up.
Robin Müller 2013

24 Shoot From The Hip SIT **6C**
Climb the wall a little right of the arete.

25 Smoke Me A Kipper SIT **6B+**
Gain a decent sloper and work into standing.

26 Hardman SIT **6B**
The big crack tackled on its left.

27 Kneebar SIT **6B**
The crack on its right.

28 Whale Of A Climb SIT **6A**
The short arete, with belly-flop potential.

Argle Bargle, 7A+ p254

258 STONY EDGE

RB Slab

The RB slab is about halfway along the crag, near the bottom path.

1 Plastic Sex Explosion ★ SIT **7A+**
Start LH crack, RH arete. One hard move leads to a technical top-out.
Robin Müller 2013

2 Beach Mechanics ★ **7A**
Climb the groove. Off the rock it's a **5**.
Robin Müller 2013

**3 Dance Me To
The End Of Time** ★ **5+** SIT **7A**
Powerful moves into a glorious finish.
Robin Müller 2013

4 RB 5+
Tip-toe up the carved letters, then smear for the top. Lankies will skip the smear.

5 Delicat ★ **6A**
Climb the slab to the right of the RB letters.

6 Elfin Safe Tea ★★ SIT **7A+**
The excellent steep arete on its right.
Robin Müller, John Wilson 2013

7 The Giant's Chamber ★ SIT **4+**
On the back of the boulder, swing to a juggy mantel from the giant low flake.

The next boulder is to the right.

8 Diceman ★ **6B**
Climb past the lofty sloper to an awkward mantel. The landing is a pad-eater.

9 School Dinner SIT **6A**
Finish over the top slab via a juggy hole.

A small wedged block is adjacent.

10 Conk Polishing SIT **6B**
Give your nose a good work out.

Just behind this is another boulder.

11 A Skirt In The Breeze 2
Waft up the easy slab.

12 Acres Of Shakers ★ **6A+**
The undercut slab, via a LH slot.

13 Ephemeral ★ **7A**
The vague right arete, on its left.
Robin Müller, John Wilson 2013

STONY EDGE

14 Project
A hard mantel.

15 Somebody's Chylt SIT **6A**
An awkward start and a low finish, pebbly holds and bit of a thrutch. What's not to love?

16 Project
From the obvious big slopey pocket, traverse rightwards to finish up *Somebody's Chylt*.

Sue

From the last boulder, continue at the same level until the end of the rocks. A little higher up the slope, past a very easy slab, is a boulder with carved writing on its face. This is Sue. Be sure to tell her she's looking pretty.

17 He Who Dares, Grins 4 SIT **5+**
The cheeky arete and tiny slab.

18 Rock The Ladle 5
Right of the arete.

19 Born To Love 4+ LOW **5**
From a crouching start on the undercuts, climb past the graffiti to top out with a good incut rail.

20 Lust Is A Downward Slope ★ **4+** SIT **6B+**
Start on the pockety undercuts and reach slopers and pebbles. Make a hard move to the poor incut rail and top out.

21 The Dark Side Of The Swoon 6A
A fine slopey mantel, staying away from top-out holds on problems to either side.

22 A Boy Named Bill Or George 5 SIT **5+**
Pull on using the low bobble and stay left of the arete.

23 A Girl Named Hugh? 4 SIT **5**
Use both the arete and the big bobbly thing.

Longship, 7A p254

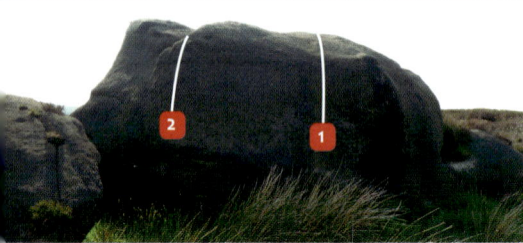

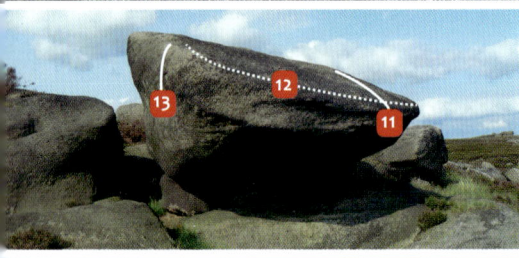

260 STONY EDGE

Scuplture Park

4 Fight Shapes With Shapes ★★ **6C+** SIT **7A+**
Use the slanting LH layaway to make progress. The sitstart adds a bit of beef.
Robin Müller 2013

5 Weakness Leaving The Boulder ★ **5+** SIT **7A+**
The wall beneath the small scoop. Make powerful moves using a sizeable LH undercling flake and a RH slopey nothing on the face.
Robin Müller 2013

6 Project

7 Zaftig SIT **7A**
Pull up slopey bumps, making full use of the giant footledge.
Robin Müller 2014

8 Penthouse Feet 5+
Mantel at the easiest point.

9 Enter The Corridor 6B
The green sidewall has a tricky bulge which leads to a scary mantel finish.

10 Amen ★ **6C**
Thrutch up the arete via the strange horizontal slot.

11 Secret Dimple 6A
There is a small hold. It does help.

12 The Epic Lip Project

13 Up With People 5

14 Inside the Wimple 5
The slightly scooped arete.

15 Fat Man's Folds 6A+
The arete, using tiered slopers. No footblock.

The Sculpture Park is the right-most area at Stony Edge, and features some worthwhile problems on attractive shapes.

1 The Hump ★ **6B**
A great little mantel problem on a small rounded boulder at the back. Stay off the footledge out right.

2 The Wink 4+
Just left of *The Hump* is an easier way up, via good holds.

3 Muscle Tussle ★ SIT **6B+**
From a slot under the roof, pull to the lip then haul up the arete.

Elfin Safe Tea, 7A+ p258

Lust Is A Downward Slope, 6B+ p259

Talking Shillbut, 7A+ p265

41 Dove Lowe

A brilliant compact collection of windswept classics with a wilderness feel. Shapes to make your fingers salivate and problems throughout the grades. Though the walk-in is on the longer side, it is flat and easy. Do yourself a favour and have a grand day out.

APPROACH 40 min
Turn off the A58 onto the B6138 Turvin Road. After half a mile, park on the left (don't block the gate). Follow the footpath to the reservoir, then turn right. Continue round the reservoir to a water channel, cross this when it becomes small enough to jump, then strike across the moor to the obvious outcrop. If the water is too high, continue to the concrete bridge a little further on. The path up to the concrete bridge is flat and a bicycle would make the approach much quicker.

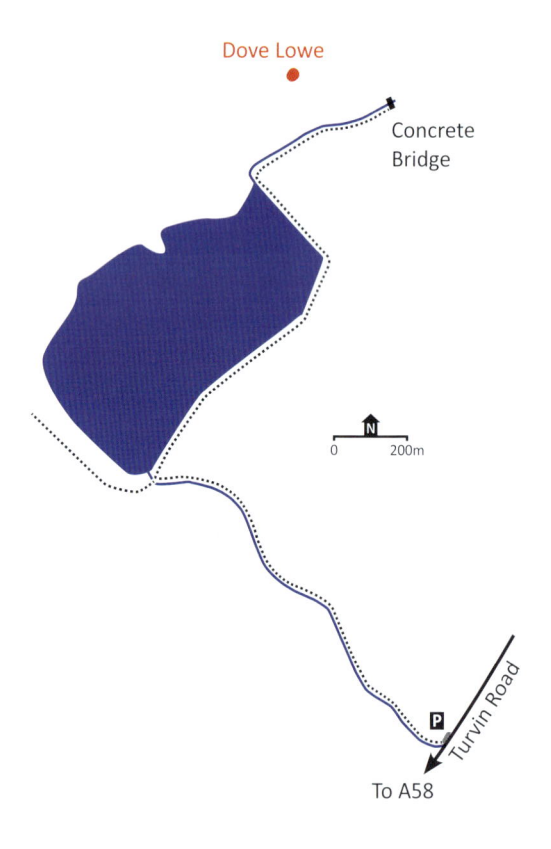

Extemporise, 7B p265

DOVE LOWE

Dove Lowe works well as a clockwise circuit of problems, starting from the easy slab. The short wall at a right-angle to the slab is **No Wonder 6B** - sitstart and stay off aretes.

1 Crenellations ★ **3**
Climb all over the lovely slab at around the same grade. The arete is nice too.

2 Boogaloo 3 SIT **5+**
The right arete on its left.

3 Whisky Drinker SIT **6B**
Sitstart the wall without aretes.

4 Maybe 5 SIT **6A**
Use the left arete to start.

5 Some Other Country ★★ **4** SIT **4+**
Swarthy laybacking. Keep going until you can rockover leftwards.

6 Project
The nice little pockets were scared off by the big bad top-out.

7 Project

8 Home Skillet ★ SIT **7A+**
Sitstart the perfect rising lip.
Robin Müller 2013

9 Project
Sitstart the steep left arete.

10 Doodlebumps SIT **6B**
Sitstart the big nobbles.

11 Umph SIT **6C**
Sitstart from hands on the lower section.

12 Grunt SIT **7A+**
Sitstart and slap.
Robin Müller 2013

13 Udge SIT **6B+**
Sitstart the arete.

14 Tufa From Home ★★ **6C+**
Style up the unusual grit tufa.
Robin Müller, John Wilson 2013

15 Extemporise ★★ **7B**
The sexy arete with a dynamic finish.
Robin Müller 2013

16 Project
Up the middle, from undercuts.

17 Mistress Distress 6B SIT **6B+**
Stay off the arete.

18 Sweat-Gang ★ **6A** SIT **6A+**
The left arete might make you work.

19 Clamber Party 5

20 Grin And Smear It 5
Smear up the tallest bit of slab.

21 Two Pebbles And One Pop ★ **6B+**
Pull onto the green wall and pop for the top.

22a Round Embrace 5+ SIT **6B+**
Sequency slapping enables progress.

22b Lonesome Dove SIT **7A**
This time, use only the right arete.
John Wilson 2013

23 Talking Shillbut ★ **7A+**
Pull on using a high LH pebble and make a hard move for the top.
Robin Müller 2013

24 Tangled Up In Blue ★★ **7A**
Climbing inside a prism? This comes close. And it's not over till the fat lady belly-flops.
Robin Müller 2013

25 The Last Dance 5+ SIT **6C**
Sitstart from the break and make a big move to gain easier climbing.

26 Go Gentle 3
The green slab round the back.

Sladen Roof, 7B

42 Sladen Roof

Sladen Roof isn't all that big, but it's just a short amble from the car. There are a couple of decent power moves and the wooded setting makes it a pleasant spot on sunny days.

APPROACH 2 min
On Todmorden Road, park in the large car park next to Sladen Wood Mill. The car park is usually open, though sometimes shut at night. Cross the canal and follow the uphill track signposted as a public bridleway. Head straight into the woods at the top. The Sladen Roof soon becomes obvious.

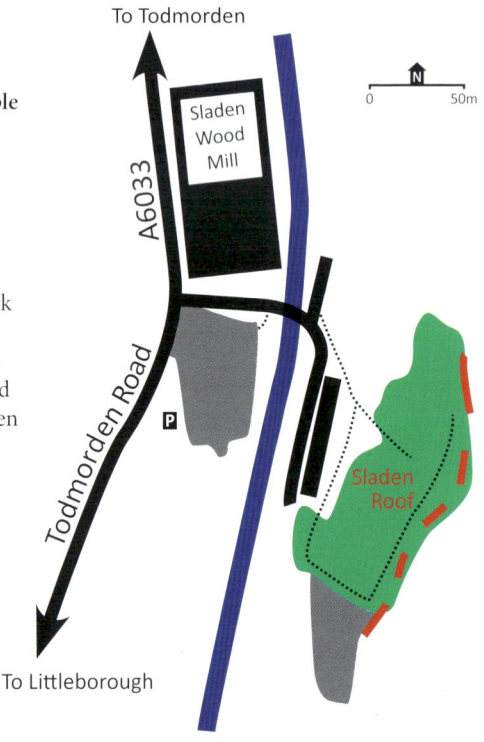

To Todmorden

Sladen Wood Mill

A6033

Todmorden Road

Sladen Roof

To Littleborough

1 Simple Sladen 6B SIT 6C
From the shelf at the back, undercling the crack and reach the lip. Go for the arete jug (hang this for the standing start) and finish upwards. The footblocks to either side of the starting block are off-limits.

2 Go Jayce 6C SIT 6C+
As before, but from the arete jug, traverse crimps right to a big ledge.

3 Sladen Roof SIT 7B
As per *Simple Sladen*, but eliminate the arete jug.
Robin Müller 2013

4 The Lightning League SIT 7A+
From the same start, reach the lip with LH but move RH up the left edge of the crack until you can make a big move to the ledge. The right edge of the crack (and everything right of the crack) is off-limits.
Robin Müller 2013

43 Cow's Mouth

A good combination of quarried and natural grit in an exposed and sunny position. There are several excellent highballs and a fine roof block.

APPROACH 20 min
Park below the White House pub on the A58. Walk uphill past the pub and turn left onto the footpath in front of the reservoir. Follow this to a small stone bridge and cross here to access the rocks without having to jump the ditch. The path is flat and a bicycle would make the approach much quicker.

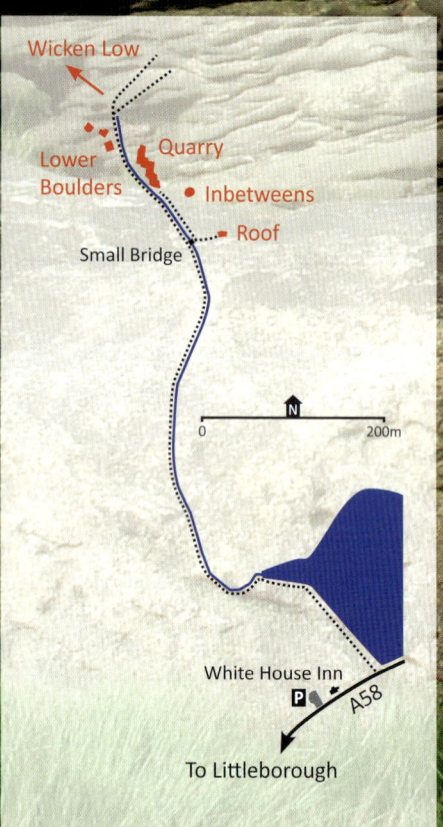

Wicken Low
Quarry
Lower Boulders
Inbetweens
Roof
Small Bridge

0   200m

White House Inn
A58
To Littleborough

Ticket To Slide, 7A+ p270

COW'S MOUTH

Cow's Mouth's star attraction is the obvious roof visible on the approach. None of the problems use the big ledge for feet.

1 Might As Well SIT **4**
Sitstart off the rock.

2 Five O'Clock Shadow SIT **5**
The obvious central line.

3 Winding The Spring SIT **6B**
Stay left of the sidepull.

4 Starter For Ten ★ SIT **6B+**
The arete, from a good low jug.

5 Get Your Fingers Out ★ SIT **7A**
From the low jug, snatch up the wall on crimps. Stay left of the arete.
Robin Müller 2013

6 Project

7 Don't Use Vaseline LOW **6C**
From matched on the jug beneath the arete, head up and right to the slopey notch.

8 Big Holds For Big Boys LOW **6C**
Start matched on the low jug and pull up the arete.

9 Project

10 Ticket To Slide ★★ LOW **7A+**
From the low jug, pull up the centre of the wall, navigating via a slopey sidepull. Worth the price of admission.

11 Project

12 Project
Desperate climbing right of the arete.

13 Happy Hands SIT **4+**
Haul up huge holds.

14 Baby Slaps SIT **7A+**
Sitstart the awkward hugfest. The foothold has always been crumbly.
Robin Müller, John Wilson 2013

COW'S MOUTH 271

15 Short Stuff SIT **6B**
The burly prow. The giant footledges are out.

16 Mantels For Dummies SIT **5**

Further along the hillside are two boulders called The Inbetweens. The first looks quite big...until you get closer.

17 Muster SIT **7A**
Without using the footledge, pull over the slopey lip. With the footledge it's **5**.
Robin Müller 2013

18 The Man From Unclean SIT **6C**
Start matched on the lip, with feet on the footledge. Traverse rightwards around the arete and step onto the ramp to finish.

19 Arsetronaut SIT **6B**
From matched on slopers, move right into the arete.

20 Project
The wall left of the arete. For masochists only.

21 The Waxing Hour SIT **6A+**
The arete.

22 Licking The Barrel SIT **6B+**
From matched on the low slanting edge, head to the arete and pull onto the slab.

Just downhill is a short boulder with an entertaining sitstart.

23 The Magic Hole SIT **6A**
Sitstart on weird holds and do something wizardly to gain the enchanted feature. No left arete.

24 The Not Quite So Magic Hole SIT **5**
Sitstart LH arete and make a move to the magic hole.

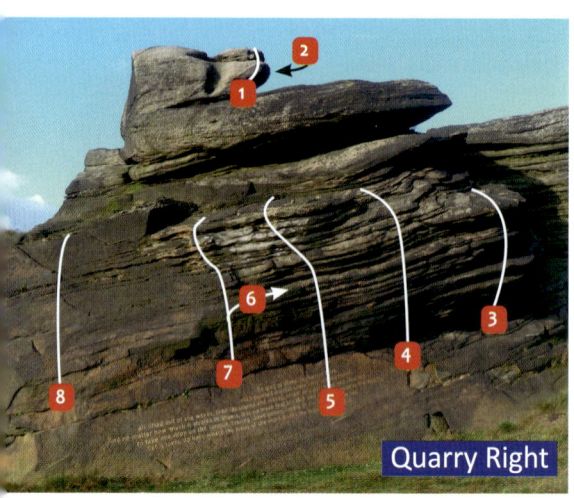

COW'S MOUTH

6 Project
Traverse the mid-height sloper line.

7 Flopper ★ 5
From a big undercling, go up and left a bit.

8 Flipper ★ 4+
The wall right of the arete.

9 Los Endos Right 5 SIT **6B+**
Sitstart the arete on its right, to the ledge.

10 Los Endos ★ 5+
The arete on its left. Finish at the ledge. Or keep going if you prefer.

11 The Don ★ 6B SIT **6B+**
Sitstart LH flatty, RH sidepull.

12 Thug-Zag 7A
From matched on the flatty, traverse left below the big holds on *The Don*. Finish at the jug on the next wall.
Robin Müller 2013

13 Not The Don Thing SIT **6C+**
Sitstart RH sharp sidepull, LH small crimp. Power up to the big holds and continue as usual.

14 Project
A hard continutation of *Thug-Zag*. Climb into the arete, still avoiding the big holds on *The Don*. Finish at the chockstone jug.

15 Hi, Feet 6C
French start to the face jug, then crimp and rockover to gain the jug above. No holds on the arete.

16 Pumper Nickel ★ 7A+
From the jug on the left end of the wall, traverse all the way to the arete. Pull round this, staying low. Finish up *Los Endos Right*.
Robin Müller 2013

17 Project
All the holds are backwards.

Quarry Right

1 Boulderers Get High SIT **6A**
Is it a low sitstart or a high sitstart? Slap up the arete...

2 King Of The Hill SIT **4+**
Another one, on the back of the boulder.

The next problems are best enjoyed with a spotter and a few pads. Otherwise, be prepared to wibble.

3 Flak ★★ 6B+
The arete is a sublime stack of slopey shelves. The top-out does not disappoint.

4 Flook ★★ 6A
In the sea of slopers is one real handhold. It's not big, but it is clever.

5 Flapper ★★ 5+
From the large foothold, quest into slopiness.

The next area is a tall, steep wall at a higher level in the centre of the quarry. In winter, large snow drifts can make the landings of the higher problems far more palatable.

18 Project
Sitstart the vague arete to gain the break.

19 Three Little Piggies ★ **6C**
The centre of the wall is intimidating. Bring more pads!

20 Nyan Cat ★★ **7A**
From the long juggy hold, pull to pockets in the break, then crimp upwards to victory. The crux is not high, but the top is.
Robin Müller 2013

21 Project

22 Project
The wall right of the arete, from underclings and a small sidepull.

23 Escalate ★ **6C**
Starting LH arete, RH undercling, climb upwards via a huge gaston. Use anything right of the crack.

The Daytona wall is further left.

24 Morph ★ **6C**
From big sidepulls in the crack, get into position, then launch for the obvious hold. Easier if you don't have to jump.

25 Project
From either side, step into the good holds, then climb straight up to the jug without the crack out right.

At the end of the quarry is a small wall, just left of the big slab.

26 End Wall 4+
Straight up the middle.

Over the top of the end wall is a long low wall that offers good super easy bouldering all down its length. Only one problem is described.

27 Last of All 4+
The left arete has a good move.

274 COW'S MOUTH

Lower Boulders

The Lower Boulders are a collection of sitstart problems located just below the main path, 50m from the quarry. The first problems are in a rough line very close to the path.

1 Weather Face SIT **6B+**
Up the middle.

2 Project
From slopers on the left, traverse to the arete and up.

3 Cheek To Jowel SIT **6A**
Pull over the lip.

4 Navel Grazing SIT **5+**
From hands in the low break, gain the lip and roll over.

5 Turn SIT **6A+**
Sitstart from hands on slopers and pull up to good holds.

6 Humpty SIT **6B**
Sitstart from the slot.

7 Little Big Cheeks ★ SIT **7B**
Sitstart left of the step up in ground level. A foot cam enables higher holds to be reached.
Robin Müller 2013

8 The Trumpeteer ★ SIT **7A+**
The wall right of the arete. A heel-toe is useful.
John Wilson 2013

9 Bugle Practice ★ SIT **7A**
The arete is tricky. Best to start with hands above the low shelf, because the end of the shelf may not take your weight.
Robin Müller 2013

10 Take The Biscuit SIT **6A**
Scuffle up the arete.

11 Tiskit SIT **6C+**
Start just left of the arete on small slopers below the middle shelf. Gain the top via a helpful edge out left.

12 Fugly SIT **6C**
A one-lurch wonder.

COW'S MOUTH   275

The next boulder is 40m left.

13 The Slug ★ sit 7A
Sitstart and battle rightwards, without the footblock. An extension should be possible, starting as far left as possible.

Next is a low bulge with distinctive veins. It's located about 40m downhill.

14 Awe Coward sit 7A
Mantel onto the attractive bulge.
Robin Müller 2013

15 Project
Flexy hips needed.

20m further downhill is a perched block.

16 Last Lips sit 6C
Sitstart off the middle rock, then grind out the mantel.

17 Glorious Bumset sit 5+
On the backside of the block. Sitstart off the middle rock, then pull up and over.

The Trumpeteer, 7A+ p274

The Eternal, 7A+

Wicken Low

Hidden in a miniature clough, this is a secretive sort of place, nestled in long grass and soundtracked by the stream beneath tumbled rocks. The boulders here are small and scrittly, but if you enjoy your esoterica they might make you smile. There is not much to do, but this tiny circuit combines well with the bouldering at Cow's Mouth.

APPROACH 25 min
Park below the White House pub on the A58. Walk uphill past the pub and turn left at the footpath in front of the reservoir. Follow this past Cow's Mouth Quarry, then strike downhill to a point roughly 50m down and left of the square structure that looks a bit like a swimming pool. The boulders only become visible when you get very close.

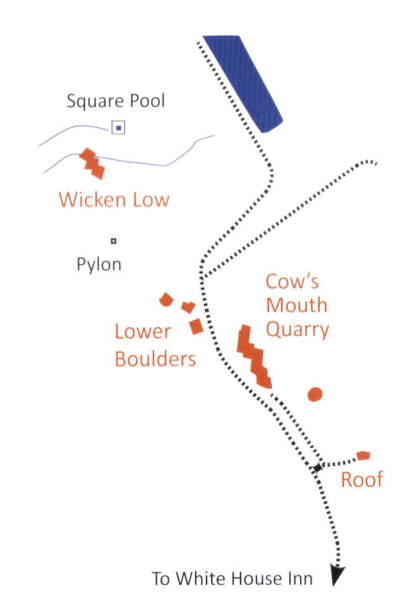

Square Pool
Wicken Low
Pylon
Lower Boulders
Cow's Mouth Quarry
Roof
To White House Inn

WICKEN LOW 277

1 Project
Sitstart the hanging nose. Very frustrating.

2 Chin Tickler ★ **4+** SIT **5**
A big sidepull allows you to sitstart.

3 Strictly Come Prancing 4
The slab left of centre, into a scoop.

4 Wheel On A Wave 2 SIT **6A**
Sitstart the arete without the back crack (the undercling is allowed).

5 Body Scrub 4 SIT **5**
The right side of the slab.

6 Riding The Sloth 4
The left side of the slab.

7 The Eternal ★ **6B** SIT **7A+**
A splendid move from sidepull and arete to a slopey lip boss. Mantel the top, or go to the back arete for an easier finish.
Robin Müller 2013

8 Apple Grumble 5 LOW **6B**
The low start is from undercuts. Reach a good hold and pull over the top.

9 Trained Fighter ★ **6A** LOW **7A**
From undercuts, slap up the arete to a slopey top-out. Stay off the good hold on the problem to the right.

The wall to the left may offer some problems, but is green and slow to dry. The next problems are on the lone boulder behind you.

10 Project
Sitstart the centre of the wall.

11 Triple Pop ★ SIT **7A+**
Only just right of the arete, start LH sidepull, RH pocket. No arete.
Robin Müller, John Wilson 2013

12 A Little Sitstart SIT **4**
The arete on its right.

13 A Little Slab 4+
The downhill-facing slab.

44 Higher Chelburn

A friendly backwater of a venue, with a summer evening's worth of mainly lower grade problems, plus a couple of more desperate moves to keep the crankers busy. The boulders catch a fair breeze and are fast-drying. They are also a good option if the wind is too fierce at Blackstone Edge and Cow's Mouth.

APPROACH   12 min
Turn off Rochdale Road at the Summit Inn. Cross the bridge and park in the obvious bay. Walk up the road until the rocks come into sight, then take the first left turn onto a footpath, which leads to the Path End boulders.

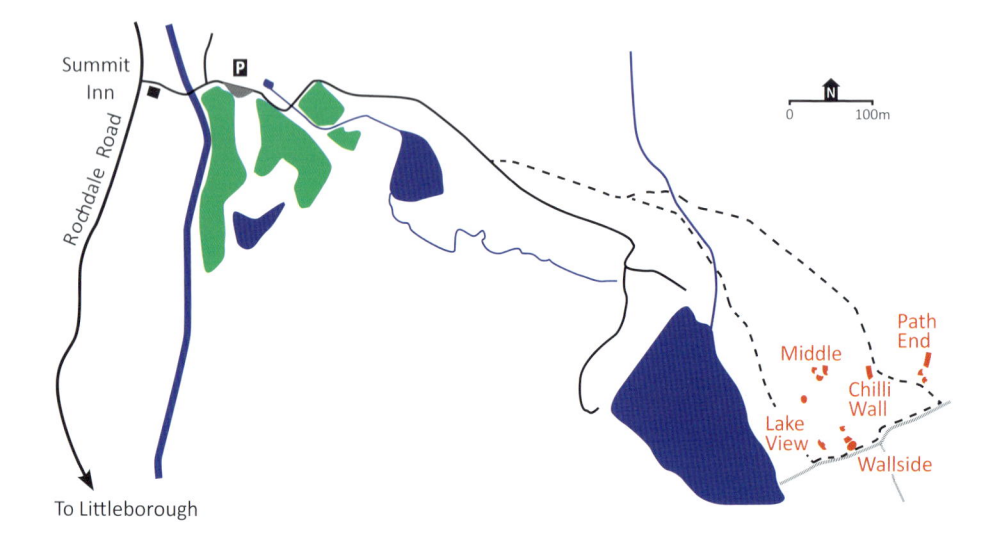

Chilli Burn, 7C p283

HIGHER CHELBURN

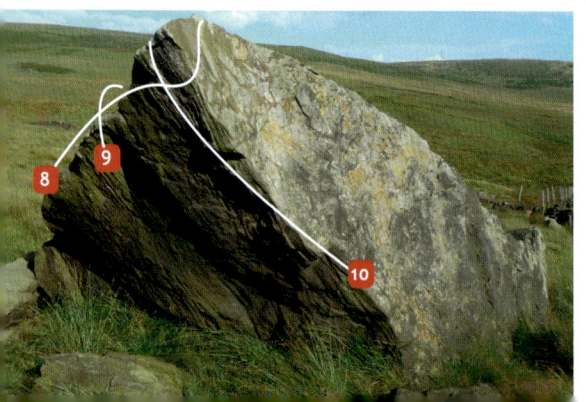

Path End

The upper footpath deposits eager climbers at a good warm-up spot, with nice grassy landings and lots of easy movement on small blocks.

1 Steady Body 2
The slabby right side of the wall.

2 Grass Abounding SIT **4**
The little block from sitting.

3 Shadow Start SIT **4**
The pillar.

4 Flow Chart 3
The slab and arete.

5 Naughty Crompton SIT **4+**
The arete.

6 Tinkle Toes 4+
From the ledge, pull round the arete and cross the slab, to finish round the far arete.

7 Slender Days 3
The gentle slab.

8 Lover's Lip SIT **6A**
From the left end, traverse the rising lip to rock onto the far slab.

9 Climbing into a Dinghy 5
Get onto the slab.

10 Small Star ★ SIT **6B**
Sitstart the arete from low matched hands. A goodun.

HIGHER CHELBURN 281

From the Path End area, follow the stone wall towards the reservoir and a big boulder becomes obvious.

1 Project
An easy looking line from the pit, with a worrying landing.

2 Ledgelopes SIT **5**
Sitstart from the rock.

3 Crimpellies SIT **4+**
The short arete.

There are some short problems directly opposite the big boulder.

4 Tilting Deck SIT **6A**
Sitstart on the left. Work upwards, with or without the arete.

5 The Harder They Come SIT **6A**
The left arete.

6 Trojan SIT **5**
Romp up big holds.

7 Gideon SIT **6A+**
From the low ledge on the right, head left and up the arete.

8 Travolta SIT **4+**
Shimmy to the ledge and dance over the top.

The next short block is tucked away 10m behind problems 4-8.

9 Expletive SIT **7A+**
From the break, pull up the protruding block via unhelpful holds. The big sidepull on the right of the break is out - using this reduces the grade to **6A**.

Robin Müller 2012

HIGHER CHELBURN

Continue on the footpath from the Wallside Blocks, until past the small hill. Turn right for the Lake View boulders, and a splendid trio of problems.

1 Deep Eyes ★★ **5+**
The pocketed wall is excellent.

2 Rockflection ★★ **6A**
The arete on its right. Great.

3 Clarion Call ★ **6A** SIT **6B**
The arete on its left.

The next block is a little further along the ridge.

4 On the Tiles SIT **6A**
Start matched on the lip. The foot-slab is out.

5 Tangentiles SIT **6A**
Start matched on the lip. Use the foot-slab and rock round to the left.

The Middle Blocks are a stone's throw away, amongst the central cluster.

6 Little Body SIT **5+**
Climb the small wall from sitting, with feet starting on the lower block. The side block is out.

7 Limber Skin SIT **7A**
Start with feet on the large side block. Cross the lip and grunt up the arete. The lower block is out.
Robin Müller 2012

8 Fool Me Twice SIT **5+**
The left-hand flakeline. Not as easy as it looks.

9 Tiny Treat SIT **6A**
Tackle the right-hand flakeline.

10 Hangalimp 5
Start hanging, slap the ledge, keep going.

HIGHER CHELBURN 283

11 Do I Have To? 5+
Hang the lip, then swing up a heel and mantel onto the slab.

12 Top Of The World SIT 6A
A neat arete.

Behind the Middle Blocks is a wall with a built up landing. This is Chilli Wall.

13 Pappa Rika 5 SIT 6B
The sitter has a tricky move to a flatty. Not the best landing.

14 Chilli Burn ★ SIT 7C
Sitstart matched on the rounded sidewards undercling. Make a hard pull-on and bump up poor holds to finish via the flake.
Robin Müller, Dawid Skoczylas 2012

15 Sergeant Pepper ★ 5 SIT 7A
Sitstart LH on the *Chilli Burn* hold, RH on a curving sidepull below the roof.
Robin Müller, Dawid Skoczylas 2012

16 Hellopeno SIT 6A
Sitstart from roof underclings. Eliminating the arete is **6B**.

Chilli Burn, 7C p283

45 White House Quarry

This is by every definition a minor venue, but its proximity to the road makes it a good easy option. Although there is some loose rock on the steeper walls, the slabs are solid with pleasant climbing.

APPROACH   1 min
Park below the White House Inn on the A58. Cross the road to the obvious large footpath just downhill. Follow this uphill and the quarry soon comes into view.

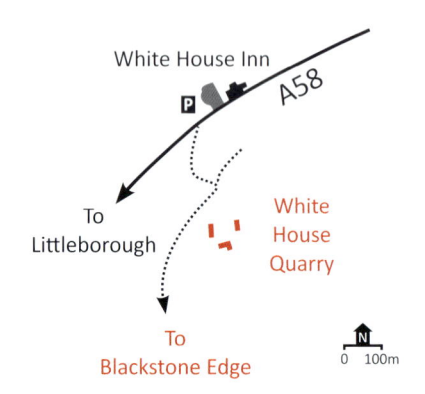

WHITE HOUSE

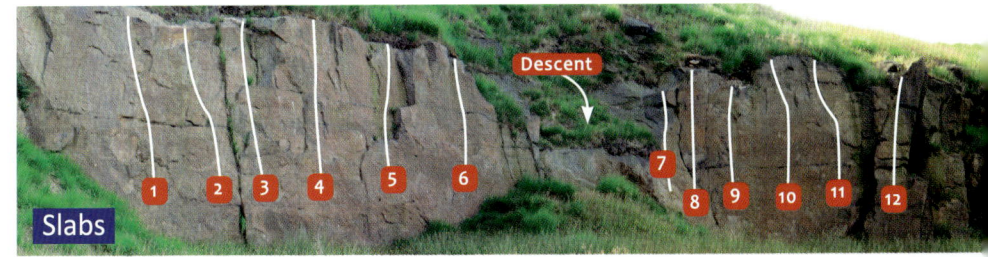

Slabs

The Slabs are on the right as you enter, and contain the best climbing here.

1 Roadside Savage 4+
Climb the wall on good edges.

2 Basement Dolphin 4+
The crack and wall to the left.

3 Cult Storm 4
The crack on its right.

4 Heaven Of Serpentine 4+
The wall left of the large ledges.

5 Escaping Chaos And The Roller 3
Large stepped ledges.

6 Crafty Freedom 2
Mantel the large ledge.

7 Lard Of The Coconut 4+
The arete and crack. Sans crack it's 5.

8 Rump Crunch 5
Use both cracks.

9 Rampant Mortal 5+
The right crack and wall to the right.

10 Ecstasy Of Yearning ★ 6A+
Go straight up from the big slot. You can make a big reach to eliminate the chipped crimp - this is **6B+**.

11 Perfectly Corona 5
The arete, trending left at the top.

12 Spork Of Meaty Madness 4
The pillar. Without the right arete it's **5**.

Traverses of both walls are possible, graded at **5** for the left wall and **6A** for the right wall.

Back Wall

The Back Wall is grotty, but has some good moves.

13 The House That Grot Built 7B
Start from large holds at the bottom of a small groove. Traverse left below the break, with a crux sequence passing an angular pinch on the bottom corner of the high flake. Rock around the arete to finish. Stay off the big footledge at the bottom of the wall.

The Final Wall is somewhat friable so take care when climbing. It's best to downclimb and drop off rather than attempt a top-out. More than one pad is useful.

14 Tribal Pork Of The Self-Inflicted Mishap 7A
From a high RH undercling and LH edge, gain the sidepull, then readjust to get the top. The broken footledge is off limits.

15 The Horny Thief 6A
The crack on its left. Be careful - it may not be solid.

16 Epitaph Of The Downwardly Inclined 7A
From slopey holds in the break, make a hard rockover to gain little edges on the face, then the top. Stay off the big detached flakes to the right.

45 Blackstone Edge

A varied and extensive collection of problems on a windswept ridge. Given a breeze, good conditions can be found even in the middle of summer. Equally, it can be hard work on windy days. The best problems are spread out, so first time visitors will get more value by touring the crag rather than concentrating on one area.

If you fancy a different type of challenge, there is also an abnormal abundancy of short boulders which require proficiency in S&M - slap and mantel. If you are open-minded to the cult of the lowball, your bum will never grow bored at Blackstone.

APPROACH 25 min
1. Park below the White House Inn on the A58. Cross the road to the obvious large footpath just downhill. Follow this uphill and turn right. Walk alongside the drainage ditch to a crossroad. Continue to follow the ditch until you can head uphill to the crag.

2. There is an alternative approach from the south. From J22 of the M6, exit south onto the A672 and park at a large layby on the right after 500m. Follow the Pennine Way towards the motorway, cross the bridge and continue on the main path to the crag.

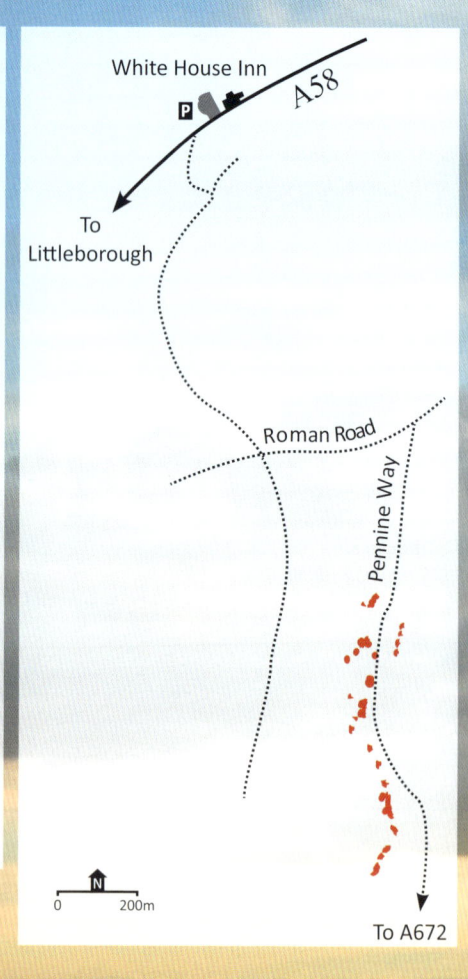

The Underdog, 7A+ p298

Map

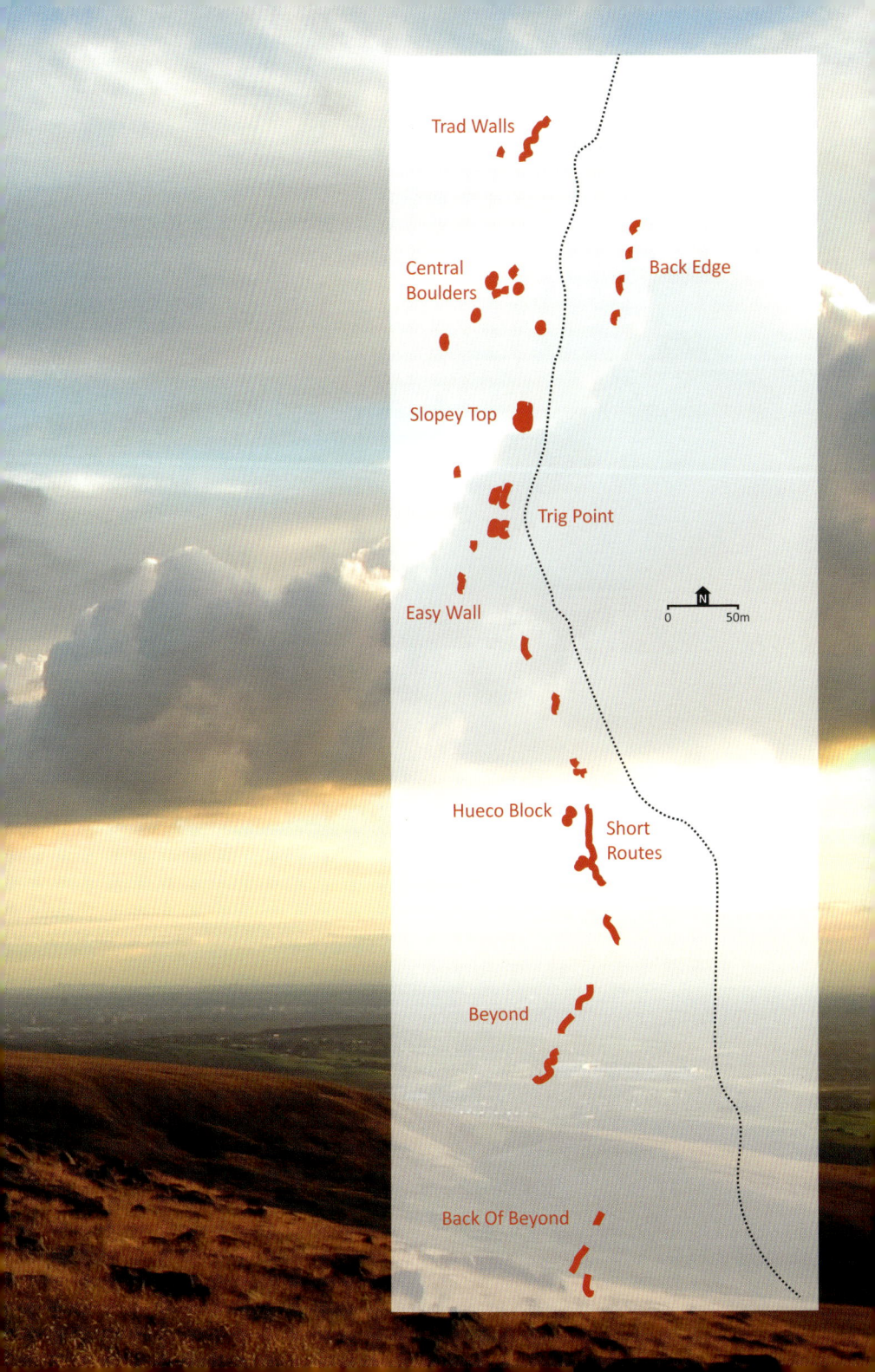

- Trad Walls
- Central Boulders
- Back Edge
- Slopey Top
- Trig Point
- Easy Wall
- Hueco Block
- Short Routes
- Beyond
- Back Of Beyond

N
0 — 50m

Trad Walls

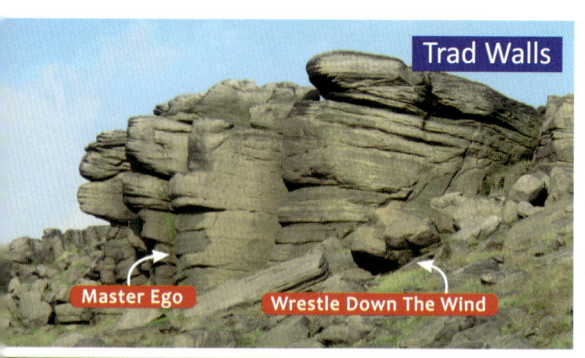

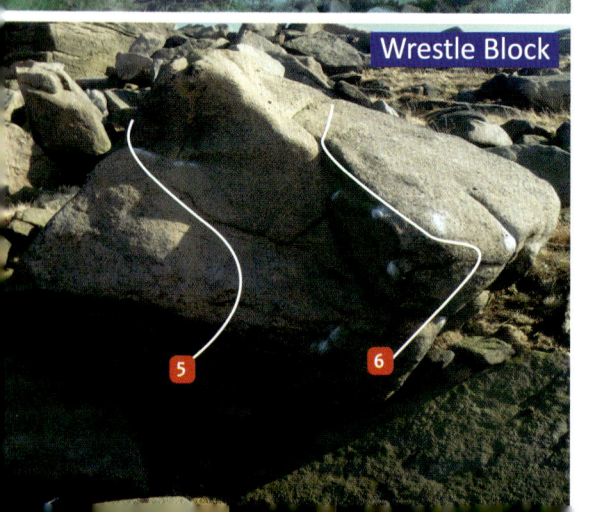

The first problems are on the tallest section of the crag, which contains Blackstone's trad routes.

1 Master Ego Trav 6A SIT 6B
Climb the arete on its right to slopey holds, then head right to finishing jugs.

2 1975 ★ LOW 7A
A crouching start from hands on the low seam. Climb the wall right of the arete.
John Wilson 2013

3 Project
Sitstart from the low crimp in the centre of the wall.

4 Recalibrate ★ 6A SIT 7B
Start from crimps just right of centre.
Robin Müller 2012

A little to the right and slightly downhill is an oddly shaped boulder.

5 Project
There aren't many holds.

6 Wrestle Down the Wind ★ SIT 7B
Sitstart matched from the low handholds (try a high heel out left) then gain the lip, pull left into the groove and battle through it to the top.
Robin Müller 2012

BLACKSTONE EDGE

The Twins are the first of the Central Boulders reached from the Trad Walls.

The Twins

1 Get Set 5
Go!

2 Diversion and On 5+
From the left arete, follow the break to jugs at its end.

3 Concavity Cons Gravity ★ 6B
Concentrate: contains confusing contours.

4 Robin's Dyno 6C
Dyno from low crimps to the top break jug.

5 Underway ★ 5+
The right arete.

6 Fridge Hugger ★ 6A+ SIT 7B+
Start matched on the low RH rail and make hard moves to get established on the arete.
Nik Jennings 2009

7 We Are Not Amused 5+
The poor groove.

8 We Are Not Confused 5
The other one.

9 Blackstone Best ★ 6B
Climb the arete from the ground, not from the rock. Bring your grit finesse.

10 Nosey Thing SIT 5+
Sitstart from crimps.

11 The Easy Mantel SIT 6A
Sitstart at an edge. One of Blackstone's easier turn-the-lip challenges.

12 Backside Slab 5+
Don't use the arete.

13 Lippy Traverse ★ 6C
Traverse the lip in either direction.

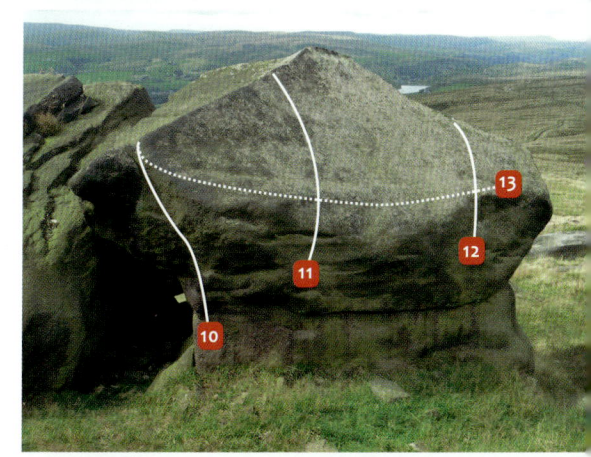

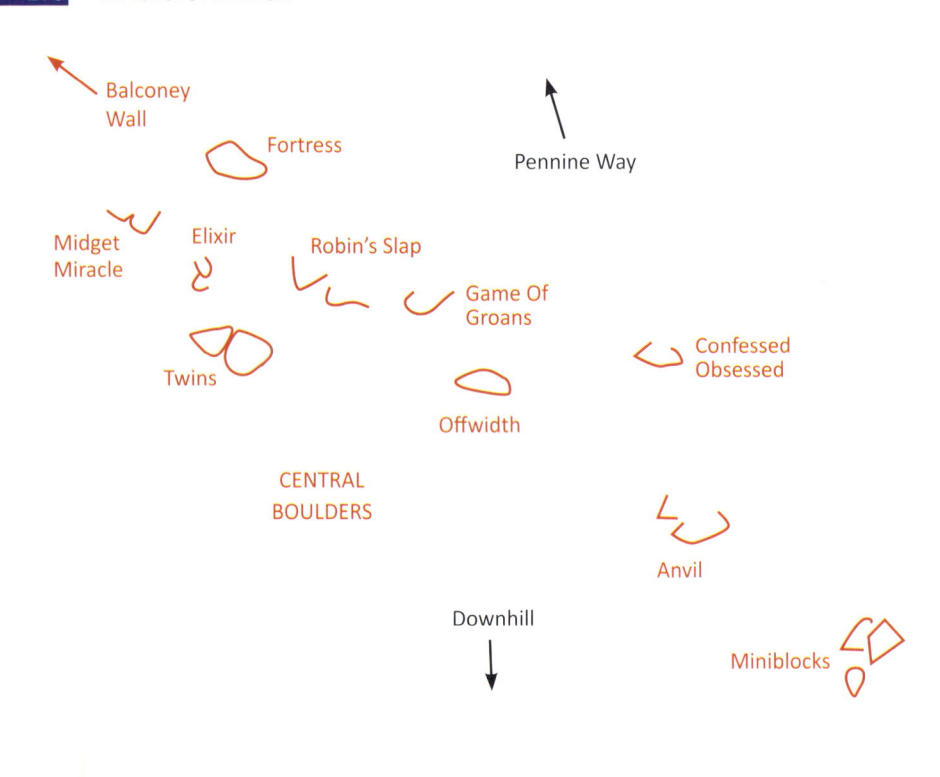

290 BLACKSTONE EDGE

- Balconey Wall
- Fortress
- Pennine Way
- Midget Miracle
- Elixir
- Robin's Slap
- Game Of Groans
- Confessed Obsessed
- Twins
- Offwidth
- CENTRAL BOULDERS
- Anvil
- Downhill
- Miniblocks

Balconey Wall

The Fortress

BLACKSTONE EDGE 291

The Twins

Midget Miracle

Robin's Slap

Behind The Twins are a rough line of small blocks. These are described from left to right, as you look uphill.

1 Sturlup 4 SIT 5
Sitstart, rocking onto the footledge.

2 Greenflint 4+ SIT 6A
Sitstart, staying right of the footledge.

3 Dansten 3

4 Naradame 4 SIT 5+
Traverse left, using the top if you want, to top out past *Sturlup*.

5 Argel 4 SIT 5+
A funny sitter up big holds.

6 Riffless 3 SIT 4+
Sitstart the layback flake.

7 Purousten 3+ SIT 6B
Pull up the middle of the wall, feet anywhere.

8 Shalling 3 SIT 6C
The arete. Feet out right are key.

9 Ugly Duckling 3 SIT 7A
The arete from sitting, starting with hands on or around the lip.
Robin Müller 2012

10 The Fortress 5
The downhill face of the fortress block.

11 The Fortress Arete ★ 4
The uphill face and arete.

12 Short and Salty SIT 5
The small arete.

13 The Midget Miracle SIT 6C
Start the short wall from pockets.

14 Eilixir ★ SIT 7A+
Sitstart the green lip and pull right to the arete. Harder than it looks - clamping the low undercling is key.
Robin Müller, John Wilson 2013

15 Robin's Slap ★ SIT 6B
From the obvious RH eye and LH sidepull, slap the top and pull over.

16 One Mover SIT 5
Another one mover, but not as good.

The Offwidth

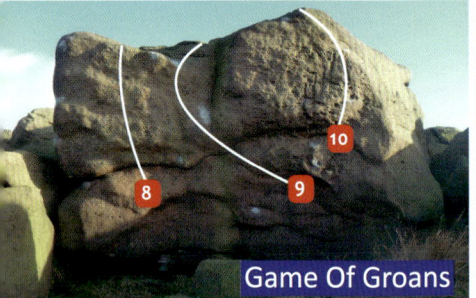

Game Of Groans

Confessed Obsessed

1 Yee-Ha SIT **6B+**
Sitstart the arete and swing right to pull up at the offwidth. No footblock.

2 Off-Side ★ SIT **5+**
From hands on the footblock, climb into the arete.

3 Offwidth Your Head ★ **6B** SIT **6B**
From the block, pull through the offwidth. The standing start eliminates the footblock.

4 Proper Job ★ **6C** SIT **6C+**
A proper mantel job. The sitter starts with feet on the footblock, LH sidepull, RH undercling.

5 Pony Club ★★ SIT **7A**
Sitstart using the lip dimple and big foothold. Ride the slopes leftwards to finish via the offwidth. Using the footblock is **6C**.
Robin Müller 2012

6 Fall And Chains SIT **6C+**
Sitstart and stand up. Now what?

7 Recess SIT **6B+**
A sitter on the back of the block. Start matched on the lip, go right to the arete and then the top.

8 Game of Groans SIT **6C+**
Sitstart LH slot, RH groove. Clamp upwards. Without the arete, this is *Game Of Stones*, **7A**.
Robin Müller, John Wilson 2013

9 Poundsaver SIT **7A**
Sitstart from RH pocket. Gaston the groove and go for the jug up and left.
Robin Müller 2012

10 Basic Tech SIT **6B**
Sitstart and up the edges.

11 Confessed Obsessed SIT **6C**
Up the awkward arete from sitting. Thank goodness for the foothold.

12 Project

13 Project
LH two-finger dimple, RH arete, slap for the top.

BLACKSTONE EDGE

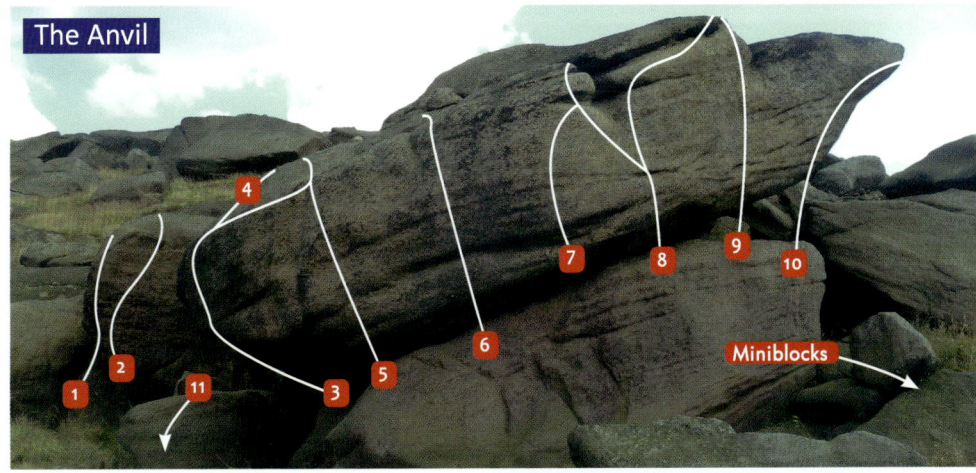

The Anvil

Miniblocks

1 Gnome Arete SIT **5+**
The little arete would fit in your garden.

2 Project
Use anything right of the arete. Proper tough.

3 Project
From hands and feet on the small detached slab, tackle the arete and slopey lip. Don't use the low boulder that makes the bottom half of the anvil.

4 Hero ★★ 7A
Step off a rock to climb the arete on its right.
Robin Müller 2013

5 Tricepatops 6C
Undercut up and left to the lip and mantel it out.

6 Newfangled Slaptop 5+

7 Happy Mole Man ★ 6C+
Jump for the high sloper from the low holds. Starting LH on arete is a bit harder - this is **7A**.

8a Lungefish ★ 5+
Head for the notch.

8b Slowfish 6B
Don't use any holds on the left side of the notch. Move right at the top to finish via better holds.

9 The Right Honourable Runnel ★ 6B

10 Anvilette 5+
The grade is for tall people.

11 Oh Dear SIT **6A**
A lying start from hands on the ledge - on a boulder downhill from the Anvil. Oh dear indeed.

12 Oh My SIT **6A**
Sitstart the arete, no footblock. Quite fun.

13 Project
Pull on to nothings and keep going.

14 Project
Desperation in the guise of a tiny arete.

15 Eager Beaver SIT **6B**
Traverse from far left. Top out at the right arete.

BLACKSTONE EDGE

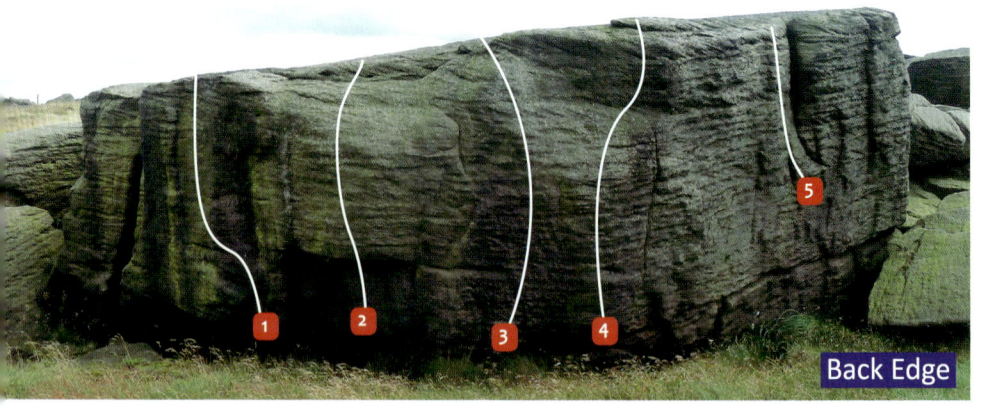

Back Edge

Set back from the top path, the Back Edge is a line of low-slung boulders with good sitstarts on often soggy ground.

1 Nik's Groove ★ SIT 7A
From sitting, somehow trick your way up the double groove, without the left arete. With the arete, it is **6B**.
Nik Jennings 2008

2 Squashed Nose SIT 6B+
The squashed nose.

3 Nik's Left ★ SIT 6B
The cunning arete on its left.

4 Nik's Arete SIT 6B+
The rounded arete and crack, with a rightwards finish using the pocket.

5 The Big Crack Thing 5
Haul up the big crack thing.

6 Nik's Slap SIT 6C
From a lying start, go for the lip.

7 Bum Fiend SIT 5+
Mantel.

8 Nibble My Grit 4 SIT 6B
Use the rib to good effect.

9 Hand Holed ★ 6B
Sitstart and gain the pocket.

10 Try Me 4 SIT 6C
Sitstart using the LH pocket.

11 Home Improvements ★ SIT 6C+
Sitstart at the big hold, then gain crimps.

12 Home Improvements Right SIT 7A
Sitstart from the big hold and head for crimps near the arete, then up.
Tom O'Rourke 2003

13 Patiopia ★ SIT 7A
From the sloper, traverse left to finish up *NMG*. Stay below the pocket - finishing via the pocket is **6C**.
Robin Müller 2012

14 Sergeant Jump SIT 6A
Undercut to a finger bucket.

15 Cocklewarmer SIT 5+
Sitstart and up you go.

16 Groove Is In The Art 5 SIT 6A
The slight groove, staying off the arete.

17 Frog Legs 4 SIT 6C
Start RH break, LH left of the arete. Weird moves to get stood up.

18 Amy Pond 4 SIT 6A

19 Ricki Lake 4 SIT 6A
The central arete.

BLACKSTONE EDGE 295

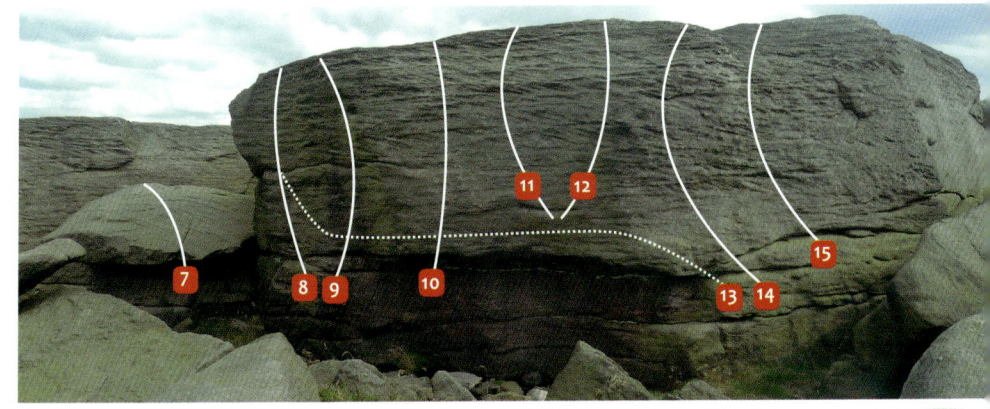

20 Billy Ocean 4 SIT **6A+**
The wall between aretes.

21 Spaghetti Limbs 3 SIT **6B**
The arete has an awkward start.

22 The Sneak 3+ SIT **6A**
The arete on its left.

23 The Runnel ★ 3 SIT **6A+**
The arete on its right.

24 Pocket Dyno ★ LOW **6B+**
Dyno from the good bit of the break to the giant pocket.

25 Polly Pocket SIT **6C**
Climb crimps, staying left of the arete.

26 Pocket Arete ★ 4+ SIT **6A**
The arete on its right.

27 No Pocket, No Cry 5 SIT **6B**
The vague central arete, without the left arete,

28 Free And Easy SIT **4+**
From the break, rock rightwards to a good sidepull.

296 BLACKSTONE EDGE

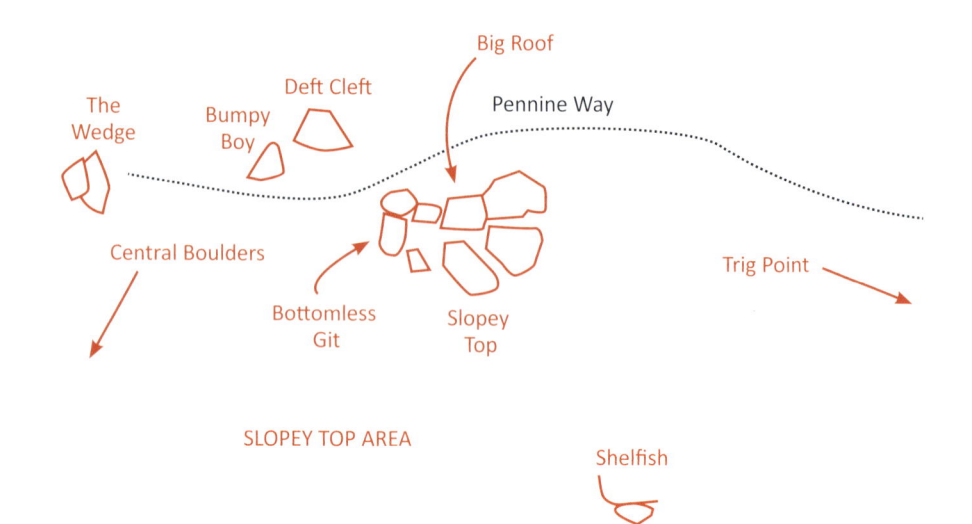

SLOPEY TOP AREA

- The Wedge
- Bumpy Boy
- Deft Cleft
- Big Roof
- Pennine Way
- Central Boulders
- Bottomless Git
- Slopey Top
- Trig Point
- Shelfish
- Little Roof

Foxy Furtlings, 7B p297

BLACKSTONE EDGE

The Wedge

The Slopey Top area is uphill and to the right of The Anvil, shortly before the Trig Point.

1 Wigeon 5+ SIT 6C
The arete on its right.

2 The Wodge ★ SIT 7A+
Start up *The Wedge* and finish *Widgeon*.
Robin Müller 2013

3 The Wedge ★★ 7A SIT 7A+
From the break, pull past the arete to a hard slopey mantel.
Robin Müller 2013

4 Wedge Witch 6A
The arete on its right. No footblock.

5 Ledge Itch SIT 6B
From the arete, traverse the slopey shelf rightwards to top out round the far arete.

6 Obstinate Bactrian SIT 6C
Start from the lower of two humps and rock left for the top. Going right is **6B**.

7 Deft Cleft SIT 6C
From a big gritty RH jug, swing up and left for the cleft.

There are some fun sitstarts on the Deft Cleft boulder, but the low rock is friable.

8 Foxy Furtlings SIT 7B
From a low start using two spaced holds and a heel out right, gain a crimp and start slapping. The right-hand footblock is allowed.
Robin Müller 2013

9 Nutrition SIT 6A+
Climb sidepulls from matched on the lowest hold. The footblock is allowed.

Bumpy Boy

Deft Cleft

Bottomless Git

Bottomless Git

10 Lock, Stock And Smoking Heel SIT 6C+
From a lying start with hands on the low lip holds, squeeze upward to big slopers.

11 Boozy Brawler ★ SIT 7A
Start matched on the main lip hold and brawl to the top.
Robin Müller, John Wilson 2013

12 Bottomless Git SIT 6B+
The right arete from low, with one tricky move to gain the scoop.

BLACKSTONE EDGE

13 Project
The arete, from roof undercuts.

14 The Lady's Not For Gurning ★★ SIT **7B**
From perched on the right side of the plinth, undercut to crimps, then use everything in a bid for the summit.
Robin Müller 2012

15 Project
As before, but a right hand exit.

Big Roof

16 Hand Me Frowns SIT **7A**
A reachy start from twin holds on the face.
Robin Müller 2012

17 Insouciance ★ SIT **7A**
Use the sidepull to gain the lip. Mantel straight up - stepping left or right to easier finishes is cheating.
Robin Müller 2012

18 Blundercut SIT **4**
Undercut and up.

19 Flip Me SIT **6C**
Sitstart using the lip and a low foothold. Gain the rib and struggle upwards. The footledge is out of bounds.

20 Leg Sandwich SIT **5+**
Sitstart the break.

The next two roofs are a little further on and downhill.

21 Stacked Like Arnie SIT **6A+**
From the ledge, slap the top.

22 The Shelfish Way SIT **6C**
From the slopey shelf, gain the top and rock left to an insecure mantel.

Slopey Top Boulder

23 Checkout SIT **6A**

24 Project
A desperate rockover.

25 The Underdog ★ SIT **7A+** LOW **7B**
Start LH arete and RH edge in the roof, then power upwards via a RH arete pinch. The low start is from both hands on your choice of left arete holds.
Robin Müller 2013

Shelfish

Little Roof

26 Sharpe SIT **7A+**
Start RH in the sharp eye hold on the lip, LH under the roof. A stiff lock off follows.
Robin Müller 2013

27 Harper SIT **6B**
Start LH undercutting the bottom of the sharp eye hold, RH just right on a slopey lip hold. The mantel is awkward!

Blackstone Slab, 6A+ p303

BLACKSTONE EDGE

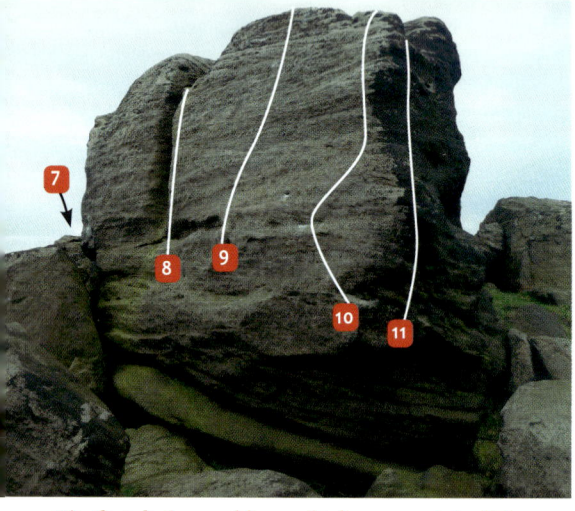

The fast-drying problems which surround the Trig Point are one of the highlights of the crag. The first problems are on the lower level boulders.

1 Fine and Dandy 4
Up the wall, stepping right up the slab.

2 Time for Tweed 3
The obvious weakness.

3 Pockington Lane ★ 6A sit 6B
From sitting, pull up pockety things.

4 Grrr 5 sit 6B+
A deceptively fiendish sitter.

5 Finder's Fee sit 4
The arete on its left.

6 Minutiae sit 5+
The arete on its right.

The Trig Point boulder itself has some more problems.

7 Trigger sit 6B+
Wriggle between boulders and sit-start (be strict) the arete from the RH sidepull.

8 Trig Crack 3

9 Trig Slab ★★ 6A
The sublime slab isn't too hard if you trust the finger ripples. A variation stays right of the undercut and is **6B**.

10 Trig Arete ★ 6B+ sit 6C
Climb the arete on its left.

11 Trigonomy ★ 6A sit 6A+
The arete on its right.

Bouldering continues on the walls facing the trig boulder.

12 No Nonsense sit 5+
The crack.

13 The Lushering ★ sit 7A
Climb the face to move left and up using a slopey RH gaston.
Robin Müller 2012

14 Done Years Ago ★ sit 6B
Head right via a good edge.

15 Con Air ★ 7A
Dyno from the slopey hold to the top.
Nick Conway 1990s

16 Paggered sit 6B+
The arete on its left.

17 Sly Way sit 6A+
The fingery sidepulls on the sidewall, using anything except the crack.

18 Green and Black ★ 6A+
Classy clamping up twin aretes.

19 Project
The right arete only.

20 Troll Mohican sit 6B+
Start LH arete, RH pinch.

BLACKSTONE EDGE 301

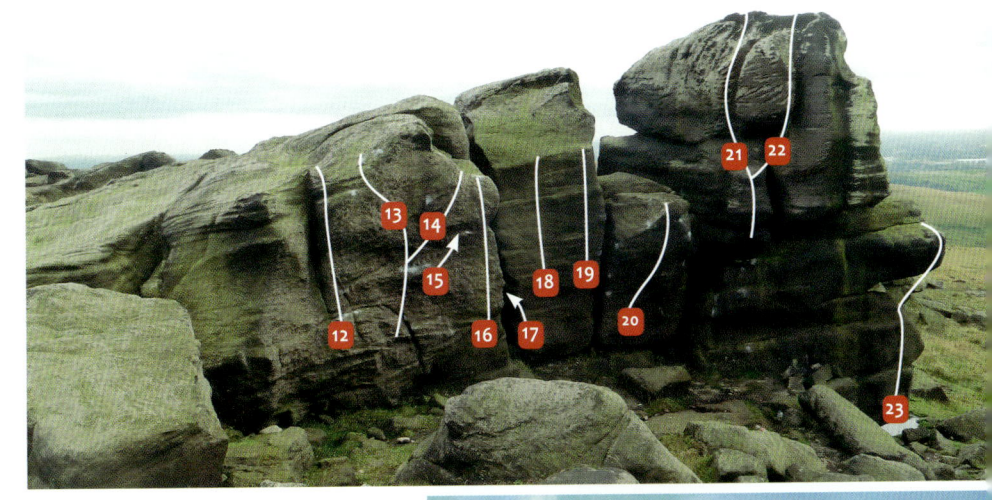

21 Cleft Of The Brave ★★ 5+
Sumptuous holds and a proper highball.

22 Fissure Of Fear ★ 6A
The right fork is a little trickier.

23 Last Lash ★ 6A SIT 6A+
The undercut wall, with a span for the juggy lip and a scary top-out.

24 Project

25 Project

26 Crackonomy 5+
Climb the crack.

27 Belly Bouncer ★ 6A
Pull up the bulge to a commiting top.

A little further right is a small tiered roof.

28 Go That Way SIT 6B
Sitstart at the arete and gain the high shelf. Traverse right to pull over at a jug.

29 Go Low SIT 6B
Sitstart from a gnarly sidepull and low crimp to grab the middle shelf. Continue to a juggy top-out.

30 Go This Way SIT 6B+
From sitting on the right, gain the middle shelf and traverse it leftwards, to finish rocking onto the far arete.

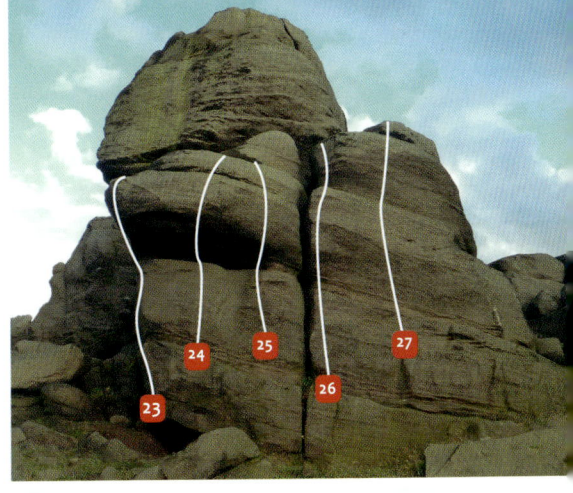

BLACKSTONE EDGE

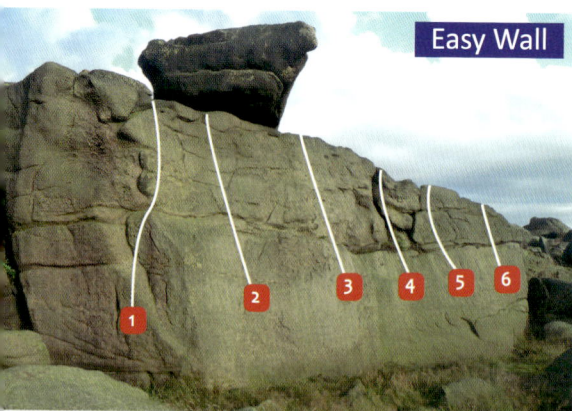

Easy Wall

The Easy Wall is a little way to the right of the small tiered roof. With a good concentration of welcoming low-grade climbing, it's an ideal spot for those in search of a more relaxed experience.

1 First Laugh 3 SIT 5+
The arete, started on the left and rocking round to the right to finish.

2 Under A Dark Dream ★ 4
Up the wall to finish left of the boulder.

3 Roaming Pleasant Hands 4
Up the wall to finish right of the boulder.

4 A Few Moves For New Love 3
Use the big crack.

5 Cutlery Creates Confusion 2
Use the right fork in the crack system.

6 Little Person's Path 3
The wall right of the cracks.

Ape Hour, 7A+ p303

BLACKSTONE EDGE

The two friendliest boulders at the crag. Fast-drying, but the ground can be boggy around the Melting Cube.

1 Uphill Arete SIT **6B**
The arete, using the right-hand seam.

2 Ape Hour ★ **7A+**
Pull on to sidepulls and a sloper, then go for the top. Stay off holds on *Hueco Arete* (including heel hooks).
Nick Conway 1990s

3 Hueco Arete 5+

4 Blackstone Slab ★★ **6A+**
The centre of the slab is splendid.

5 Be Strict 6C
The crack leads up the slab, but stay off the arete.

6 Be Skilful ★★ **6A**
The arete on its left is very good.

7 Be Less Skilful 5
The arete on its right.

8 Nothing Cubed 4

9 Cuban ★ SIT **6A+**
Climb the arete on its right.

10 Cube Root 6C
Stay off the arete.

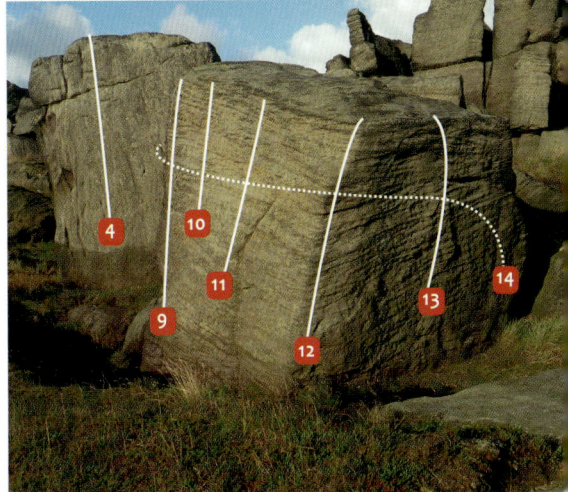

11 Cubic Crack SIT **6B+**
Stay left of the arete sloper. With this it is *Cubic Crack Right* **6B**.

12 Cube All SIT **6A**
The arete on its right.

13 Shortarse SIT **6B**
The vertically challenged wall. Missing out the slot is **7A**.

14 Nick's Traverse ★ SIT **7A+**
From the shortest arete, traverse leftwards below the top, to finish up *Nothing Cubed*.
Nick Conway 1990s

304 BLACKSTONE EDGE

Short Routes

My heart's away in the lonely hills,
  Where I would gladly be—
On the rolling ridge of Blackstone Edge,
  Where the wild wind whistles free!
There oft in careless youth I roved,
  When summer days were fine;
And the meanest flower of the heathery waste
  Delights this heart of mine!
Oh, the lonely moors, the breezy moors,
  And the stormy hills so free;
Oh, the wild, wild moors; the wild, wild moors,
  The sweet wild moors for me.

Excerpt from Oh The Wild, Wild Moors
by Edwin Waugh - "The Lancashire Burns"
(circa 1889)

BLACKSTONE EDGE

The short walls behind the Hueco Block have numerous lower grade lines. Some are bolder than others, but most are amenable to boulderers, as difficulties usually stop at the upper break.

1 The Bounder 4+
Follow the crack.

2 Rough Life 4
Escape the pod.

3 Naomi's Wall ★ 6B
From small holds, make a move to gain the slopey crack. A sitter might be possible.

4 Curving Arete SIT 5+ LOW 6A
Sitstart the curve. Harder from the low start matched on the sloper.

5 I know 3
Climb out of the scoop on its left. Exiting on the right is *Yes* 4.

6 Easy Peasy 2

7 Stay Cool 5

8 Another! 4+
Cracks lead the way.

9 Two 5
Twin cracks on the right of the wall.

10 Easier Peasier 2

11 Who? Me? 4+
Up the middle of the slab, then the upper wall.

12 Rubbery 5
The right side of the slab to a small chimney.

13 Relief 2

14 Slight 4
The thin wall. Easy at the top.

15 Porage 2
Chimney to the same finish as *Slight*.

16 Feet 4+
From the left, pull into the slab and follow this to the high crack.

17 Balance 4+
Step onto the slab from a high rock and continue past the break on pockets.

18 Steppin' Out 4+
Follow the left arete.

19 Foot Business 5
The centre of the wall, past an undercut.

20 Leaning To The Left Of Sloper ★★ 6A
Climb the wall via the crackline.

21 Softly Softly ★ 6A+
The undercut arete is entertaining.

BLACKSTONE EDGE

22 Beginning 2

23 End 2

24 Forward Straight 2

25 Cornered 2
Up the corners.

Next comes a hemmed in boulder. Nothing on it is super hard, but be wary of the landing - one pad doesn't do much.

26 Floating Wigs 4+
The left arete is airy and the landing is hairy.

27 Larn Summat 6B
A big move from a big hold.

28 Ruler Fooler ★ 6B SIT 6B+
The straight crack.

29 Old Silky ★ 6A
The right arete on its left.

30 Old Milky 5+ SIT 6A
The right arete on its right.

31 Pinnochio 6A
Climb the protruding block from the back, to pull onto its green end.

32 You There 3 SIT 6A
Sitstart the arete on its left.

33 Look Here 5 SIT 6A
Clamp up the central face from sitting. No footblocks.

34 Just Do It 4 SIT 6A
Clamp up the arete from sitting. No footblocks.

35 Pheasant Walk ★ 3
The pleasant slab.

36 Grouse Mate SIT 5
The right side of the slab.

BLACKSTONE EDGE   307

50m further right are the last problems in this cluster. They are the best of this bunch, and well worth seeking out.

37 Subtletease ★★ 4
The left-hand line up the lovely slab.

38 Paw Print ★★ 3
Beautiful easy padding.

39 Queasy Face 5 SIT 5+
Rock onto the green slab and finish. Not as good as its neighbours.

40 Look to Windward ★★ 5+ SIT 6A+
Sitstart using the right arete and climb the slight central arete on its right, with a delicate move at the top.

41 Andrex Guppy ★★ 5+ SIT 6A
Guppy gleefully up the fin.

Trig Slab, 6A p300

BLACKSTONE EDGE

Beyond

The Beyond boulders provide a cluster of perfect mini-blocks that make a great sunset circuit.

1 Crimpemup SIT **6B+**
Sitstart from the sloper. No arete.

2 Dodgem SIT **4+**
Sitstart the arete, from the sloper.

3 The Skelter LOW **6B**
Pull on with hands below the crack.

4 Merry Go Rounded 3
An easy breezy arete.

5 Backseat Climber SIT **5**
Crimpy flakes.

6 Granny's Got Moves SIT **4**
Sitstart the aretes.

7 Grandad's Hard To Hold 6C
A squeezed-in challenge: from the blob, slap the top and mantel upwards. Don't use adjacent walls.

8 Nooks And Grannies SIT **4**
The positive arete.

9 Let Loose The Lion SIT **6B**
The arete, starting from the rounded dish. Climb via the thin sidepull out right, without which it's **6C**.

10 Get Horny 3
Use the horn. Go on.

11 The Rantle ★ SIT **7A**
Slap a heel on and attempt a rockover mantel. But is it possible facing both directions? Beautifully ridiculous.

12 Something From The Attic SIT **5**
Start matched on the low block and grind up the arete.

13 Shelf Life SIT **6B**
From matched on the low block, stay right of the arete.

14 Pack Up And Go SIT **6A**
Start from the nice sidepull.

15 Udge Repellant 6C
Small holds repel unready fingers.

16 The Fop Is On Form ★ **6B+**
The arete on its left.

17 Dandy Gets Handy ★ **6A+** LOW **6C+**
The arete on its right. The low start is from hands matched on underclings.

18 Chalk The Talk ★ **7A** LOW **7A+**
The wall just right of the arete, using the slopey LH pocket and a small hold for RH. The low start is from hands matched on underclings.
Robin Müller 2013

19 Custom Eyes ★ **6C** LOW **6C+**
The right side of the face, using a small hold for LH and throwing for the notch. The low start is from hands matched on underclings. Lanky folk can reach the top from here, which is much easier.

20 Aesthete's Foot ★ **6B+** LOW **6C**
The arete on its left, with a dynamic move to the notch, then a tricky mantel. The low start is from hands matched on underclings.

21 Merci Moi 7A
The arete on its right. A worthwhile move, despite its proximity to the adjacent block.
Robin Müller 2013

310 BLACKSTONE EDGE

Back Of Beyond

The Back Of Beyond area is the last collection of boulders at Blackstone, just a little further on from the Beyond blocks. Near its left end is a baby buttress with some easy walls.

1 Fragmen **4**

2 Illustrion **3**

3 Porital **4+**

4 Scultis **3**

5 Kescate **3**

A little way to the right are twin roofs.

6a Swingers ★ LOW **7A**
Start on the left-hand slab, then use awkward holds on the upper block to reach the jug on the nose. Cut loose and finish up and left.
Robin Müller, John Wilson 2013

6b Return Of The Swing ★ LOW **7A+**
Climb *Swingers* to the jug, then traverse right to finish up *Luna*.
Robin Müller 2013

7 Luna ★ SIT **6B+**
Start below the roof, on the low left block, then move past undercuts to better holds. The right hand roof is off limits.

8 Kraken ★ SIT **6A+**
From the shelf at the back, pull through the crack, using any holds you can reach.

9 Leviathan SIT **6B+**
From the back, pull through the right-hand roof without using the left-hand roof.

On a higher level, in the middle of the jumble, is a line of short, perched blocks.

10 Handwarmer SIT **6A**
Follow the lip rightwards and rock round the arete. No footblock.

11 Legwarmer SIT **4+**
The small arete on its left, using the footblock.

BLACKSTONE EDGE 311

12 Ribbed For Applause sit **4+**
Sitstart the short rib.

13 Step Into The Light sit **6B**
Start from the break and fight past slopers to the top. The rib is off-limits.

14 Sneak Up The Right sit **6B+**
The wall left of the arete, without the arete. Stay off the low right footblock.

15 Don't Stop To Fight sit **6B**
The arete, using any holds on the face. Stay off the low right footblock.

And finally, a little to the right...

16 The Butcher sit **6B**
Sitstart the low prow.

Swingers, 7A p310

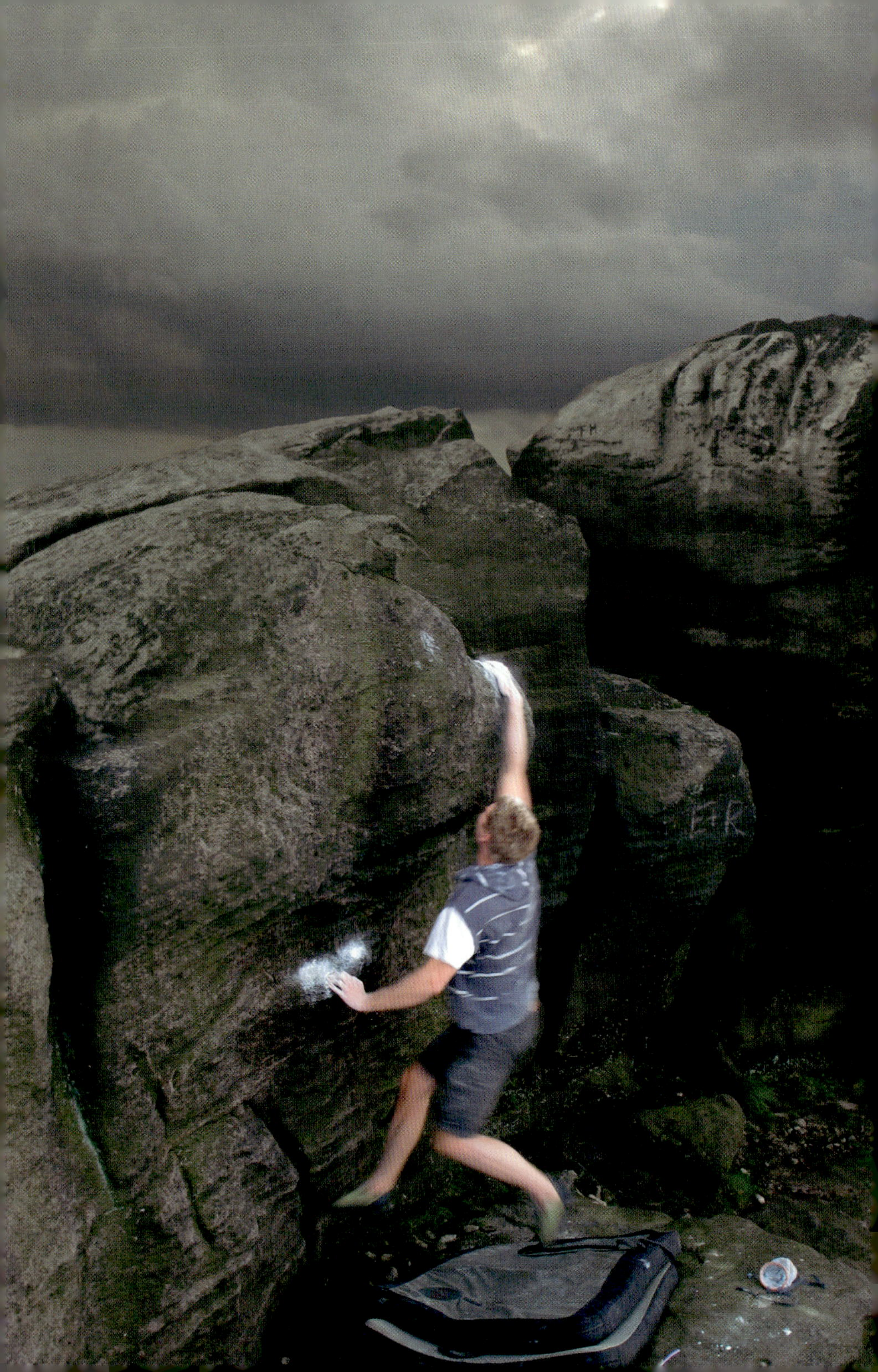

Con Air, 7A **p300**

Tilting For Champions, 7A

47 Withens Buckstones

Here is a scenic spot with curvaceous formations. The rock is mostly solid, but some areas seem a bit more fragile, so it's best to visit only on dry days. The position above the reservoir and flat grassy landings make this worth a trip. Expect lots of sitstarts and tricky mantels.

APPROACH 25 min
Drive along the B6138 which runs between Mytholmroyd on the A646 and Blackstone Edge reservoir on the A58. Take the downhill turn-off which is signposted to St John's Church. Follow this road through a small village and onto Rudd Lane. Park in the free car park at the end of the road. Walk to the reservoir and turn left. Continue round the reservoir to a break in the water channel. Cross here, where you can easily step over the small section of wooden fence on the left. Follow the vague track which leads along the edge of the brook to the right then turns left uphill.

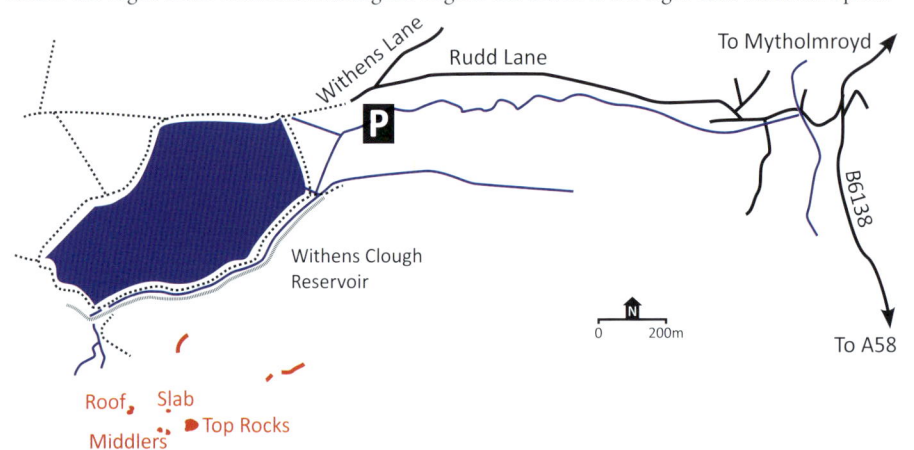

WITHENS BUCKSTONES | 315

Top Rocks

1 See No Mantel 6B+
The left-hand line, with a crimpy runnel on top.

2 Hear No Mantel ★ LOW 7A
The centre, from crouched on the shelf.

3 Speak No Mantel 6A+

4 The Oldest New Thing 6B
Pull right from the lip. The sitstart is a project.

5 Tilting For Champions ★ SIT 7A
Climb the arete and rock round to finish.

6 The Masticator 5+ SIT 6C
Pull onto the slab via the cleft.

7 Project
The full lip traverse.

8 Scooch SIT 6B+
Start on lip holds left of the arete.

9 Mooch SIT 6A
Start on the low boss. Use the arete.

10 Pooch With A Punch SIT 6C
The arete on its right.

11 The Wart Whisperer SIT 7A
Pull up dimples, staying off adjacent jugs.

12 Rail Enthusiast SIT 6A
Follow the rail.

13 Hip-Pop Music SIT 7A+
Start matched on the lip. Use the arete.

14 Cream Of The Flop 5+
The scoop.

Middlers

Low Roof

Slab

15 Stacked Like A Body-Building Gnome SIT 6C
From low slopers, head left to a hold, then mantel.

16 Project

17 Cheesy Rider 7A
The arete on its left.

18 Tworettes 6A
Twin aretes.

19 Millions Of Tiny Black Teeth SIT 6B
Use the big groove hold round the arete.

20 Relief 4
The slab. Also the way down.

Project - Healey Nab p119

WARDENS OF ROCK

Climbers stalk a small corner of existence, the domain of wild mineral matter. Though it may not figure largely in the collective consciousness of mankind, it is our playground, our dreamworld, and also our ward. Our parents and their parents have danced and clawed and styled their forms upon these cliffs and boulders, and in their place we shall do the same, then one day our children, and another day their children. It would be a good thing if each generation could pass on their pleasures and challenges, the arena for which has been many eons in the making. Some wear and tear will inevitably occur – a small imprint of our activities cannot be denied – but there are steps that each of us can take to ensure that our ward, this sacred realm of rock, is cared for and protected to the best of our abilities. It's a small way to say thanks for the good times.

LITTER
...Is bad. Don't do it. That should go without saying. Sadly, not everyone is as careful as most climbers. Sometimes litter is also carried off unseen by mischievous winds. Blame is usually unproductive, but one thing we can all do is take litter home, even if it came from someone else. Try to leave the crag a little cleaner than when you arrived.

CHIPPING
...Don't chip holds into the rock. It leaves an ugly mess and it ruins the challenge for others. Once the surface layer (the patina) is broken, the soft rock underneath crumbles and erodes rapidly.

WET ROCK
...Is often more fragile than dry rock. It's also not much fun to climb.

BRUSHING
...Is best done carefully. Use a soft brush. Don't use a wire brush.

RAGGING
...Is often a better option than brushing. Whack holds with a rag, and you'll find it effectively removes scrittle and chalk, without damaging the surface.

DIRTY CLIMBING SHOES
...Are bad for the rock and can cause eroded footholds, as well as making the rock much less pleasant to climb for anyone else. If you can't be bothered to take your climbing shoes off when you walk between problems, then please make a proper effort to clean them before you climb. A beer towel is ideal for this purpose. You may not want to carry a bouldering mat (aka the deluxe foot-wiper), but a beer towel weighs nothing and will do the job.

VEGETATION
...Grows quickly, especially in esoteric spots. If footholds, cracks or top-outs are overgrown, then pulling away some greenery will be doing everyone a favour. Climbers only use a small part of the natural world, so keeping this part tidy should not cause any environmental problems. That said, take care not to interfere with any rare plants.

TIMELINE

1948-49 Parr's Crack 6A
Eric Parr and friends

Pre 1969 Unjust 6B
Hank Pasquill

1977 Rusty Wall 6C+
Dave Hollows, Hank Pasquill

1979-83 Hank's Wall 7A+
Hanks Pasquill

1983 Pigswill Sitstart 7A
Andy Kay

1984 Rodin's Requiem 7B
John Hartley

1987 Renal Failure 7B+
Paul Pritchard

1985-89 Traverse Of The Gods Fr. 8b+
Dave Kenyon

1995-96 Going Down Fr. 8c+
Neil Carson

2001 Colt 7C
Paul Robins

2001 Snatch 8A
Nik Jennings

2001 Endangered Species 8A+
John Gaskins

2005 Endless Nameless 8B
John Gaskins

2006 Moment Of Clarity 8B
John Gaskins

2007 Super Submarine 8A+
Gareth Parry

INTERVIEWS

A FOREWORD ON HISTORY

This may be the first bouldering guidebook to the area, but people have been bouldering here for many years, often by accident. In an attempt to convey not just the bones of this history, but also flesh out some of the characters who created it, here is a series of short interviews with some of the area's movers and shakers. To lend a bit of context, I'll start with an overview of some of what happened, and when.

The crucible of Lancashire bouldering is undoubtedly Brownstones. Throughout the 20th Century, Lancashire's finest fingers have fondled every inch. It was a key training ground for local climbers, who worked their way through all the obvious lines. Hank Pasquill's big-boot ascent of **Hank's Wall, 7A+** was perhaps the end of an era in which talented trad climbers made their mark (probably whilst imagining what each move would be like on top of a 20ft runout). Andy Kay's 80s sitstart to **Pigswill, 7A** was the sign of a younger generation with visionary bottoms; boulderers who sought a purer physical challenge in preference to the head games of route climbing. Despite this anal revolution, it wouldn't be for another couple of decades until sitstarts really caught on in Lancashire.

Over in Wilton 3, the climbing scene's reluctance to accept new realms of difficulty was once again in evidence when John Hartley climbed **Rodin's Requiem, 7B**. It was possibly the hardest problem in Lancashire at that time, though the guidebook writer refused to put it in the guide until John proved he could climb it (see John's interview on p.386 for the full story).

As the 80s wore on, sport climbing came into vogue and stamina training became fashionable. Craig Y Longridge provided a perfect unrelentingly steep wall on which to practice. It was also a temporal and geographical hotspot for luminous lycra leggings, though there is insufficient data to calculate how this impacted on climbing standards. When Dave Kenyon completed **The Traverse Of The Gods, sport 8b+** it was a landmark event. A decade later Neil Carson's lower level traverse - **Going Down, sport 8c+** - was monumental. Straight-up problems at Longridge only took off when bouldering mats appeared and indoor training became the norm. To date, the hardest problem at the crag is Gaz Parry's **Super Submarine, 8A+**.

After 2000, standards in Lancashire reached their zenith with John Gaskins' ascents of the area's two biggest, baddest problems. **Endless Nameless, 8B** at Stanworth took him two days in 2005, and may be the hardest slab in the world. He may also have set a record by taking nearly a decade to come up with the name. Over at Thorn Crag, his highball mega arete **A Moment Of Clarity, 8B** is another phenomenal achievement and like the Stanworth slab, stands unrepeated.

While the level set by John eclipses all other efforts in Lancashire, other talented boulderers have been increasingly active. On Lancashire's northern fells, Greg Chapman has spearheaded interest with his dedication to Bowland bouldering, both documenting existing classics and adding many fine new problems, including several 8A's. Elsewhere, exploration and discovery has increased massively in the last few years. The most major developments are the East Lancs Moors crags, which have been lifted from obscurity and now boast hundreds of problems in excellent settings. Meanwhile, several crags have benefited from intense bursts of enthusiasm, such as Bull Stones, Jumbles, Deeply Vale, Ousel's Nest and the Wiltons.

HANK PASQUILL

You are well known for your hard routes in the Lancashire quarries. Was bouldering a way to train for some of these lines, or just a bit of fun?
Bouldering was purely for fun and a change from doing routes. We did train on gritstone bridges and the rings.

Is it true that you did Hank's Wall and Pigswill in big boots?
Yes, I did the first ascent of Hank's Wall in Eiger Darbla boots with hard Vibram souls - very good on tiny holds. But not Pigswill, this was a lot later.

Hank's Wall and Pigswill were probably the hardest problems in the area when they were done. Was there competition for the first ascent?
No competition on Hank's Wall, although I was inspired by John Gill's book. Pigswill did have competition from my lad Ryan & Geoff Mann.

You've been bouldering at Brownstones since the 60s. Have climbers changed over the years?
Yes, we climbed all the time and became quite fit but today's climbers train like mad - miles stronger than we were.

Technology has altered drastically since you began. Rock climbing shoes, chalk, bouldering mats. Just how different was climbing without these things?
For the first year we climbed in army boots and it took a while adapting to Masters & PA's [50s and 60s climbing shoes]. It's funny how you just get used to whatever's available at the time. Initially we preferred clay/dirt on our hands and took ages changing to chalk. [Climbing] without boulder mats sometimes made you commit more as you didn't want to hit the floor, although nowadays I'm totally addicted to them.

How did you begin?
I began climbing with schoolmates, top roping in grotty shaly quarries. Then we discovered Wilton and met proper climbers who said we must lead or solo the routes.

Author's note...
There are a couple of amusing tales surrounding Hank's Brownstones legacy. The first is that, contrary to the BMC guide's polite reinterpretation, Pigswill was not named because of an oft-quoted phrase: "Pigs will fly if this has been climbed". In fact, when Hank first climbed the problem, he was observed by Tony Preston, who exclaimed "F**king Pigswill!" then walked off. Thus it was named. Tony was by all accounts a very funny man and a great character - one of many who did not leave his name on the Brownstones first ascent list, but nonetheless added something unique to the history of the place.

Another story has it that the legendary American climber Ron Kauk once visited Brownstones. Upon attempting Hank's Wall, he announced "Hank's Wall kicks Midnight Lightning in the ass!"

Maybe.

ANDY KAY

Your sitstart to Pigswill was quite unusual for the era, and somewhat ahead of its time! How did it come about?
I did it around '83 I think after spending a bit of time working out a sequence that didn't involve controlling a big barn door going for the small edge (up left above the little 'nose' – I ended up using a toe-hook which is different from how I do it today). I was pretty stoked to complete it and gave a big shout after reaching the good holds. I was then surprised a minute later, to be confronted by two blokes who had been down at the pool, had heard the shout and came running up expecting to see someone badly injured and in pain on the deck!

Where did you learn about Pigswill - was it by word of mouth or a previous guidebook?
There was a guide supplement around at that time with the legend writ large that this wall was unclimbed. I spotted it when browsing in the now long gone Alpine Sports shop on Bradshawgate.

Given that I was particularly focused on Brownstones at the time, it seemed like something to get stuck into. It's surprising that it wasn't climbed, given the people operating at a high level around that time. To be honest, I think the history is so contestable that it would be difficult to ascribe the first ascent [of the standup] to anyone really.

Yeah, it seems Hank did the standup at around the same time. Dates are a bit vague. But you definitely did it in 1983?
... Yep, definitely '83 – left Uni in '82 and then seemed to live at Brownstones for about a year after. Indulged in monster stamina sessions down at the pool and worked a load of problems around Ash Pit Slabs. I can't remember the day or month but it was certainly '83. Thank god I had a witness for RH Hank's... Like you, I just got into the place in a big way and just looked at what looked the hardest things there and tried to climb them.

Out of interest, who were the guys climbing hard in those days? I always think it's a shame that FA details only tell half of the story.
The main guys that I can remember were Paul Pritchard, Andrew Gridley and Phil Kelly was in there too. John Hartley and John Monks were still active and of course Geoff Hibbert was always knocking about; although he never could do Hank's Wall strangely enough. Geoff Mann was a regular too – it was a pretty busy scene but those are the names I can remember. There were others but I can't remember the names unfortunately.

A lot of the focus was on Wilton around that time and bouldering was seen as something supplemental. I just loved bouldering though and started doing my own thing, travelling out to Bridestones and Widdop a lot before hooking up with Matt Leigh; maybe I was just shy and unsociable, who knows.

I imagine few other people were thinking about sitstarts in the early 80s?
Remember too that there were no pads and a beer towel and possibly a car mat served as your starting point. I came off the top of Ash Pit Slabs loads of times trying a 3 hold eliminate problem up the Digitation slab – it's a good problem but so eliminate it would be pointless considering. Here's a bit of history for you – Matt Leigh was the first person I ever came across with something that looked like a pad, a homemade affair put together with betterware gardening pads, some old cushions and lots of duck tape! It was ridiculously small but just took the edge off the landings (if your jump/fall was accurate enough that is). From there I developed a bigger pad made from a folded over children's play mat, more cushions and a shed load of tape – it weighed a ton!

PAUL ROBINS

In 2001, you did the first ascent of Colt at Brownstones. As far as I know, it's only been repeated once since then (by Mike Adams), but 7C's at Longridge are climbed all the time. Are they easier?
The thing with Colt is its probably not 7C, and maybe I could see it being hard 7C+ for some. I graded it as it felt the hardest thing at Brownstones and as V8 [7B+] was the hardest at the time it got V9. But it was and is still one of those problems that always feels really close, like you'll do it next go but never happens, so its hard to grade.

So are Longridge problems easier? Umm, one thing I can say is some of the hard Brownstones problems are proper hard and need a fair bit of technique as well as solid crimp strength. Longridge usually just needs a few visits and a bit of a power boost and most problems become ok...difficult to compare.

Tell me about Colt. What's the hard bit? Did you do it the first time you stuck the crux, or did the top spit you off?
The hard bit for me with Colt is the timing being a left handed slap. You only get about 10 goes in a session before it puts a hole in your middle finger, so you've got to be quick. Nah, the top bit was fine, I used to climb into it from Rusty Wall so had it dialled. So yes, once I hung the slap to the crimp I wasn't for falling off the top.

You've done a few FA's at Longridge. Colon Power and the The Priory stand out as the hardest. How did they come about?
It was at a time when I spent a lot of time up there and was running out of things to do. So I naturally just started looking for eliminates and odd holds that never get used. And suddenly the lines jumped out, couldn't believe they'd not been climbed really, totally independent and classics of the crag, especially Colon Power.

Has your approach to climbing changed over the years? What are you keen for in the future?
A little bit of change.. I climbed a lot of trad and soloed a lot when I was younger and developed a really static and controlled style, which is fine for exactly that but it's held me back especially on sport routes, so I have over the last few years tried to address this...

I also just really try to enjoy climbing and not get too focused on training. Ironically, I'm probably more psyched now than ever. The future... whatever tomorrow brings. I'd love to crack a few hard boulder problems *before I git too owd*, but I'm also really keen to travel and do some more big alpine style rock routes.

You used to run a bouldering wall and now you make fingerboards (crusherholds.co.uk). Training is obviously a big part of your life. How did you train to get strong for Colt?
I didn't really, at the time I was climbing a lot of trad and had been climbing at Pex quite a bit, so was really dialled into thin technical wall climbing.

Do you get more out of climbing hard problems than easier ones?
Not really, its good to get your teeth into something and train specifically for it, but I also love knocking problems off quickly or flashing them. Some of my best days bouldering have been doing some of the circuits in font, just moving and flowing, reading the rock spontaneously, turning it on when you need and backing off equally. Very Zen, haha.

GAZ PARRY

You did the first ascent of one of Lancashire's hardest problems - Super Submarine at Longridge. You look pretty chuffed in the video of your ascent – is it something you'd worked on before?
I think it took a couple of sessions but in the end it came down to better conditions. Yeah I was pretty happy, I think it came from the past when Big Marine was a massive challenge for me and now I could do this super low start.

Since the ground level has lowered, getting set up for the throw can be done with a more straightforward sequence. Do you think the difficulty has changed?
I haven't been on it recently. It does sound easier, a grade or two lower maybe.

In Lancashire you've left your mark on the trad scene. With FA's of Toxic Bilberries and Darwen Weasel at the Wiltons, you've produced the area's two E8 7a routes. How do they compare? To entice (or scare off) the boulderers, could you guess at a font grade for the cruxes?
Don't forget the one at Hoghton too - can't remember the name. I think this and Toxic are unrepeated by local beast Jordan Buys and Toxic has only been done by taller climbers who can leave their foot in the break. Toxic is nails without the break, but in reality probably only comes in at around 7B ish as a total guess. As for Darwen, we compared it to a short 8b sport route at the time.

You're one of the people responsible for creating BoulderUK, located in Blackburn. It was one of the first dedicated bouldering walls in the country, and must have gone some way to improving the average finger strength of Lancastrian boulderers. Were you responding to demand, or hoping that the wall would help grow the scene?
It started as something for us to train on but soon we thought it would work better for everyone to have access. With it producing multiple GB team members it is a facility I am proud of. Even nowadays with the boulder wall explosion I still think with Ian's setting and the volumes and surfaces, BUK is one of the best boulder walls in the country.

Over the years, you've had great success in every style of climbing – 8c+ in sport, E9 on trad and 8B in bouldering. 2007 seemed to be your best year for bouldering, with super fast ascents of several 8B's. Were you training specifically, or just on a roll?
I was training hard for the comps and living in the wall at BUK, training training and more training. Climbing outside almost every day too. Sleeping on the mats then doing it all again.

Do you still have designs on any Lancashire problems or projects?
Hmmm, there are a couple of things but that would be telling.

GARETH WALLIS

You must be one of the keenest locals around. You've made free guides, created the all-singing Brownstones wiki and filmed loads of problems. What motivates you?
I've climbed and pursued outdoor interests since I was ten. The things I did when I was younger (alpine, winter climbing, trad multipitch) gradually gave way to bouldering by necessity of time. Then I came into bouldering as an independent entity.

What keeps me going varies. I think I must have an obsessive personality; I can end up thinking about one problem or line all the time. Finding new problems, and the process from exploration and discovery to completion, is something I find very rewarding. Going somewhere that few people have bothered with and finding a hidden gem is its own reward. The other motivation is trying to put to bed some of the problems that become nemeses, although the to-do list always seems to expand.

What place does climbing have in your life, and has that changed over the years?
I went to university in Glasgow, mainly due to the proximity of rock. I would skip lectures and be out a couple of times per week and at weekends. Now with children and work, the time I have is more limited and therefore more precious so I have to focus more carefully on what I want to achieve. Where I used to go out a lot and not have specific aims, now I know exactly what I want to do. Wanting to get things ticked inevitably means narrowing one's perspective whilst trying to stay open-minded about possibilities.

There is an abundance of rock in Lancashire, but some people dismiss it as mostly esoteric rubbish. Is there really anything worth climbing outside Brownstones, Longridge and Thorn Crag?
Lancashire suffers from a perception of poor rock and low quality problems. The result of that is that there are some amazing problems around that get ignored. Many people can't be bothered going to a venue that has many reasonable problems and two or three classics, but that's their loss. I suppose that is part of the appeal of the bouldering around here, it has less traffic so there is certainly a feeling of adventure and excitement about climbing the best problems. There is a great deal of satisfaction to be had.

There are a lot of great problems in lesser Lancashire venues, and I mean great in comparison to the Peak, Yorkshire etc. The minority have known about them and developed them over time. There are plenty more good lines to be climbed, if you know where to look (or dare to explore).

You've sieged a few problems in your time. Which problem did you become most obsessed with?
There are a couple of problems that don't suit me and subsequently feel really hard. **Hank's Wall** always felt impossible (and sharp), and I would try it on each visit to Brownstones. One day I did it twice in a row, but I've never done it again. The planets aligned that day. **Big Marine** (Longridge) is still resisting after ten years - the move to the right hand pocket doesn't like me.

A couple of my first ascents became obsessions. **David Vetter** (Stronstrey) took many visits to abseil down and clean it, then to commit to the solo on my own one afternoon. I'd looked at it a number of times with Nik [Jennings], but on the day I just popped out with two mats and did it, scaring myself silly in the process. Another stand out is **The Crescent of Embrace** (Jumbles). I'd seen the line that people had tried and failed on, dwelled upon it for weeks, then spent three long visits trying it. My sequence was pretty duff and consisted of a sequence of four hard, low percentage moves and I constantly dropped one or the other. When I did it, it was by the skin of my teeth.

It was a similar, but much longer story for **Rivers of Blood** sitter (Cadshaw) - one of the hardest sets of moves I've ever done. The Red Wall is very fickle with conditions and seems to have its own micro-climate (and midges). Each move on that problem was near my limit at the time, so to link them took a long time. I gave it 7B+ because I didn't want to stick my neck out and say 7C, although in retrospect it's probably a bit of a sandbag.

Any problems in particular that you have enjoyed more than the rest?
Other than those mentioned already, I love Thorn crag for the problems and the scenery. And For My Next Trick is great, but suffering from traffic. Mothership Reconnection is another classic.

Other stand out problems would be: Nick's Traverse, The Slab and Blacktone Best (Blackstone Edge), Ridiculous Dyno, Nexus Dyno (I love dynos), Pigswill (so simple once you know how) (Brownstones), Mirth of the Ducks and the Phat Haendel block (Stronstrey), Pick Pocket (Denham), Clown's Pocket and Sit Thee Down (Jumbles), Dinosaur Adventure 3D (Lower Montcliffe), Snakey B (Wilton One).

Seek and thou shalt find.

JOHN HARTLEY

Rodin's Requiem was possibly the hardest problem in Lancashire when you did it in 1984. Tell me about that...
On the day of the first ascent, I was bouldering with a group that included (if my memory serves me correctly) Mick Lovatt, John Monks, Gerry Peel and Joe Healey. The small vertical crimp was actually a small flake but I pulled this off as I cranked on it. I spun off, just cleared Gerry Peel and landed (on my feet fortunately) on the very edge of the drop to the left of the boulder. I succeeded on the problem on my next try. None of the rest of the team could repeat the problem and Phil Kelly would not include it in the guide until he had seen me do it.

I was there one night some years ago when Ryan Pasquill climbed it direct without the rockover move but he is very tall (especially in comparison to me) and not without talent. At the time I thought it was English 6a/6b as I found it realatively easy (it suited my physique) and could always repeat it first time, every time. It is certainly not E5 and 6m long as Phil described it in the old guide.

That grade seems a little low!
Rodin's is possibly harder than 6c as, to the best of my knowledge, it hasn't had many ascents. I only thought it was English 6a/6b because it suited my style of climbing and in those days I was pretty flexible as I taught martial arts. Ryan is the only person I have seen do the route but only by his direct start. If my memory serves me correctly, he had his left foot on the block where I started from but pulled up directly (because of his long reach) with a high step for his right foot.

It's a very unusual problem. What was your sequence?
I started on the low block to the left using a small vertical crimp above the overhang for my left hand and a high rockover for my right foot on the end of the thin horizontal break. I reached up with my right hand into the small shallow corner [the gaston] and using both holds in opposition, rotated on my right foot to face left. I placed my left toe on a small hold on the very edge of the roof (I placed my head on my left hand to help me do this, hence the name [which refers to Rodin's Scuplture, *The Thinker*]) and pressing with my left hand and leg I started to stand up until I could use the small undercut just left of my right hand (the small overlap as described above) to enable me to fully extend. I finished the problem using the large sloping hold for my right hand and a smear for my left foot.

Author's note...
John mentions that Phil Kelly wouldn't put the problem in the guidebook until he proved he could climb it. There's more to the story. Phil decided to tease John by telling him he still wasn't going to include it, and continued the wind-up by showing him the draft script for the new guidebook on a weekly basis - Rodin's Requiem was always notably absent. When the day came to send the script to the printers, Phil forgot to rectify the omission. The route did find its way into subsequent editions, but confusion over the exact line and grade meant it probably didn't get the attention it deserved. Phil did eventually apologise!

JOHN GASKINS

You've done the FA of several impressive lines on Lancashire grit, some in the quarries and some on Bowland crags. Was it your mission to seek out unclimbed lines, or were there certain features that just called out to you?

I started my climbing on the South Lakes limestone crags of Farleton, Hutton Roof etc and also the Lancashire Quarries so I was aware of where and what a lot of the unclimbed lines were. I've always been more into the "project" approach of picking a specific line or number of lines that I wanted to climb and seeking out difficulty, which then led to trying the unclimbed lines.

How did you get into climbing, and why do you think you got hooked?

I got into it as a progression from walking and scrambling in the mountains and had a few years of trad climbing before I got into bouldering and sport climbing. I liked, and still do like, the physical movement and problem solving aspects of climbing.

When you found an inspiring project, did you focus on it exclusively or did you rotate sessions on various problems?

Usually weather depending I tended to focus on specific projects at a time, although I would still train in conjunction with working the line and I'd have days where I went out and climbed at other venues. But my primary objective would be "the project" whatever that was.

You've done a massive ammount of limestone bouldering, which is often short and fingery. Does gritstone demand different strengths, or is it fairly easy to switch between the two?

I think it depends on the type of gritstone you are talking about (natural or quarried). There is a much greater crossover into quarried grit with its crimpy edges. Whilst a lot of my bouldering focused on short, steep limestone problems, my early climbing was on roughly vertical limestone and grit and I think that that combined with just getting out climbing made it fairly ok to switch.

Exploring and developing new areas takes a lot of time. How did you balance this with training?

In general I'd explore and clean lines when the weather wasn't great either on non-climbing days or after training. I generally trained, and still do, in a morning so it was straightforward to do that then go out and explore/clean off new lines in the afternoon. The other bit is that most of my new problems/venues were at places in the area that I'd both grown up in and also started climbing in so it wasn't "blind exploration", rather it was remembering the unclimbed lines/crags I'd seen then.

A Moment Of Clarity stands out as one of the most attractive and challenging highballs in the area. What was the experience like?

Strange one really, I worked it on a number of occasions and at first it was just a technical challenge on a top rope with no intention of trying to lead it. It was only when I realised that because of how you climb it that a fall would land you on the flat ground on the Last Temptation side of the arête and that the hardest moves were relatively low down that I viewed it as a potential boulder problem. The climbing is a lot about body position and getting good conditions as the crag sits in a bit of a suntrap. The day I did it everything just clicked and it didn't feel that hard but I think that was a combination of learning the body positions and good friction. I climbed it in a period when climbing really wasn't that important to me, I knew that my dad only had a matter of weeks or months to live, and the relative unimportance of climbing was why I never publicised it.

Your slab Endless Nameless at Stanworth is another incredible piece of rock, and not the usual angle for something of this difficulty! Did it take many visits, and is the climbing comparable to anything else you've done?

The only other things that I could really compare it to are the 8B version of Enigma at Isatis (before the hold broke), but even that differs a lot, or something like Coral Sea Supersuper Direct at Trowbarrow or maybe in style to a slate route. I'd been and scoped it out (on a rope) on a prior visit but not really tried it and then I came down, worked a sequence on a top rope and then bouldered it out taking a few falls prior to success. So 1 day of trying it properly plus some hold/sequence inspection a few weeks earlier.

Information Highway Revisited at Lower Montcliffe is another last great problem that has been looked at for years. It's not one of your hardest, but it's an outstanding line. What's the climbing on this one like?

I can't remember a huge amount about it to be honest, it only took me an hour or so from arriving at the crag. My memories of it are of an easy couple of moves to small crimps and slightly out of balance climbing, again I looked at it from a top rope to clean it, try the moves and work a sequence and then I bouldered it out.

Are you still climbing?

Yes, I still train 3 or 4 times week on my board, the difficult bit has been getting out climbing with a full time job and a family but as the children (I've got three, aged between 2½ and 8½) get a bit older it is easier to go out as a family which means I get to climb outside and we still get to spend time together (they also do some climbing).

NIK JENNINGS

Your hardest problem in Lancashire is Snatch, an unrepeated highball slab at Denham Quarry. You've done lots of other hard slabs too, mostly trad routes. What drew you to slabs in the first place?

I always felt I was quite weak and so tended to avoid steeper ground. Also where some people are drawn to the striking lines of aretes and cracks, I've always been pulled in by those almost blank faces that make you think "is that possible?". In retrospect I think that the truth is I wasn't weak (I remember having an early finger board and a friend of decent climbing ability trying to hang the poorest slopey two finger edges and struggling two handed, and then I could hang them one handed. Ooooo look at me...) but rather that I had, and to an extent still have, woeful stamina so steep ground was a bit intimidating.

You made a special hands-free slab board to help you train. Can you describe it, and how you used it?

It was simply a piece of ply at a slab-sequel angle covered in various foothold edges and smears. I used to just stand on it (no hands) and then would move my feet around and then move on to jumping onto footholds. It helped develop balance and also let me find the limits of what I could stand on in a controlled-ish environment (or it just kept me entertained in the evening...)

What do you remember about climbing Snatch? Can you compare it to other slabs you've done?

It's very thin, I worked it on a rope and then fell off a fair few times going for it. I initially gave it E5 7a which is nonsense as a grade, it's mentioned in Grit List 2 as E8 which is equally amusing. Maybe 8A/+ but pretty highball? Also it's barely a slab, very much on the cusp of wall climbing. Taking it as a slab it's the hardest slab I've done, and possibly the second hardest boulder problem I've done.

In 2005 John Gaskins climbed a line on the Stanworth slab, which he graded 8B, making it maybe the hardest slab in the world. It's a stunning sweep of rock, and there is potential for more than one line. Previous to John's ascent, you put some effort into one of those other lines, striking straight up the left side of the slab. What are the moves like?

Hard, very hard and thin. I sort of did all the moves but was a wayyyyyy off linking them. The hardest slab I've ever been on. Hardest slab in the world? May well be... It would be good to get a definitive description of where John climbed the slab. There is certainly space for two (or three) lines on that slab, they'd start at current cutting edge slab climbing and head north grade-wise from there. :)

You wrote on ukbouldering that you fell hundreds of times trying that project. Can you see yourself returning for a rematch, or are you letting this one go?

Living on the Isle of Man coupled with the access awkwardness at Stanworth, I imagine a serious rematch is not on the cards...

...but...

...I'd never say never, and I certainly haven't ruled out a rematch.

CREDITS

These people helped make this guidebook happen. They are great.

Photograhpers - photos by page
Oliver Müller - COVER, 18, 101, 105, 109, 129, 130, 131, 140-141, 144, 148-149, 155, 160, 168, 176, 192, 196, 199, 206-207, 232, 233, 247, 268, 278, 288-289
Greg Chapman - 48
Mike Binks - 63-64
Alan Holden - 68
Neil Herbert - 75
Peter Wilkinson - 76
Joe Dobson - 120, 126, 316
Tim Greenhalgh - 191
Owen Mcshane - 202
John Wilson - 259
Dawid Skoczylas - 285
All non-credited photos by the author.

Photographed Climbers
Mike Binks, Jordan Buys, Greg Chapman, Gareth Cokell, Joe Dobson, Luke Donaldson, Rich Draisey, Andy Emery, Elliot France, Robbie Gardiner, Rick Ginns, Tim Greenhalgh, Ivan Guardia, Will Harris, Neil Herbert, Simon Huthwaite, Derek Kenyon, Oliver Müller, Robin Müller, Matt Nuttall, John Proud, Dawid Skoczylas, Graham Stevens, Gareth Wallis, Peter Wilkinson, James Williamson, John Wilson.

Proof-Readers
Liz Buchanan, Greg Chapman, Joe Dobson, Tom Coulthard, Arran Deakin, Andrew Emery, Rick Ginns, Tim Greenhalgh, Niall Grimes, John Hartley, Phil Kelly, David Kettle, Oliver Müller, Matt Nuttall, Tom O'Rourke, John Proud, Paul Robins, Graham Stevens, Gareth Wallis, John Wilson.

Other People
Loads more people than I have space to list have helped with advice and encouragement. I thank you all. A special big thanks to my brother and my parents, without whom this guidebook probably wouldn't exist. Many thanks to Peter Clayton for hosting the website. Thanks to Niall Grimes, who knows a lot about guidebooks. Thanks to Matt Nuttall for providing me with pub knowledge. For info on various crags thanks to Greg Chapman, Bruce Goodwin, John Proud, Gareth Wallis, the Bury MOB and everyone else who told me something I didn't know or gave me something I could use in the guidebook.

And the BMC
Who loaned me the money to cover the printing costs. Join the BMC, your membership helps them to represent climbers, protect access and care for the places we like to climb on. You can find out more at www.thebmc.co.uk

Rocksucker, 7A - Lee

Locate your favourite ticking pen, here are the 250 undisputed best problems in the book, grade by grade.

THE TOP 250

8B
Endless Nameless
Moment of Clarity

8A+
Endangered Species
Super Submarine

8A
Lone Wolf
Outer Reach
Pot Of Gold
Snatch
Vector

7C+
Another World
Colt
Fracking
Information Highway Revisited
No Tome For Losers
Resistance Is Futile Sitstart
Return Of The Fly
Submarine
The Priory Sitstart

7C
Afterlife Direct
Chilli Burn
Colon Power
Copernicus
Excess Force
Fingertoe
Hellebore
Legs Not Included
Magic Beans
Rivers Of Blood
Something Under The Bed Is Drooling
The Noisy Cricket
The Plumbers Link
The Priory
The Starship Wilton

7B+
Afterlife
Bad Moon Rising
Bone Down
Double Dutch
Fire Wall
Fridge Hugger
Groundhog Sitstart
In Excess Sitstart
Limbo
Mentalist Direct
Mind Storm
No Country For Old Men
Private Press
Right Hand Hank
Undercut Problem
Vickers' Eliminate

7B
Barbara's Man
Body Bionics
Broken Jokes
Extemporise
Fanfare
Fix My Sink
Gaz's Traverse
Giganticus
Grow Wings
Meat In The Middle
Mind Over Matter
Monochimp
Moor Beast
Mothership Right Hand
Naiad
Patricky
Ping
Positions Of Strength
Purple Feel
Race To Base
Recalibrate
Resurgence
Rodin's Requiem
Teen Wolf
The Bignag
The Knockdown
The Lady's Not For Gurning
Thunder
Wrestle Down the Wind

7A+
Ape Hour
Argle Bargle
Berth Of A Tool
Big Marine
Big Muff
Cascadia
Chocolate Popsicle
David Vetter
Eldritch Sigh
Elfin Safe Tea
Facehugger
Faith And Energy
Fertile Delta
Fight Shapes With Shapes
Gristle Test
Hank's Wall
Home Skillet
Knee Butt
Lie 'n' Cling
Midgesquito Crimpelopes
Mothership Reconnection
Nick's Traverse
Ninja Fingers
Return Of The Swing
Ridiculous Eliminate
Shuffle Generation
Slice Of Life
Slipstream
Superfly
Talking Shillbut
The Eternal
The Grit Exam
The Man From Del Monte
The Trumpeteer
The Wedge
Ticket To Slide
Veteran Cosmic Rocker
Weakness Leaving The Boulder

7A
And For My Next Trick
Armajesty
Backslash
Bend Of The Rainbow
Black Beauty
Black Whirlwind
Brian Jacques
Con Air
Cordless Power
Ephemeral
Flywalk Slab
Grandad's Chin
Groundhog
Hero
JR's Soft Shoe Shuffle
Laissez Faire Stare
Longship
Mirth of the Ducks
Bleak House
Nik's Groove
Nyan Cat
Pigswill
Pony Club
Resurrection
Rocksucker
Sans Arete
Scream
Shed Seven
Sit Thee Down
Swingers
Sword Song
Tangled Up In Blue
The Lushering
The Move
The Rantle
Two For The Price Of One
Whisker
Zendik

6C+
Dinosaur Adventure 3D
Future Light Cone
Guns N' Ammo
Red Rose Addict
Rusty Wall
Summer Rain
The Gauntlet
The Soot Monkey
Top Hat
Tufa From Home

6C
2001 A Grit Odyssey
Common Knowledge
Elemental
Ell's Arete
Goldkick
Hawkeye
Knights Of The Turntables
L'Arete Traverse
Lifeline
Pond Traverse
Push To Prolapse
Slanting Hats And Spooky Cats
Snakey B
The Jeff Bomb
Two Mat Attack

6B+
Armscliff Wall
Cackhanded Compliment
Don't Go Yet
Flak
Innominate
Muscle Tussle
Scorched Earth
The Kingdom Of Slope
The Swine
Trig Arete

6B
Blackstone Best
Boopers
Burnt Heather
Camille Claudel
Catfoot
Concavity Cons Gravity
Done Years Ago
From Ape To Aardvark
Fundamentalist
Here I Am Again
Neat Whisky
Orchasm
Ouzel Thorn
Ribblesdale High
Small Star
The Undercut

6A+
Black Hole
Blackstone Slab
Dynamo
Ecstasy Of Yearning
Flook
Jalapeno Arete
Kraken
Look To Windward

6A
Andrex Guppy
Be Skilful
Bogette
Digitation
Directissima
Leaning To The Left Of Sloper
Parr's Crack
Pickpocket Direct
Rockflection
The Postman's Daughter
The Square
Toro Loco
Trig Slab
Who Left The Tap On?

5+
Bull Run
Cleft Of The Brave
Dance Me To The End Of Time
Deep Eyes
Flapper
Lungefish
Midvale School For The Gifted
Pickpocket
Zaggin'

5
Action And Refraction
Layback
Perving Arete
Pipe Dream
Take The Bull By The Horns

4+
Gold Bullion
Lower Slab Direct
Pillow Talk

4
Some Other Country
Subtletease
The Bum At The End Of The World

3
Ash Pit Slab
Paw Print
Score

INDEX OF STARRED PROBLEMS

1975 288
2001 A Grit Odyssey 41

A

Ace Of Diamonds 55
Acres Of Shakers 258
Action And Refraction 247
Aesthete's Foot 309
Afterlife 47
Afterlife Direct 47
A Is For Aardvark 256
Alan's Acme 53
Alison's Route 195
All Or Nothing 51
Amen 260
And 51
And For My Next Trick 35
Andrex Guppy 307
Another World 101
Ape Hour 303
Argle Bargle 254
Armajesty 30
Armscliff Wall 30
Ash Pit Slab 156
Ash Pit Traverse 156

B

Baby Bouncer 254
Backslash 101
Bad Lad 233
Bad Moon Rising 39
Barbara's Man 176
Bastille Traverse 218
Beach Mechanics 258
Belly Bouncer 301
Bend Of The Rainbow 71
Bend To The End 75
Bend To The End Low 75
Berth Of A Tool 249
Be Skilful 303
Beware Of The Bull 54
Big Butt 151
Big Marine 70
Big Muff 151
Big Wind 246
Black Beauty 231
Black Hole 58
Blackstone Best 289

Blackstone Slab 303
Black Whirlwind 64
Blacky Woo Woo
 Bon Bon Pipkins 103
Bleak House 23
Blister 125
Blurt 157
Body Bionics 242
Bog Chic 23
Bogette 23
Bone Down 178
Boopers 157
Boozy Brawler 297
Bounty Hunter 53
Brash Slab 53
Brian Jacques 132
Broken Jokes 191
Brownstones Crack 148
Bugle Practice 274
Bullet Proof 56
Bull Ring 56
Bull Run 56
Bully Beef 56
Burnt Heather 35

C

Cackhanded Compliment 116
Cadger 133
Camille Claudel 181
Cascadia 56
Catfoot 141
Chalk The Talk 309
Chicken Wings 195
Chilli Burn 283
Chocolate Popsicle 72
Clarion Call 282
Cleft Of The Brave 301
Clown's Pocket 199
Clown's Pocket Direct 199
Colon Power 71
Colt 151
Common Knowledge 182
Company Of Wolves 69
Con Air 300
Concavity Cons Gravity 289
Conniption 193
Copernicus 134
Cordless Power 76
Corn Mantel 156

Cowbell 51
Cowslip 50
Crackpot 94
Crawl From Your Hole 206
Creased Up 65
Crenellations 264
Crescent Of Embrace 199
Cruel Country 68
Crumple Stiltskin 37
Cuban 303
Cubic Zirconium 36
Custom Eyes 309
Cut Diamond 55

D

Dance Me To The
 End Of Time 258
Dandy Gets Handy 309
David Vetter 115
Deep Eyes 282
Delicat 258
Dezertion 157
Diceman 258
Digging For Deeply 229
Digitation 156
Dinosaur Adventure 3D 144
Directissima 156
Dirty Crack 224
Done Years Ago 300
Don't Go Yet 56
Doozy 187
Double Dutch 120
Dreamcatcher 57
Dynamo 101

E

Ecstasy Of Yearning 285
Edge Game 105
Eilixir 291
Eldritch Sigh 90
Elemental 41
Elfin Safe Tea 258
Elliot's Traverse 195
Ell's Arete 176
Endless Nameless 104
Ephemeral 258
Escalate 273
Excavator Wall 229

Excess Force 71
Extemporise 265
Extra Bacon 242

F

Facehugger 105
Facial Flaring 208
Faintline 151
Faith And Energy 195
Fanfare 251
Farthing Arete 229
Feet Of Strength 251
Fertile Delta 71
Fifty Flyers 47
Fight Shapes With Shapes 260
Fingertoe 171
Fire Wall 35
First Bit 75
Fishface 140
Fishing For Compliments 126
Fissure Of Fear 301
Fix My Sink 35
Flak 272
Flapper 272
Flipper 272
Flook 272
Flopper 272
Flute Note 256
Flying Truck 61
Flywalk 169
Flywalk Slab 169
Footloose And Fancy Free 242
Fraud 156
Fridge Hugger 289
From Ape To Aardvark 72
Full Sail 91
Fundamentalist 201
Funhouse 111
Funkatronic 242
Future Light Cone 55

G

Gary's Arete 30
Gaucho 50
Gauntlet Failure 70
Gaz's Traverse 71
Get Down On It 185
Get Your Fingers Out 270
Giganticus 133
Glue Wave 90
Going Down 75
Gold Bullion 53

Goldkick 213
Good Lass 233
Grabadabadoo 119
Grandad's Chin 166
Gravitational Experiment 175
Green and Black 300
Green Angle 65
Gristle Test 249
Gritworm 256
Groundhog 152
Grow Wings 68
Gruts 69
Grüvy 226
Guns N' Ammo 41

H

Haig 188
Halfway 75
Hand Holed 294
Hank's Wall 154
Happy Mole Man 293
Hardline 151
Hash Lee 108
Hawkeye 133
Head Butt Wall 175
Hear No Mantel 315
Heel The World 214
Hellebore 116
Here I Am Again 36
Hernia 148
Hero 293
Hidden Prowler 178
Hit The Buzzer 192
Home Improvements 294
Home Skillet 264
Hoplite 28
Hopper 156
Horror Arete 162
Horrorbix 162
Horwich Haul 144

I

I'm Not Going 51
Indian Face 144
In Excess 71
Inflexion Direct Start 229
Information
   Highway Revisited 143
Innominate 143
Insouciance 298
Intent 252

J

Jalapeno Arete 42
Jiggery Slopery 256
JR's Soft Shoe Shuffle 185
Jubilee Tower 34

K

Kiss The Razor's Edge 67
Knee Butt 175
Knights Of The Turntables 41
Kraken 310

L

Laissez Faire Stare 125
L'Arete Traverse 171
Last Lash 301
Layback 154
Leaning To The
   Left Of Sloper 305
Learning To Wave 79
Legs Not Included 119
Licking The Barrel 141
Lie 'n' Cling 246
Lifeline 150
Limbo 47
Lippy Traverse 289
Little Big Cheeks 274
Live Evil 26
Lone Wolf 47
Long John 188
Longship 254
Look to Windward 307
Los Endos 272
Lost Propriety 241
Lovehandle 115
Lower Slab Direct 39
Low Life 72
Luna 310
Lungefish 293
Lurch 123
Lust Is A Downward Slope 259

M

Madcows 51
Madman's Paradise 221
Magic Beans 209
Magic Goods 135
Maid In Stone 144
Manbumps for Geese 186
Man Up 120

Meat In The Middle 209
Mentalist Direct 201
Middle Bit 75
Middle Bit Plus 75
Middle Third 75
Midgesquito Crimpelopes 166
Midsummer Nights 56
Midvale School
   For The Gifted 30
Mind Over Matter 109
Mind Storm 47
Mirth of the Ducks 112
Moment of Clarity 37
Monochimp 91
Monty Blonx 221
Moor Beast 64
Morph 273
Moss Wall 148
Mothership Reconnection 43
Mothership Right Hand 43
Mr Owl Ate My Metal Worm 26
Mr. Skin 69
Mr Tumnus 114
Mucky Pup 99
Munchies 51
Muscles In Their Imagination 69
Muscle Tussle 260

N

Naiad 135
Naomi's Wall 305
Nexus 155
Nick's Traverse 303
Nik's Groove 294
Nik's Left 294
Ninja Fingers 151
No Country For Old Men 27
Nostriloquy 182
No Tome For Losers 99
Not The Don Thing 272
Nyan Cat 273

O

Obscenity 158
Off-Side 292
Offwidth Your Head 292
Old Silky 306
One Pebble Slab 53
Orchasm 239
Origami 65
Outer Reach 44
Ouzel Thorn 36

Over The Hill 213

P

Pandora's Box Left Hand 91
Parabola 154
Parboiled 201
Parr's Crack 154
Patiopia 294
Patricky 38
Paw Print 307
Pendulum 221
Perving Arete 34
Pheasant Walk 306
Pickpocket 94
Pickpocket Direct 94
Pigs On The Hoof 179
Pigswill 154
Pillow Talk 247
Ping 72
Pipe Dream 57
Pit Bull 55
Plastic Sex Explosion 258
Poblano 43
Pocket Arete 295
Pocket Dyno 295
Pocket Pull 178
Pockington Lane 300
Pond Traverse 148
Pony Club 292
Positions Of Strength 44
Pot Of Gold 71
Private Press 36
Proper Job 292
Pumper Nickel 272
Pump 'Til You Jump 68
Purple Feel 181
Pursuit Of Slappiness 199
Push To Prolapse 70

Q

Quiver 180
Quiver Upriver 140

R

Race to Base 109
Race To Base 109
RB 258
Reach For The Stars 193
Recalibrate 288
Red Rose Addict 41
Remembarete 167

Renal Failure 70
Reservoir Slab 252
Resistance Is Futile 41
ress For Success 242
Resurgence 229
Resurrection 229
Return Of The Fly 37
Return Of The Swing 310
Reunion Wilderness 114
Ribblesdale High 79
Ridiculous Eliminate 158
Right Hand Hank 154
Rivers Of Blood 132
Road House 23
Robin's Slap 291
Rockflection 282
Rocksucker 233
Rock This Country 225
Rodin's Requiem 182
Rough Diamond 55
Ruler Fooler 306
Rustication 78
Rusty Wall 151

S

Sandman 102
Sans Arete 115
Satisfying Sloper Problem 152
Saxon 28
Scorched August 71
Scorched Earth 103
Score 34
Scream 82
Scrunch 120
Second Fifth 75
Sergeant Pepper 283
Seven A 68
Shed Seven 87
Shuffle Generation 101
Sidewalk 169
Simon's Starter 51
Sit Thee Down 199
Sketch Artist 214
Slanting Hats
   And Spooky Cats 166
Slap 247
Slice Of Life 39
Slip 247
Slipstream 178
Slope 247
Slope-Em-Up 83
Slower Montcliffe 144
Small Star 280

Smash Patrol 252
Smeg City Plus 70
Snakey B 165
Snatch 94
Softly Softly 305
Some Other Country 264
Something Under
    The Bed Is Drooling 239
Sons Of Pioneers 61
Spitsbergen 103
Squirreling Dervishes 39
Starter For Ten 270
Start To High Break 75
Strawbogen 227
Submarine 70
Subtletease 307
Suction 55
Sultans Of Squirm 247
Summer Rain 126
Summit Fever 256
Sunken Gold 214
Superfly 217
Super Submarine 70
Sweat-Gang 265
Swingers 310
Sword Song 28

T

Take The Bull By The Horns 52
Talking Shillbut 265
Tangled Up In Blue 265
Tarot Plane 68
Teen Wolf 47
The Back Of Beyond 140
The Bignag 152
The Bum At The
    End Of The World 247
The Cherry On Top 247
The Chickens Are Restless 30
The Don 272
The Enchanted Tower 125
The Fop Is On Form 309
The Fortress Arete 291
The Gauntlet 70
The Giant's Chamber 258
The Grit Exam 254
The Hacker 170
The Hump 260
The Jeff Bomb 218
The Kingdom Of Slope 254
The Knockdown 249
The Lady's Not For Gurning 298
The Lightning Bolt 217

The Lushering 300
The Man From Del Monte 52
The Miggity Mac Daddy 91
The Move 162
The Nerds and the Knees 116
The Noisy Cricket 111
The Pincher 184
The Postman's Daughter 166
The Ranch 57
The Rantle 309
The Renaissance Men 188
There's A Ghost 97
The Right
    Honourable Runnel 293
The Runnel 295
The Slug 275
The Soot Monkey 170
The Square 182
The Square Left Hand 182
The Starship Wilton 183
The Swine 179
The Traverse Of The Gods 75
The Trumpeteer 274
The Undercut 181
The Underdog 298
The Urkling 177
The Wedge 297
The Wedge 297
The Wrong Side Of The Flaw 254
Three Little Piggies 273
Thugousity 83
Thulsa Doom 165
Thunder 151
Ticket To Slide 270
Ticketybang 124
Tilting For Champions 315
Timothy's Route 68
Toffee Nut Ice-Cream 105
Too Hard For Greg Rimmer 168
Top Hat 30
Toreador 55
Toro Loco 23
Totem Vole 26
Traverso Grande 99
Treading The Eel 102
Tree-Being 123
Trev The Trav Chav 134
Trig Arete 300
Trigonomy 300
Trig Slab 300
Troy A Little Tenderness 209
Tufa From Home 264
Twist 134
Twist And Shout 265

U

Under A Dark Dream 302
Undercut Problem 94
Underway 289
Unjust 156
Unnatural Selection 72

V

Vector 38
Veteran Cosmic Rocker 169
Vickers' Eliminate 68

W

Warland Slabside 252
Weakness Leaving
    The Boulder 260
Welcome To The Palindrome 26
Wellington Wall 206
Whisker 141
Who Left The Tap On? 126
Wiggling Crack 34
Wingspan 185
Wing Wang 213
Wobble Bottom 68
Woops-A-Crazy 227
Wrestle Down the Wind 288
Wurzel Gummidge 114

Z

Zaggin' 78
Zendik 195

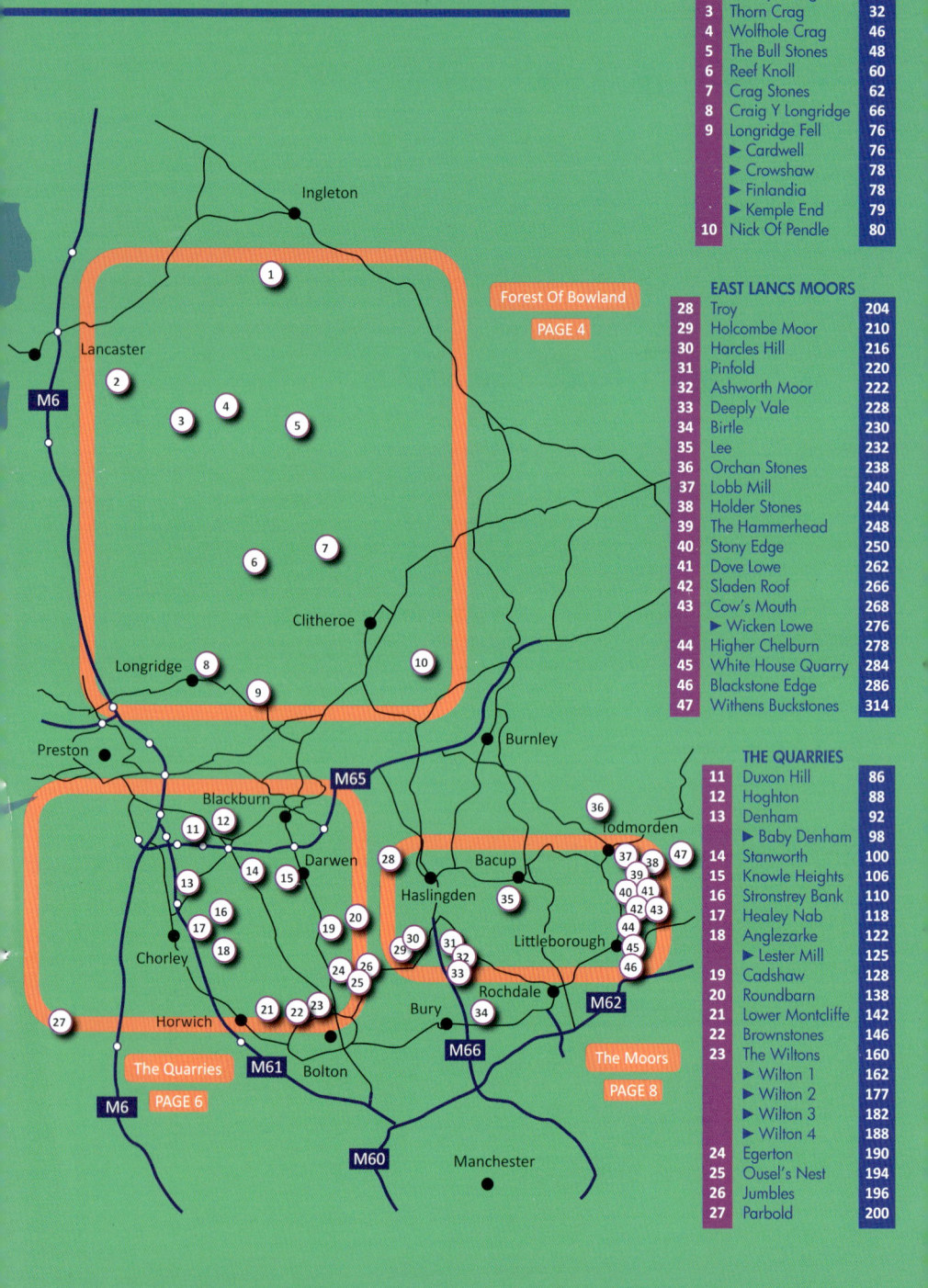

miniMAP

Forest Of Bowland
PAGE 4

The Quarries
PAGE 6

The Moors
PAGE 8

BOWLAND

1	Great Stone Of Fourstones	22
2	Windy Clough	24
3	Thorn Crag	32
4	Wolfhole Crag	46
5	The Bull Stones	48
6	Reef Knoll	60
7	Crag Stones	62
8	Craig Y Longridge	66
9	Longridge Fell	76
	▶ Cardwell	76
	▶ Crowshaw	78
	▶ Finlandia	78
	▶ Kemple End	79
10	Nick Of Pendle	80

EAST LANCS MOORS

28	Troy	204
29	Holcombe Moor	210
30	Harcles Hill	216
31	Pinfold	220
32	Ashworth Moor	222
33	Deeply Vale	228
34	Birtle	230
35	Lee	232
36	Orchan Stones	238
37	Lobb Mill	240
38	Holder Stones	244
39	The Hammerhead	248
40	Stony Edge	250
41	Dove Lowe	262
42	Sladen Roof	266
43	Cow's Mouth	268
	▶ Wicken Lowe	276
44	Higher Chelburn	278
45	White House Quarry	284
46	Blackstone Edge	286
47	Withens Buckstones	314

THE QUARRIES

11	Duxon Hill	86
12	Hoghton	88
13	Denham	92
	▶ Baby Denham	98
14	Stanworth	100
15	Knowle Heights	106
16	Stronstrey Bank	110
17	Healey Nab	118
18	Anglezarke	122
	▶ Lester Mill	125
19	Cadshaw	128
20	Roundbarn	138
21	Lower Montcliffe	142
22	Brownstones	146
23	The Wiltons	160
	▶ Wilton 1	162
	▶ Wilton 2	177
	▶ Wilton 3	182
	▶ Wilton 4	188
24	Egerton	190
25	Ousel's Nest	194
26	Jumbles	196
27	Parbold	200